The Left

C000131505

The Left Hand Path

By

B R Taylor

2019

First Printing, 2019

Pictures sourced from Creative Commons and edited by B R Taylor
Source : Creative Commons. Copyright permission expressly granted.
Pictures available for commercial purposes; pictures which can be modified,
adapted or built upon.

@ www.creativecommons.org

Cover design
by
B R Taylor

ISBN : 9781698646589

Preface

The idea for this book came about from my research into Kabbalah. During that research circumstantial evidence pointed to Kabbalah being a lot older than we are led to believe, revealing links between Kabbalah, astrology, religion and the Holy Land. Once aware of these common links, I began to explore Kabbalah, in respect to both the Tree of Life and the Tree of Death to see if any light could be shone on the direction of the globalisation project's obsession with destabilising the Middle East.

Contents

The Left Hand Path

Introduction

Trying to understand theology without a basic understanding of astrology and metaphysics is like sailing a vast ocean without a compass. During my research for this book, it became clear to me that any serious endeavour towards unveiling occult and theological matters must incorporate a basic understanding of Kabbalah. Being the benchmark for most theological and occult ideologies, kabbalah really is the key to unlocking our conscious connection to the Creator. Although evidence for Kabbalah only goes back to the 13th century, circumstantial evidence suggests it is much older and is an ancient form of astro magic which influenced some of the greatest figures throughout history. Because of the profound esoteric wisdom contained within Kabbalah's fabric, it is still relevant in today's world of globalisation and presents us with deep rooted traditions underpinning the doctrines and ideologies of many secret societies and religious cults. Most people shy away from occult matters, believing this will compromise their righteous place within creation, soiling their relationship with the All Mighty. In their ignorance they fail to appreciate the positive contribution Kabbalistic knowledge can bring to one's appreciation of the human conscious connection to the Creator/Logos. What ever level of spiritual evolution a person is at, Kabbalah can help guide them towards greater union with their Creator. As a consequence of this profound ancient wisdom, there is a negative aspect. While the righteous Kabbalah can lead one up the Tree of Life towards a powerful union with the Creator, the opposite is the case when descending down the left hand path, a place where the individual can become seduced into a spiritual vacuum, as they cast off morality and descend down the Tree of Death. Equally as powerful, the Tree of Death offers short term material rewards from the God's of the underworld, as their Qliphotic demons and Archons suck the Divine light from all who walk the left hand path.

This book tries to examine how Kabbalah is still as relevant today as it has always been. It explores how the globalisation project, as a brave new venture for all of mankind, is in fact a collective journey down the left hand path, into the abyss. Although many credible individuals sincerely believe in the merits of this brave new world, they fail to see the dangers inherent in such an all encompassing technological control grid, and only through an appreciation of Kabbalistic principles can the bigger picture come into focus. There has always been, and still are, dark spiritual forces interacting with this physical realm, using subtle suggestion, deceit and corruption to undermine Divine creation, with the potential of imitating the Creator, seducing many towards the left hand path. This perpetual ongoing battle between the forces of good and evil are once again gearing up for a show down of biblical proportions. At this poignant moment in human history, one must ask the question:

Which side are you on?

Chapter 1, What is the left hand path?

To understand what is meant by the left hand path a great deal of esoteric and occult (hidden) knowledge needs to be understood. As the word sinister in Latin means 'to the left' or even 'left handed', we find our history full of phrases and meanings which point towards this left hand path. A path opposing the preferred orthodox or official view of righteousness.

In chiromancy, commonly known as palmistry, the left hand represents the past, the feminine, our subconscious and spiritual karmic disposition. The fingers are believed to be antenna, picking up cosmic energy from the planets and the cosmos. This energy is then displayed on the hand of an individual through various lines, mounts and form. The left and right hands are connected to opposite sides of the brain, where the left hand is controlled by the right hemisphere and the right hand the left hemisphere. Each hemisphere represents our focal or subconscious mind.

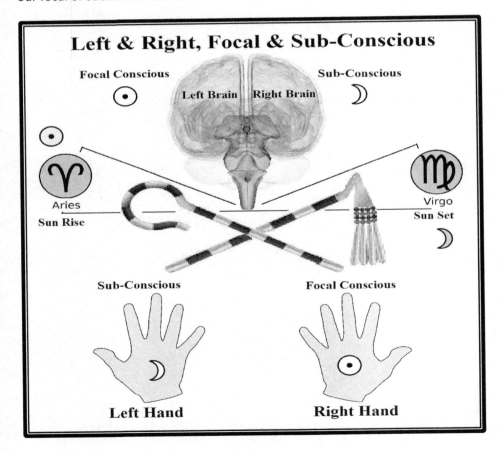

To better understand the different aspects of human awareness it becomes clearer when viewed as a triad of consciousness, with the focal, sub and higher mind (Logos) interacting together to give us the overall conscious experience.

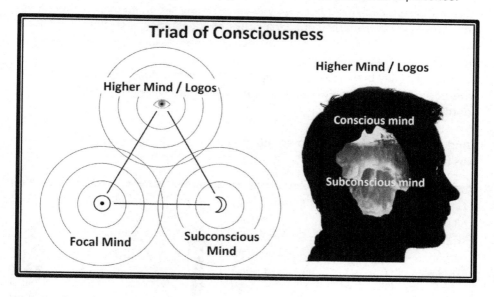

The Sun has always been associated with the Soul and is regarded as the energy source behind our focal awareness. In Latin the Sun was known as solis or sol. Our ancestors, using astrology as the benchmark for their cultural and social activities, understood the connection between the Sun and the soul consciousness. The soul is the physical earthly connection to the Logos, or universal consciousness, whereas the spirit is the subconscious connection to that higher spiritual realm. When the Sun or sol comes up in the morning most of us come back into focal awareness, energised by the Sun's electromagnetic energy. We get out of bed and stand upon the Earth with the soles of our feet.

The Moon is regarded as the subordinate luminary to the Sun. It has been associated with the human subconscious and the spirit realm for thousands of years. In ancient Mesopotamia the Moon was known as 'Sin', and worshipped by both Hebrews and Arabs. This could well be the origins of the Latin word sinister, as a connection to the Moon.

The subconscious is the greater part of the mind, being at least 70% of our conscious capacity. It is also connected to the spirit realm through its tapestry of internal emotions, feelings and habitual programming. It is the part of the mind which forgets nothing, recording everything we ever do, feel and sense. Like a digital hard drive, all our experiences are shared within the garden of the collective subconscious. The spirit realm is free from the constraints of time and

4

space, constraints which limit the soul within the restrictions of spatial awareness. It is therefore free to explore the past, present and future simultaneously. This partly explains why, after a good nights sleep, our dreams appear nonsensical. This is because you cannot view simultaneous past, present and future events from the soul perspective of lineal time constraints. The Moon, the subconscious and the spirit realm have also been associated, throughout the ages, with the feminine which leads us to the Adam and Eve concept. Women have traditionally been regarded as more spiritual than their male counterparts, whereas men are generally better at spatial awareness exercises and coordination.

"And so it is written, the first man Adam was made a living soul; the last Adam was made a quickening spirit." - 1 Corinthians 15:45 (KJV)

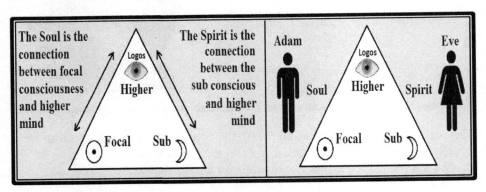

In astrology each sign of the zodiac has a ruling planet, which influences that sign with its overall metaphysical characteristics. For example Aries is ruled by the planet Mars, and Mars is the planet of proactive energy focused in a specific direction. This is reflected in the glyph for Mars, a circle with an arrow or cross pointing outwards towards its chosen direction.

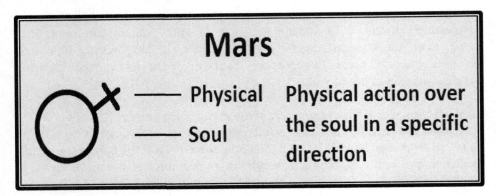

In astrology each glyph is made up of three separate components, the soul, the spirit and the physical. These are symbolised by a circle, a crescent or a cross, combined in specific ways to represent the metaphysical characteristics of the individual planet's energetic construct and personality. This allows those who understand the language of astrology to interpret what is taking place.

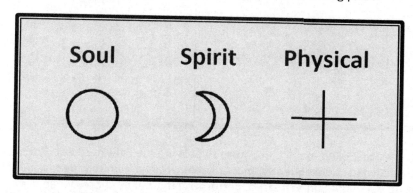

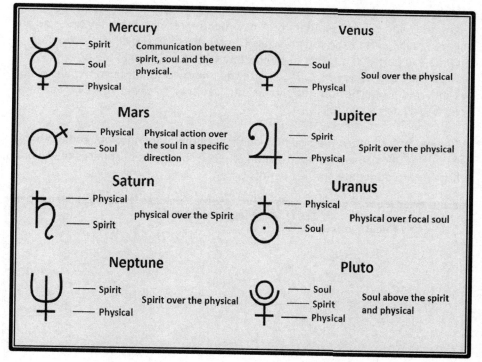

When the zodiac is divided up into day and night polarities, where the day is ruled by the Sun/soul and the night is ruled by the Moon/spirit, some interesting observations can be made.

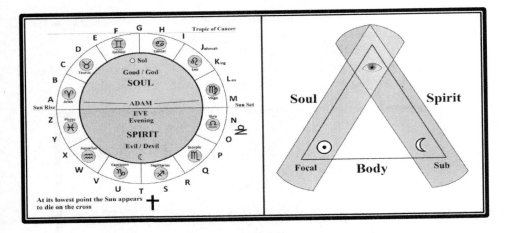

Our ancestors relied mainly on nature to provide the light necessary for their day to day activities. Consequently, most people, who had limited means, would wake up when the Sun appeared, perform all their daily chores while it was light and then sleep when the Sun went down. They saw the darkness as a cold, frightening and evil place. Adam or A-day-man represented the day, the soul and the masculine part of the zodiac, while Eve represented the evening, the dark, and the evil part of the night. Our ancestors therefore, lived in the day and viewed the night as a grim doorway into the underworld, far from the life giving warmth and properties offered by the Sun. Live spelt backwards is evil, and lived spelt backwards is the Devil.

When we superimpose the two hemispheres of the brain onto our zodiac chart we find specific planets dominate and influence specific hemispheres of the brain, which in turn dominate specific hands.

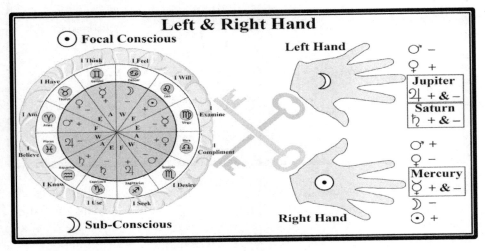

As can be seen from the above diagram, the planetary rulers of each zodiacal hemisphere of the brain influence each hand accordingly. The right hand which is associated with left brain activity is very much to do with the present moment, or the now; whereas the right brain, with its subconscious and spiritual bias, has influence over the left hand. Here we see certain planets dominate each hemisphere along with each hand. The right hand contains both masculine and feminine polarities of the planet Mercury, giving it significant influence over the present moment. To appreciate living in the now, to its full potential, one must optimise good communication between all levels of consciousness, where Mercury, the messenger and planet of communication plays a leading role. The planet Mercury was and is still known as Budha in Sanskrit. Gautama Buddha, the sage, is often depicted with his right hand held out as he teachers the path to enlightenment and the art of living in the now. It is also not uncommon to see Buddha's right hand displaying a spiral symbol denoting the Sun.

Buddha's Right Hand

The flag of the Vatican is quite revealing in a variety of subtle ways, it reflects the Catholic Church's understanding of this triad of human consciousness. The symbolism of crossed keys suggest that the organisation behind the church see themselves as gate keepers to unlocking the human collective's soul and spiritual connection to the Logos. The gold key represents the Sun/soul connection and the silver key reflects the Moon/spiritual connection.

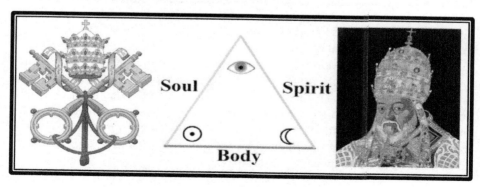

The planets dominating the left hand are Saturn, Jupiter and the Moon. It is the spiritual hand of karmic disposition and past tense. All these planets have personified spiritual characters assigned to them. These characters are known as Satan, Jesus and Gabriel, all of a spiritual nature. Satan takes the leading role within the left hand due to his ruler-ship over Capricorn and Aquarius, that is, the two signs associated with the depths of the night, from midnight to 4am. Jesus on the other hand, a polar opposite of Satan, in a metaphysical context, could not be seen sharing the same platform as the prince of darkness, so was assigned to be the Son (Sun) of God sitting on his right hand.

"He exerted when he raised Christ from the dead and seated him at his right hand in the heavenly realms." Ephesians 1:20 (NIV)

"But Stephen, full of the Holy Spirit, looked up to heaven and saw the glory of God, and Jesus standing at the right hand of God. "Look," he said, "I see heaven open and the Son of Man standing at the right hand of God." Acts 7:55-56 (NIV)

Because Saturn is the main ruler of the left hand, Satan, its personified deity has been associated with the left hand path together with the old name for the Moon 'Sin'.

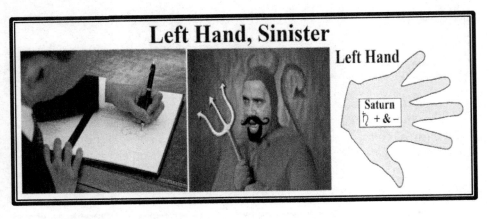

As stated in my previous book *Language of the Gods*,[2] Archangel Michael represents the angle of the Sun in the sky, and therefore the right hand, while Gabriel represents the Moon and therefore the left hand. All the Archangels are personifications of the planetary angles in the heavens. They make up the Elohim (plural for more than one God/El). This is why most Archangel's names end with the letters EL. Their influence on human consciousness is an accumulation of electromagnetic stimulation reaching us at different angles from out in the solar system. According to the Jewish encyclopaedia, both Michael and Gabriel are told which side of God they should stand.

"Michael stands at the right hand of God, Gabriel at his left (Jellinek, "B. H." v. 166)" Jewish encyclopaedia[1]

"A wise man's heart is at his right hand; but a fool's heart at his left." Ecclesiastes 10:2 (KJV)

"Length of days is in her right hand; and in her left hand riches and honour." Proverbs 3:16 (KJV)

When we look closely at the glyph for Saturn we see it is a cross over a crescent. This tells us that the energetic metaphysical influence of Saturn promotes the cross of materialism over the crescent of spirituality. A 180 degree opposition to Jupiter's optimistic energy of hope and good will.

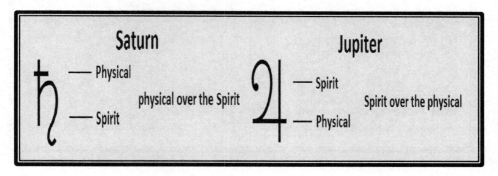

Satan is the old Persian word for the planet Saturn, and as a personified ambassador for that planet he is the God or El of this material earthly realm, and consequently the ruler over the left hand path.

"Satan, who is the God of this world, has blinded the minds of those who don't believe. They are unable to see the glorious light of the Good News. They don't understand this message about the glory of Christ, who is the exact likeness of God. " - 2 Corinthians 4:4 (NLT)

In tarot, each card has a specific relationship to astrology and the zodiac. The cards relating to both Saturn and Jupiter are revealing in a subtle yet profound way. Saturn is the judgement card depicting the cross over dead spirits which are awakening into the material world. According to the website Shrivinayaka Astrology, it states:

"Saturn is the planet of Judgment. He works as a judge and punishes a person based on his karma done by him". - Shrivinayaka Astrology[3]

Jupiter on the other hand is the crescent of spirituality over the cross of materialism, it is the planet of optimism, good fortune and abundance. In tarot it is represented as the wheel of fortune card, where the devil of materialism can be seen under the wheel of fortune. Jesus (Jupiter/Zeus), the ambassador for the Age of Pisces and also its ruling planet, reflects much of the optimistic, hopeful and good will values associated with the planet's energetic metaphysical characteristics. The Bible clearly states that Jesus's kingdom is not of this world, meaning it is not of the physical material realm. His kingdom is spiritual, reflecting the crescent of spirituality over the material cross.

"My kingdom is not of this world; if it were, my servants would fight to prevent my arrest by the Jews. But now, my kingdom is not of this realm." John 18-36 (NIV)

Saturn

Saturn is the 6th planet from the Sun and the 2nd largest after Jupiter. It takes 29 years to perform one full orbit around the Sun and return back to its initial position. It is a gaseous giant, 9 times bigger than the Earth, comprising mainly of hydrogen and helium. It has 62 moons, and a visible ring system made from ice particles. Together Jupiter and Saturn account for 92% of the total planetary mass in our solar system. Saturn has for many years been depicted as a black cube and synonymous with the number six. An astronomical explanation for this came about in 1981 when the voyager space craft sent back photographs of Saturn's bazaar hexagonal shaped weather pattern at its north pole. For our ancestors to know about this is another mystery, or just another unacknowledged anomaly suggesting they once had advanced in-depth knowledge of the stars and planets within our solar system.

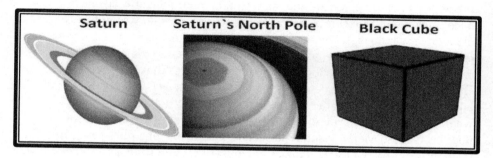

The astrological and metaphysical characteristics of Saturn are, to some extent, a reflection of its position out in the solar system. Being the furthest planet visible to the naked eye, its slow progression across the heavens gives it the title of master or father of time. Its restrictions and constraints in the physical realm give us the opportunity to learn valuable lessons during the course of our lives. Other characteristics of Saturn are as follows:

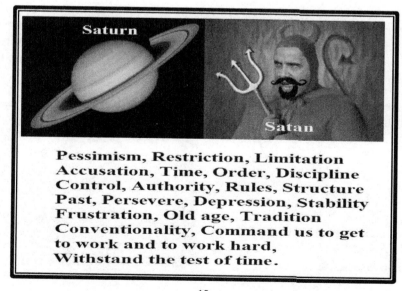

12

In our distant past, before the days of monotheism, our ancestors left us detailed clues as to their understanding of the constellations, planets and the solar system as a whole, giving us the impression that they were far more sophisticated than modern established historians would have us believe. Before monotheism it appears that a general appreciation of all the planets, in a polytheistic fashion, was preferred, harmonising each culture's conscious connection to the Logos, while keeping a balance between nature and planetary rhythms and cycles. As humanity evolved various forms of monotheism sprang up worshipping different singular deities. Modern academia, universities and theologians fail to appreciate that all the main monotheistic religions of today have singled out a specific planet as their focus of worship, promoting that planet over all the rest. The result of this single planet worship restricts each religious cult with the energetic characteristics of that single planet at the expense of all the others. Consequently, it submerges that society within the characteristics of that single planet's energetic construct, eventually precipitating and promoting those characteristics out into the cultural consciousness as a whole. Christianity chose Jupiter as its primary planet; Islam chose Venus; Buddhism chose Mercury and Judaism chose Saturn. If one pulls away from these religions or philosophical ideologies and observes them from a distance. With the aid of ancient astrology as a benchmark, the true foundations to these religions become a great deal clearer.

Christianity and Jupiter

The Christians are people associated with Jupiter, the planet which ruled Pisces throughout the 2160 year epoch of the two fish. The Pope sits on the throne of Peter (Jupiter) focusing mainly on the energetic frequencies given off by this planet and the luminaries of the Sun and Moon, giving a Christian perspective of the triad of consciousness. Using the law of attraction they align their whole belief system with the energetic characteristics of this enormous planetary body, bringing forth and emphasising its unique potential.

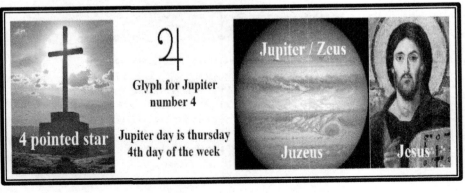

4 pointed star — Glyph for Jupiter number 4 — Jupiter day is thursday 4th day of the week — Jupiter / Zeus — Juzeus — Jesus

Jupiter is the 5th planet from the Sun, the biggest planet in our solar system, 1/10 the diameter of the Sun and 11 times the diameter of the Earth, a gas giant comprising mainly of hydrogen and helium. Jupiter takes approximately 12 earthly years to perform a full orbit of the Sun, this means Jupiter will stay in each zodiac house for approximately 1 year before moving into the next. The planet has a red spot, a giant storm the size of the Earth, which was observed as far back as the 17th century. Jupiter is not alone, it is accompanied by 67 moons, the biggest, Ganymede, has a diameter greater than Mercury. One of its moons is called Europa, which mainly consists of an ice covered liquid ocean.

Jupiter's astrological characteristics are a reflection of its size and physical nature. It is the King of the Gods, the planet of plenty, it is tolerant and expansive. Attributes include good luck, bounty, optimism and growth. It comes with morality, gratitude, hope and honour. Jupiter can guide you to a sense of purpose and high ideals. Some of its pathways towards fulfilment come through learning, travel, challenges and philosophy. The planet's energy does have a negative side, due to its size, which can lead to blind optimism, excess and overindulgence. Jupiter was the chief deity of the Roman State religion, along with his wife Juno. Jupiter was also known as Jove, Luppiter, Lovis, Diespiter and Zeus in Greek. When humanity entered the Age of Pisces, Jupiter the ruling planet, became the new focus of spiritual energy emanating from the cosmos. It would naturally dominate during this epoch of 2160 years. The Romans understood how this all worked, hence why Jupiter became their chief deity offered by the ruling classes as the new state religion. Any form of grass roots spirituality which preached the truth, the light and universal wisdom, were targeted as a threat to Rome's new established authorised religion. The early Christians and Jews, possibly understood holistic wisdom and its origins better than we do today, consequently, their position posed a threat to the establishment's doctrine, with many of them unwilling to depart from the science of light and their knowledge of universal teachings. As the state took control over the running of this New Age Christianity, they undermined its potential by offering a perverted and diluted version of the truth, organising a new religion taming Jupiterian energies for their own benefit.

The Romans threw the early unreformed Christians to the lions, but once the Christian religion was under the control of the ruling classes, they no longer needed to inflict cruelty upon those poor animals, their new weapon was to use suggestions which would alter the subconscious beliefs in the minds of the masses, steering them on a safe manipulated path, a path keeping them in obedience and under control.

The vice for Jupiter is gluttony. A recent study for the Journal of Religion and Health, found that Christians are more likely to have a larger BMI (body mass index) than atheists and other religious groups.

"Evidence of this association was strongest among those affiliated to a Christian religion." Dr Deborah Lycett, a senior lecturer in dietetics at Coventry University.[4]

Aligning one's community or nation with the expansive energy of Jupiter will in time manifest these traits in a culture's reality, contributing to the Christian's expansive domination around the world. Roman Catholicism has become one of the wealthiest institutions on Earth. The Christian faith expanded to nearly every nook and cranny on the planet, leaving no stone unturned. Sunday became the preferred holy day in the Christian week. Seven is their most highly regarded number, it symbolises completeness and perfection, both spiritually and physically. The number 7 appears over 700 times in the Bible and is the foundation of God's word. Although Christians are associated with Jupiter, they are also equally aligned with the Sun and the Moon, in a triad of Father, Son and Holy Spirit, choosing the day of the Sun to focus on their faith.

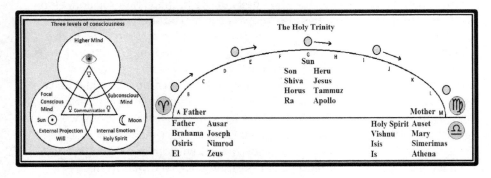

Thursday, Jupiter's day is not entirely neglected. Holy Thursday is one of the most important days on the calendar of the Catholic religion. During the Last Supper Ju-zeus offered himself as the sacrificial lamb, he bid farewell to his followers before prophesying of his betrayal and subsequent death. All around the world bishops and priests celebrate what is known as the institution of the priesthood (Holy Thursday), where a mass is held in which a senior bishop washes the feet of 12 catholic priests. The feet are associated with the zodiac house of Pisces, and there are 12 priests one for each house. This is a symbolic reconstruction of the moment when Christ washed the feet of the 12 Apostles. The cross can also represent a 4 pointed star, symbolising the day of Jupiter. There is no greater example of Jupiter's expansive gluttony, expressed in the physical realm, than the Christian festival known as Thanksgiving, and it is no coincidence that this festival is celebrated on the fourth Thursday in November. Jupiter rules over two signs of the Zodiac, Pisces and Sagittarius, the motto's of

15

which are "I believe and I seek".

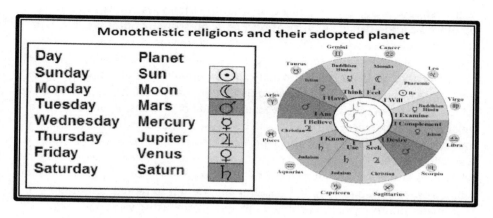

Monotheistic religions and their adopted planet

Day	Planet	
Sunday	Sun	☉
Monday	Moon	☽
Tuesday	Mars	♂
Wednesday	Mercury	☿
Thursday	Jupiter	♃
Friday	Venus	♀
Saturday	Saturn	♄

Although Sunday has been adopted by the Christians as the first day of the week, probably due to the importance of the Sun as the prime luminary in the heavens, in the ancient world the day of the Moon was considered as day one. The Moon being the closest and fastest moving body in the solar system relative to the Earth, it gives us words like mono, Luna or unus, signifying the first day of the week. Many cultures and countries outside the Christian tradition also consider Monday as the first day of the week. This is backed up by the international standard ISO 8601.

Islam and Venus

Muslims make up approximately 23% of the world's population. They follow the religion of Islam, based on a book called the Quran, which is considered to be the word of God, revealed by the prophet Muhammad. Muslim is Arabic for "one who submits to God". The planet adopted by this religion is Venus; the planet of love and liking. The number associated with Venus is five along with their holy day of Friday. They pray five times a day and adhere to "the five pillars of Islam". On top of some mosques you will see a crescent moon and a five pointed star. The top of the mosque roof could represent the trinity of consciousness, with the Sun, the crescent Moon and the five pointed star of Venus.

Muslims and Venus

Venus is the second planet from the Sun with an orbit of 224.7 days. It is the brightest natural object in the night sky after the Moon. Its atmosphere is made up of 92% carbon dioxide with an atmospheric pressure 92 times greater than the Earth. It is the hottest planet in our solar system with an average surface temperature of approximately 460 degrees centigrade. The astrological energetic characteristics of Venus include love, liking and the pleasures we take from life, along with our appreciation of the exquisite nature of all things, especially things which make us happy, including our luxuries and possessions. Venus also has a negative aspect or vice; this energy can be misused, transpiring as self-indulgence, self-centred, vain and superficial. The traditional vice for Venus is lust, which is understandable once you comprehend the characteristics of Venus, which was also linked to Aphrodite. This could be one reason why some Muslim women are required to wear the Burka, in an attempt to reduce temptation in their male counterparts by keeping them away from lustful vices. Venus rules Taurus (I have) and Libra (I complement), one is a fixed earth sign and the other is a cardinal air sign. Libra is associated with law and justice, a balance of right and wrong. Sharia law a term which means the "path or way", is a legal framework to regulate those who live within the Islamic system. It deals with many aspects of life handing out some extreme and harsh penalties. Today's propagandised view of Muslims, by western powers, is an attempt to demonise them for economic and political reasons, and the picture they portray is largely an inversion of Venus' planetary energies.

Prior to Muhammad, much of the Arab world were still involved in polytheism or paganism, participating in the Arabian star family worshipping cults. The Assyrians considered Athtar/Venus to be the supreme deity who suddenly appeared around 2500 BCE. Assyria and Syria means "the land of Venus". According to Dr Rafat Amari, in his book *Islam in light of history* he suggests that Venus stole the title of Allah from the Moon, and both the Moon and the Sun became subjects to Allah, the brightest star.[5]

"If you asked them, who created the heavens and Earth and subjected the Sun and the Moon? They would surely say, Allah. Then how are they deluded?"- Sura 29:61

The Muslim scholar and historian Al Masudi 896 – 956 CE, reveals that Venus was the star of choice worshipped in Mecca, Tathrib and Yemen, which also hosts a Kaaba similar to the one found in Mecca, the Kaaba in Yemen was built specifically for the worship of Venus. Allah became a great and high star which descended every third part of the night to appear to his worshippers. In *Islam in light of history* Dr Rafat Amari cites a source from Ali Bin Burnan al-Din al-Halabi, known as the author of Halabieh:

"Allah descends to the heaven of this world when it is the last part of the night. It is clear that, by the word Allah, they meant the morning star which they saw in the third portion of each night."- *Islam in light of history*[5]

In the book *Sahih Bukhari*, the book containing the authorised hadith of the Prophet Muhammad, we find a subtle but clear indication of the morning star Venus.

"Our Lord, the Blessed, the Superior, comes every night down on the nearest heaven to us when the last third of the night remains," Volume 2, book 21, number 246, *Sahih Bukhari*, translated by M. Muhsin Khan.

The worship of Venus suddenly appears around the early time of the Assyrian Empire. Modern theories concerning the birth of Venus are in tune with the work of Immanuel Velikovsky, in his book *Worlds in collision*,[6] his hypothesis has been partially corroborated by recent scientific discoveries. It is now believed that around 2500 BCE, Venus entered our solar system, pulled in by Jupiter's immense gravitational force, propelling it towards the position and orbit it occupies today. On its journey, Venus took on all the characteristics of a huge comet, like the horns of a bull, with a distinct, bright tail trailing from both sides of its mass. As it moved towards its new position it is thought that it interacted with the Earth on 4 separate occasions, a 52 year cycle of unprecedented upheaval and catastrophe ensued affecting various parts of the Earth. During this time it has been suspected that the Earth's gravitation turned over, the Sun rose in the west and set in the east, and the North Pole flipped to become the South Pole.[7]

"Four times in this period (so they told me) the Sun rose contrary to experience; twice he came up where he now goes down, and twice went down where he now comes up; yet Egypt at these times underwent no change, either in the produce of the river and the land, or in the matter of sickness and death." Herodotus Book 2 of his histories, chapter 142.

"I mean the change in the rising and setting of the Sun and the other heavenly bodies, how in those times they used to set in the quarter where they now rise, and used to rise where they now set" Plato, *The Statesman*, p.49-53.

Due to its time as a comet, Venus has been associated with a beard or "one with hair", Venus Barbata,[8] Venus worshippers would grow their beards to symbolise the comet's tail. The Kaaba in Mecca houses a very important stone. it is a meteorite which fell to Earth, supposedly at the time of Adam, possibly from Venus as it passed by. It was set into the wall of the Kaaba by Muhammad in 605 CE. The stone was believed to have been white, the same colour as Venus when it was first discovered, but went black over time when combined with the bad energy of humans touching it.

Venus Comet

Some scholars have suggested that the crescent moon on the top of the mosque represents the comet Venus, not the Moon. However, the overall picture is clear that Venus played a major role in the lives of the people who witnessed its birth and entry into our solar system, a new God was born and thus a new religion.

Muslims pray five times a day, their first pre-dawn prayer meeting is known as the Fajr. Coincidently, this takes place when Venus appears on the horizon at Mecca in Saudi Arabia.

Venus Appears On The Horizon At Mecca During The Fajr

Venus

Buddhism and Mercury

Buddhism emerged from Hinduism. It is a nontheistic religion/philosophy. In Sanskrit the word Budha refers to the planet Mercury,[9] the planet of intellect and communication. In Buddhism it could be considered, by some, as impertinent to confuse this Budha with the Buddha or Gautama Buddha who was a Sage (someone who has attained wisdom). The word Buddha, with two d's, in this context, means "awakened one or enlightened one". Gautama Buddha was a man born into a wealthy family. His father was elected chief of the Shakya clan and expected his son to follow in his footsteps. When Gautama was 29 years old he left the comforts of the palace to pursue a journey of discovery, understanding and enlightenment. In Buddhism there is no creator and no supreme God, the only way to salvation is through your own spiritual improvement. The Buddha teaches you to question everything including the Buddha. Through Buddha's teachings (Dharma), he will show the "way or path". It is up to the individual to decide their own route to Nirvana. The Buddhist also believes in reincarnation, the cycle of birth, death and rebirth.

Mercury is the smallest and closest planet to the Sun with an 88 day orbit. The planet has virtually no atmosphere, creating an environment where the surface temperature fluctuates from −173 degrees centigrade during the night to +427 degrees during the day. Its surface is similar in appearance to our Moon having a large number of varying sized craters scattered across it.

Looking at Buddhism from an astrological perspective, we find correlations between Mercury, Wednesday and the number three throughout Buddhist traditions and practices. The number three is a common occurrence in Buddhism:

The three precious Jewels (Buddha (Teacher), Dharma (Teachings), Sangha (Community)).

- Three poisons (Ignorance, Attachment, Aversion).
- The three baskets of the Pali Canon.
- Three aspects of the eight fold path (Morality, Meditation, Wisdom).
- At the Buddhist temple, when bowing one makes three prostrations with three sticks of incense.
- When making a ceremonial procession around a temple or tomb it is done three times.

The astrological characteristics associated with Mercury, the planet known as the messenger to the Gods, are as follows:

- Communication.
- Intellect.
- Awareness.
- logic & Reasoning.
- Thinking.
- How we express our thoughts.
- To get answers on the physical and psychological level.
- Dexterous and Perceptive.

- Things happen fast with Mercury energy prompting us to move from one thing to the next.
- To express ourselves in all kinds of ways.

Buddhism is a religious philosophy. Through meditation and self-discipline one can achieve enlightenment. The whole mechanism behind this participatory philosophy fits perfectly well within the characteristics of Mercurian energy. The meditation process facilitates a communicative balance between all levels of consciousness. In peaceful stillness one can be in the space between thoughts where all possibility exists. Buddha teaches that the unawakened mind falls into the trap of the three poisons, and through the Dharma, the teachings of the Buddha, mind training can be achieved, leading one towards a righteous path, eliminating suffering which is caused by the three poisons greed, hatred and delusions.

Buddhist monks or moonks are instantly recognisable in their orange robes and shaved heads. One explanation for their appearance can be deduced from their role as Moon watchers. Like all monks they are responsible for observing the cycles of the Moon. They shave their heads to symbolise the Moon and their orange robes are thought to represents the colour of the sky during sunset, a time when the Moon slowly becomes the dominant luminary in the sky. Unlike other religions the Buddhists do not focus on an artificially created holy day of the week, instead they base their holy days on the four main phases of the Moon, full moon, new moon and half-moons, harmonising their spiritual connection to nature. Moon days in the Theravadan calendar of Thailand are called "Wan Phra – (Monk Days)", all monks are expected to stay in the temple on these holy days. "Wan Phuth" is Thai for Wednesday and "Phut" is another word sometimes used for Buddha.

Mercury and Buddhism

Mercury rules over two signs of the zodiac, Gemini and Virgo. The energetic mottos for these two signs are "I think" and "I examine", a perfect reflection of the philosophical approach of the Buddhist. Bangkok, the capitol of Thailand is at the heart of this Buddhist nation, the etymology of the name Bangkok is uncertain, although Bang is Thai for "a village situated on a stream", kok could be derived from the Hebrew word "Kokhav ", which means the planet Mercury.

Judaism and Saturn

As already mentioned Saturn has for many years been depicted as a black cube and is synonymous with the number six. Saturday is the Jewish Sabbath, the 6th day of the week, they also use the six pointed star of David to represent the Jewish faith.

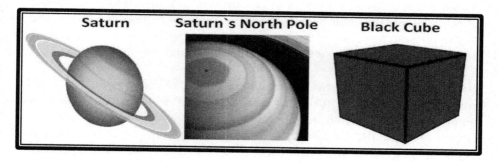

Saturn   Saturn`s North Pole   Black Cube

The orthodox story of the Jews is as follows: During the Age of Aries and Pharaonic Egypt, the tribes to the north east, between the Nile and the Euphrates were known as Canaanites. A city state system evolved around 1500 BCE in Egypt, Mesopotamia and Canaan. The story of the beginnings of the Israelites start around this time with each city state using the Canaanite people as economical slaves. A man named Moses appeared to liberate these slaves from the exploits of the Egyptians, an Exodus of 600,000 men and their families followed, leading them back to the land of Canaan, the Promised Land. They wandered through the desert for 40 years before finally settling in the hills of the West Bank, here they grew from small villages into towns and cities, conquering the old cities of Canaan, they also built a temple in Jerusalem, the First Temple, honouring their single deity, a monotheistic religion with the one God, YHWH. They called themselves Israelites, God's chosen people. Unlike other religions at the time who were worshipping many gods, the Israelites taught against polytheism.

The First Holy Temple was sacked by Pharaoh Shoshenq I, around 930 BCE, who carted away most of the treasures. It was stripped again around 700 BCE by the Sennacherib King of Assyria, but finally destroyed by the Babylonians in 586 BCE. At this point the upper classes of the Israelites, the priests, prophets and scribes were marched off to Babylon as captives. Here they organised themselves with their scrolls into writing the first five books of the Bible, known as the Torah. Without a city or a temple they wrote their Bible to keep their faith and traditions alive. Although in exile in Babylon they could still worship, pray, perform rituals and keep the Sabbath alive. When Babylon fell in 539 BCE the Israelites went back to Jerusalem to build their Second Holy Temple, which was no where near as grand as the first but allowed them to focus on their religious practices. When Alexander the Great took control around 332 BCE, the Second Temple narrowly escaped being destroyed. It wasn't until 198 BCE when Antiochus the Great came along with the Ptolemaic Army that a rebellion ensued. Antiochus wanted to Hellenise the Jews by converting them to Greek polytheism, but the rebellion was quashed. Later under Antiochus IV an official ban was placed on circumcision and the religious observance of the Sabbath, plus a statue of Zeus was erected in the Second Holy Temple. When a Greek official ordered a Jewish priest to perform a Hellenistic sacrifice on a pig, the priest killed the Greek officer and with his five sons fought off the Greeks and won their freedom.

The Romans eventually arrived and took control of the city, their military might was just too much for most cities to resist. Around 20 BC the Second Temple was renovated and extended by King Herod the Great, a stooge for the Roman Empire. Finally during the Siege of Jerusalem in 70 AD the Romans flattened the city destroying the temple and much of the Jewish culture. In 132-135 AD during the Bar Kokhba revolt against the Romans, the Jews wanted to rebuild the temple, but when the revolt failed, they were banished from the city, cast out into surrounding villages and towns. In the 7th century during the expansion of the Muslim faith a shrine was built on the site of the Jewish temple. This became known as the Dome of the Rock, and has stood in the same place since 691 AD. The Al Aqsa Mosque now stands in the temple courtyard. After WW1 the Zionists were given land in Palestine, the Promised Land. Many Jews settled their before, during and after WW2, with a huge number perishing throughout this turbulent period. After WW2, with overwhelming sympathy for the deaths of six million Jews, a recommendation was put forward by the United Nations to form the legitimate "State of Israel". On 14th May 1948 this came into effect, but it came under criticism because some felt that the borders of this new state were not clearly defined in the declaration.[10][11][12]

In 1967 a war broke out. The Temple Mount and old city of Jerusalem was captured from Jordan by the Israelis, this became known as the "Six Day War". In 1980 Israel unified East Jerusalem and the Temple Mount with the rest of the city, against opposition from the United Nations Security Council. The Zionist Jews had a brave ambition to unite all the Jews together within the Promised Land, an area put aside for God's chosen people, from the Nile to the Euphrates. The flag of Israel reflects that ambition. The Star of David, the six pointed star of Saturn is between two blue lines, representing the Nile and the Euphrates.

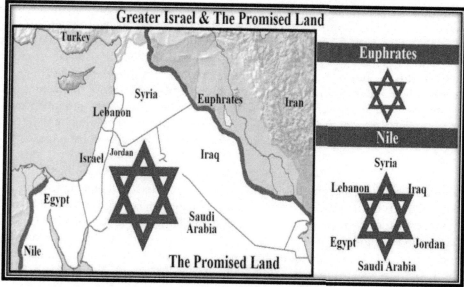

From an astrological perspective more light can be shone on this story, in order to understand its significance. The first five books of the Old Testament, Genesis through to Deuteronomy, the Judaic Torah, are purported to have been written by Moses. It is their version of human history, which according to their timeline began in the Age of Taurus, hence the name Torah. The legend mentions 600,000 men escaping slavery in Egypt under the leadership of a man named Moses, this Exodus happened in the time of Aries ruled by Mars (Marses), a time of hope and liberation, a new beginning with a new set of rules, laws which Moses brought down from Mt Sinai as Ten Commandments from God.

"And the glory of the Lord abode upon Mt Sinai, and the clouds covered it for six days" Exodus X 24:16

They wandered throughout the desert for 40 years before settling in the hills of the Promised Land. The energy of the planet Mars, is a proactive, physical energy, one of movement, motivation and physical doing. They couldn't have chosen a better character to lead them to freedom. Israel has many archaeologists working to find evidence to support the ancient biblical events found in the Torah, events which would legitimise their claim to the Promised Land and a Greater Israel. Unfortunately, the physical evidence uncovered to date does not support the entire biblical hypothesis. The findings lead towards a slow decline in the city state system around the time the Exodus was supposed to have happened. As conditions deteriorated in Egypt, Canaan and Mesopotamia, many of the lower classes, the serfs, slaves and common Canaanites moved out. They took the opportunity to move into the hills to form small communities; these communities grew and united together under common goals and values, creating the early Israelites. Contrary to what the Torah suggests, they were the result of a collapse in the Canaanite city state structure not the cause of it. With a desire to break away from their suppressed lives, under the old polytheistic city states and elitist rule, they had the opportunity to create a fresh, new ideology, cementing it under the worship of one God; the Bible called them "a mixed multitude". A new version of history was put together, painting a romantic view of a people's struggle and liberation under the guidance and helping hand of God, a chosen people selected for a chosen purpose and promised a chosen piece of land.

During these early years many people were still polytheistic, unwilling to give up the traditions of the past. As each generation emerged, coerced by their leaders, a slow transition took place to create the Jewish faith we see today, a faith which has singled out the energy of Saturn as their primary focus. The combination of energetic frequencies emanating from Saturn are unique. Submerging oneself in these energies will result in a specific character trait. The energies and characteristics of Saturn are:

- Order, structure and control.
- Commands us to get to work and work hard.
- Discipline and responsibility.
- Limitations, frustrations, loss and restrictions.
- Organising one's time.
- Governs time from birth to death.
- Sense of tradition and conventionality.
- Perseverance and withstanding the test of time.
- Senior status brings authority.
- Pessimism and depression.
- The past.

It takes 29 years for Saturn to perform one full orbit around the Sun and return back to one's natal chart position; this may be the reason why, in Jewish tradition, one could not enter into public ministry until the age of 30. Saturn is the 6th planet from the Sun and the 2nd largest after Jupiter, a gaseous giant, 9 times bigger than the Earth, comprising mainly of hydrogen and helium. Together Jupiter and Saturn account for 92% of the total planetary mass in our solar system. When one looks closely at the lives and habits of practising Jews, it is possible to identify many of Saturn's energetic characteristics, some being of an admirable quality. Maybe the reason why we see a disproportionate number of Jews in positions of importance and authority is because they align themselves with the characteristics and qualities of this planet, they are the people of Saturn. Being without a homeland for most of their existence the Jews have had a sense of insecurity forcing them to organise themselves well, to work hard and be responsibly disciplined while helping to keep their faith and traditions together. This has brought restrictions and limitations to many areas of their everyday lives, their kosher food preparations and consumption requirements can be frustrating and restrictive unless you are habitually accustomed to them. They have a huge sense of tradition and must be applauded for preserving their heritage which has withstood the test of time. They have great respect for their elders and are conventional within the boundaries of time. These are all Saturn's characteristics. A culture aligned with this energetic frequency will inevitably reflect this in their reality. The number six is very important to the Jews, being the number associated with Saturn, it is found in many of their myths, writings and history.

- Sabbath (Saturn's day).
- Saturn is represented as a six pointed star or a hexagon.
- Six Day War in the 1960s.
- Exodus 600,000 men.
- ISRAEL has 6 letters.
- There are 6 Jewish fasting days per year.
- Noah was 600 years old when the flood of the waters fell onto the Earth.
- Six million Jews died in the Holocaust.
- Siege of Jerusalem (1099), 60,000 people were massacred, 6,000 Jews.
- Exodus V 14:7 "And he took 600 chosen chariots".
- Exodus VI 16:5 "And it shall come to pass on the 6th day, that thy shall prepare that which thy bring in".
- Exodus VII 20:8 "6 days shall thy labour and do all thy work".
- Exodus VIII 21:2 "If thy buy a Hebrew servant, 6 years he shall serve".
- Exodus IX 23:10 "& 6 years thou shalt sow thy land and gather in the increase thereof".
- Exodus X 24:16 "& the glory of the Lord abode upon Mt Sinai, and the cloud covered it 6 days".

- Exodus XI 26:9 "And thou shalt couple fine curtains by themselves and 6 curtains by themselves and shall double over the 6th curtain in the forefront of the tent".

Some people have speculated that the war in the Middle East, essentially comes from the desire of the powerful Zionist factions inside the Israeli government, to expand their borders to the biblical boundaries of the Promised Land, and that ISIS is a private mercenary army helping to facilitate this outcome. The name ISRAEL is a construct of ISIS, RA and EL, the Jewish triad of consciousness.

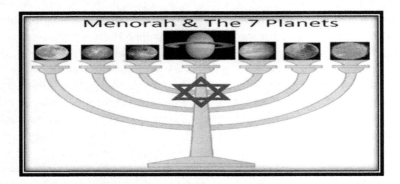

The Jewish triad consists of Saturn, Sun and Moon worship. The Moon was favoured and worshipped by ancient Hebrews, Arabs and many other cultures in our distant past. The Mesopotamians named their Moon God "Sin or Nanna". This is where the name for Mount Sinai originated, it is Moon worship. The Jews who pray three times a day call their place of worship a SINagog (Synagogue), AGOG means (eagerly, expectantly or merry mood). The interesting thing here is the Christian use of negative terminology to undermine Orthodox Saturn and Moon worship. Saturn has become Satan, Nanna or Sin is the opposite of good and the El of EVE, the evening or night time is considered as evil.

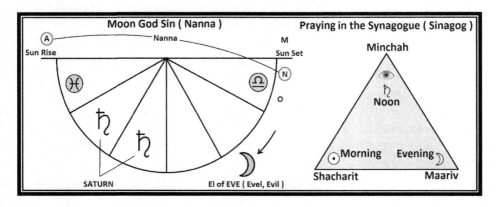

27

Black has, for a very long time, been used to symbolize the planet Saturn along with the shape of a cube. In traditional Judaism the practice of wearing the tefillin is observed during weekday morning prayers. Two black leather cubes containing scrolls from the Torah are joined by leather straps, one cube is placed over the third eye and the other is placed on the subordinate arm with the straps wrapped around the arm like Saturnian rings, they go all the way down to the left hand and around the Saturn finger. This whole practice is a physical symbolic ceremony aligning oneself with the energetic frequencies of the planet Saturn along with all its characteristics. It is also a common practice for Jewish worshippers to rock (rocks and stones are ruled by Saturn) backwards and forwards, at the western wall in Jerusalem. The wall is made from stone, the domain of Saturn, rocking is a pseudo sexual act, thrusting the base chakra forward, this is also Saturnian in nature. The worshippers also write notes which are placed within the cracks of the western wall's stone structure, these are prayer offerings of intent to Saturn's energetic consciousness. The wall faces west, opposite to what most religions practice, preferring the energies associated with the Sun rising in the east. The west is where the Sun sets, and gives way to the underworld, ruled by Saturn.

Jewish Tefillin

From their initial foundations most of these monotheistic religions developed creating many offshoots, and splinter groups, perverting and deviating from the underlining philosophy and ideology which the original root religion adhered to. Just as a tree grows branches further and further away from the roots, some of these religious offshoots became unrecognisable to their parent foundation religion.

Jupiter is king of the planets but its domain has greater scope within the spiritual realm as opposed to Saturn which rules the physical, material world; this is why the Jews, Saturn worshippers, had to be the ones who initiated the end of the physical Ju-zeus. This is part of the ongoing battle between the two opposing energies.

It is important to point out the houses associated with both Jupiter and Saturn, when trying to piece together the astrological forces at play concerning the modern world. Jupiter rules both Pisces and Sagittarius, the signs of (I believe) and (I Seek), the 9th house of travel, higher learning, religion and philosophy; and the 12th house of karma and the subconscious. Saturn on the other hand rules Capricorn (I use) and Aquarius (I know), the 10th house of career and the 11th house of groups/friends. This is important when trying to understand the differences between Jupitarian Christianity and Saturnian Judaism. Saturn is also considered to be Old Father Time and the Teacher, and as the 10th house is the house of career, it is no surprise to discover, although Jews are only 2-3% of the American population, they make up almost half of the country's billionaires.[13]

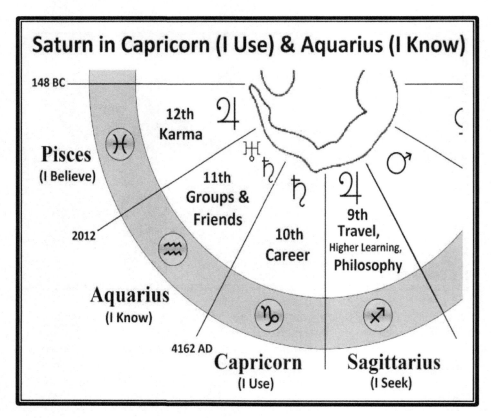

Saturn in Capricorn (I Use) & Aquarius (I Know)

148 BC

12th
Karma

Pisces
(I Believe)

11th
Groups &
Friends

2012

9th
Travel,
Higher Learning,
Philosophy

10th
Career

Aquarius
(I Know)

4162 AD

Capricorn
(I Use)

Sagittarius
(I Seek)

Christianity has generally been associated with seeking philosophical answers, higher learning, belief and spiritual wisdom, while Judaism has been associated with Capricorn's (I use) usury, career, business and hard work. Judaism is also synonymous with the 11th house of groups and friends, i.e. (friends of Israel).

As we move further away from the Age of Pisces, materialism will take over from the crescent of spirituality, leaving the cross of the physical realm to take precedence. Saturn will take over from Jupiter, and we will no doubt see the Messiah of the Old Age being replaced by a new one; an individual who represents all the characteristics of the new Aquarian Age of the water bearer. It will eventually become clear that Jesus, the personification of Jupiter/Zeus will only be with us till the end of the Piscean Age.

"Therefore go and make disciples of all nations, baptizing them in the name of the Father and of the Son and of the Holy Spirit, and teaching them to obey everything I have commanded you. And surely I am with you always, to the very end of the Age." - Matthew 28 : 19-20 (NIV)

Usury

Saturn (materialism over spirituality) is the planet associated with order, control, restriction, limitation and austerity. Ruling Capricorn, a sign who's energetic characteristics are reflected in its motto 'I use'. The tenth house of career is part of one's social identity, concerned with how we appear in the eyes of the community.

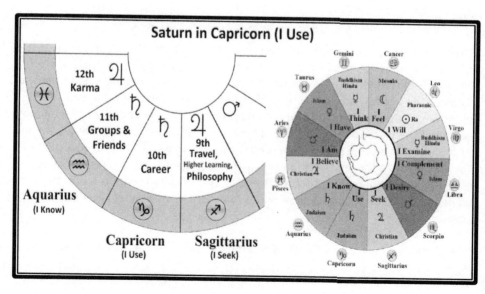

Baphomet the goat of Capricorn

Baphomet, the goat of Capricorn is depicted in the Tarot's Devil card. It holds its right hand skywards, towards the heavens and the spiritual realm, while the left hand points down towards the more earthly material realm. The Devil card represents the zodiac house of Capricorn, especially the aspect of "I use". The card shows two people shackled at the feet of Baphomet as he controls them utilising the energies associated with the planet Saturn.

Money

The word money is derived from the silver Moon, it is essentially mooney. Throughout most of history gold and silver has been used as a method of storing wealth. Their scarcity and resistance to corrosion made them ideal as a means of transferring wealth. And because gold was rare, common low value coins were made from silver, giving rise to the name mooney. Our recent concept of money evolved from an amount or weight of high grade silver. The word sterling means 92.5% pure silver, and a pound sterling is a pound in weight of that silver purity. The same is true for the Dollar and many other names used as a reference to currency, it is all derived from the silver moon and sin. The Moon is also the planet associated with the subconscious, which, in astrology, represents our emotional needs.

"For the love of money is a root of all kinds of evil." - 1 Timothy 6:10 (NIV)

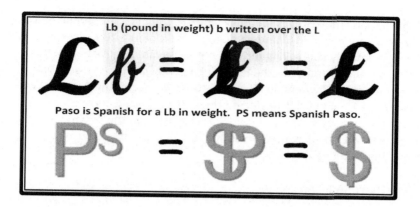

Lb (pound in weight) b written over the L

$$\mathcal{L}b = \pounds = \pounds$$

Paso is Spanish for a Lb in weight. PS means Spanish Paso.

$$PS = \$ = \$$$

Most people believe the evolution of the control system has their best interests at heart. They consider the monetary system to be a carefully oiled machine, which is designed to benefit the majority. When a nation borrows itself into debt, no matter how hard its citizen's work, it can only sink further into debt. Each generation finds itself paying more tax for fewer services because of its inherent obligation to pay off the compounding interest on huge government borrowing. Disguised through inflation the debt can never be repaid as only the principle is sent into circulation. Eventually, when there is not enough money, due to inflation/deflation manipulation, bankruptcies ensue, transferring tangible assets into the hands of the international financiers connected to the Ponzi scheme. History is full of examples of the dangers inherent in usury, where money changers and goldsmiths were regularly thrown out for exploiting their host nations. The Romans eventually allowed usury with careful restrictions, while Christianity was opposed to it for quite some time, this all changed in England under Henry VIII, with his 1545 Act, allowing usury of up to 10%, meanwhile Muslims have always been against usury. The modern banking system can be linked to the creation of the Bank Of England in 1694, a private central bank which was set up to stabilise pricing and lend money to the government. With a panel of shareholders the BOE would lend money on interest for empire building, while making the shareholders richer, the citizens were not only asked to fight in numerous conquests but also required to pay the tax burden for the privilege. The partnership between the City of London's financiers and the government, allowed the British Empire to eventually influence 1/3 of the globe, becoming the benchmark for other competing empires, all financed by a handful of banksters. This process turned the world's empires into tools for the objectives of the global financiers. Wars and invasions were encouraged to line the pockets of the shareholders and to export influence. Like all loans, conditions would be attached making the financiers masters over the borrower, in this case it was the governments of each nation. Incidentally, the City Of London is a private corporation owned primarily by large financiers, outside the normal controls of the host nation. The Rothschild family who are the most influential banking family in history began in a modest building in Frankfurt during the mid-17th century, eventually controlling most, if not all private central banks. In 1946, after the Second World War, the Bank of England was nationalised, with all stock brought into public ownership. This only took place after the Bretton-Woods agreement of 1944 which transferred the baton of world currency and financial global dominance over to the United States Dollar and the private Federal Reserve, a private bank which was set up in 1913, and owned by the international banking cartel.

The New Age of Aquarius.

Every 2160 years the great astrological clock moves from one Age into another. Eventually moving through all twelve signs of the zodiac, in an anticlockwise precession, over 25,920 years, this is known as a Great Year. As we move through this latest transition from Pisces into Aquarius, cosmic changes are taking place. It is a natural and inevitable cycle for the universe and humanity. New electromagnetic frequencies will stimulate our consciousness, and therefore our perception of reality, as we move steadily into this new epoch of "knowing". Many people at this moment feel the world around them is changing, but are confused as to what is really behind the changes. Frustrated by the system they have been living under and supporting throughout their lives, people are feeling the strain under the pressure of these new changes. Humanity is awakening from a naive daze of Piscean belief which it has been living under for thousands of years. People all over the world are beginning to see things in a different light, undermining what they previously believed to be real. Many have become suspicious of the control system and sense a greater force behind global events and Earth changes, they don't know what it is but they feel it.

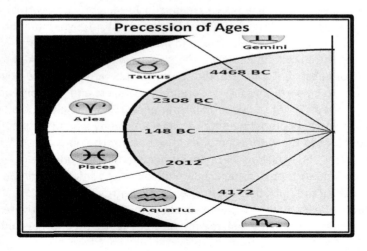

Egyptian Bull and Ram Gods during Taurus and Aries

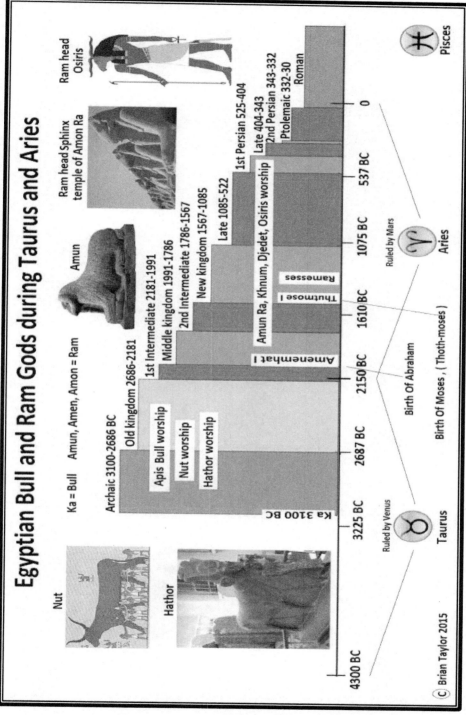

Ka = Bull   Amun, Amen, Amon = Ram

Nut

Hathor

Ram head Osiris

Ram head Sphinx temple of Amon Ra

Amun

Archaic 3100-2686 BC

Old kingdom 2686-2181

Apis Bull worship

Nut worship

Hathor worship

1st Intermediate 2181-1991

Middle kingdom 1991-1786

2nd Intermediate 1786-1567

New kingdom 1567-1085

Late 1085-522

1st Persian 525-404

Late 404-343

2nd Persian 343-332

Ptolemaic 332-30

Roman

Amun Ra, Khnum, Djedet, Osiris worship

Ramesses

Thutmose I

Amenemhat I

Ka 3100 BC   3225 BC   2687 BC   2150 BC   1610 BC   1075 BC   537 BC   0

Ruled by Venus

Taurus

Ruled by Mars

Aries

Pisces

Birth Of Abraham

Birth Of Moses , (Thoth-moses)

© Brian Taylor 2015

34

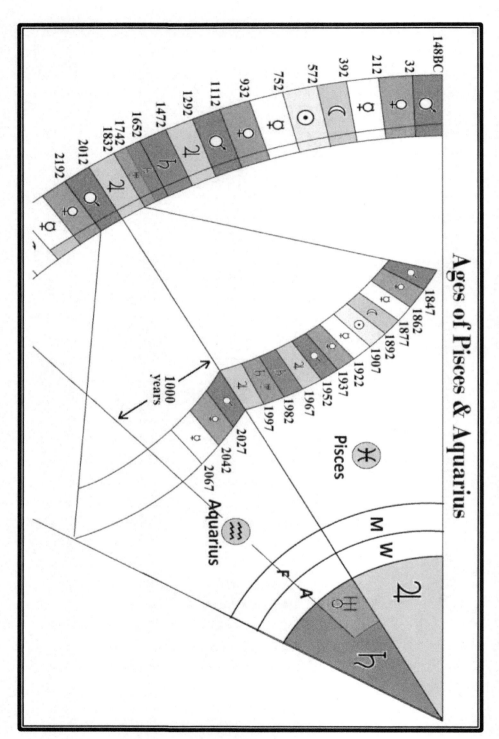

Ages of Pisces & Aquarius

35

This transition into Aquarius, from a metaphysical perspective, is basically turning our whole concept of perceived reality upside down. The Piscean Jupitarian crescent of spirituality over the cross of materialism is making way for Saturn's materialism over spirituality. It is essentially a 180 degree paradigm shift in human consciousness.

"Everything is backwards, everything is upside down. Doctors destroy health, lawyers destroy justice, psychiatrists destroy minds, scientists destroy truth, major media destroys information, religions destroy spirituality and governments destroy freedom." — Michael Ellner.

The New Age of Aquarius is the Age of "Knowing", traditional astrologers considered the whole age, all 2160 years, to belong to Saturn, but recent astrologers, since the rediscovery of Uranus, have placed the daddy of Saturn as the ruler for the first half or 1000 years of this new epoch. This makes for a very interesting contrast of planetary energies influencing humanity. While the controlling elite, predominantly aligned with Saturn, are expanding their restrictive Saturnian control grid; Uranus, the planet of rebellion, revolution and unpredictability will be pouring out cosmic frequencies over human consciousness. Energetic vibrations of freedom, new technology and a need to break with tradition will certainly promote interesting times.

The Saturnine control system, which comprises of anyone who has a vested interest in Saturn and those aligned with Saturn's energies, include:

- People with strong natural Saturnian karmic dispositions.
- Practising traditional Judaism.
- Saturn worshipping cults, and Satanists
- Organisations of control.
- Corporations or rigid organised institutions.
- Traditional structures of control within the establishment.

All these players will work together, using all the latest technology, tightening the straps on humanity's straight jacket, preventing any outbreak of Uranus energy from threatening the stranglehold of the globalisation (Saturnisation) project.

Uranus shares its rulership with Saturn, for the first 1000 years of this Aquarian Age, the planet of out of the blue events, technology and rebellious revolutions. This should create a great deal of spontaneous rebellion towards a saturnian control system imposing its will and authority. With Uranus being associated with uranium and new technology, along with out of the blue events, we may, sometime in the future, come up against problems regarding uranium and nuclear weapons. After 1000 years of joint rulership, Saturn will dominate in full, pushing Uranus out of the picture for a very long time.

"When the thousand years are over, Satan will be released from his prison" - Revelations 20:7

With Satan's disposition in tune with the energetic characteristics of the planet Saturn. A great deal of wisdom can be deduced by looking at ancient descriptions and accounts associated with Saturn's various personified characters. Bearing in mind that Saturn is the planet of pessimism, loss, order, control, restriction, austerity, hard work and anything relating to the past.

The Devil was known as "DIABOLOS" in ancient Greek, a name derived from two words divide and abolish. With a mind set and disposition in tune with Saturn's pessimistic obsession with the past one can see how an individual can create a very bleak future for themselves. Satan is the accuser, divisive acquisitions which abolish the individual's ability to live in the now forgoing abundance and the good fortunes associated with the energies of Jupiter and the teachings of Jesus Christ.

"But I am afraid that just as Eve was deceived by the serpent's cunning, your minds may somehow be led astray from your sincere and pure devotion to Christ." 2 Corinthians 11:3

"Get behind me, Satan! You are a hindrance to me. For you are not setting your mind on the things of God, but on the things of man." Matthew 16:23

"We know that we are children of God, and that the whole world is under the control of the evil one." 1 John 5:19

A Saturnian disposition of self-doubt and self-accusation can suck an individual down into a bottomless spiral of unresolved depression, trapped by spontaneous reflections of past events, blame and division. This is hell, burning inside under Saturn's suffocating energy of self-inflicted accusations which lack Jupiterian optimism, taking all those who succumb down the left hand path and into the abyss.

Eve was seduced by the serpent in the garden, to set a seed of doubt in her mind, a mental process pulling her away from jovial harmony of living in the now, like children they were innocent until Diabolos came along. Serpents are nocturnal feeders and have throughout the ages been used to symbolise the night, the evil evening and our spiritual subconscious.

The globalisation project is controlled and organised by those who are well aligned with Saturn's energetic characteristics. This will only grow, spreading Saturnian traits throughout this brave new world of the Aquarian Age. Diabolos, divide and abolish will manifest throughout society, in various forms. While the control system offers us, in their right hand, the fruits from the tree of knowledge, using their left hand, they will utilise all the latest technology to ring fence and restrict most people's freedoms into a narrow band of politically correct possibilities. We will be controlled from cradle to grave, with digital devices storing our every waking moment within a technological control grid.

Notes for chapter 1

(1) B R Taylor, Language of the Gods, Chapter 15, page 334, Createspace publishing, 2016, ISBN-10: 1533157685, https://www.amazon.com/Language-Gods-B-R-Taylor/dp/1533157685

(2) Solomon Schechter, Ludwig Blau, Emil G. Hirsch, GABRIEL (נבריאל Γαβριήλ, "man of God"), http://jewishencyclopedia.com/articles/6450-gabriel

(3) Dev Kaushik, Shrivinayaka Astrology, Saturn is planet of scarcity and disputes. http://www.shrivinayakaastrology.com/Planets/saturnplanetofscarcity.html

(4) Lianna Brinded, Christians are more likely to be fat than atheists, December 2014, International Business Times, http://www.ibtimes.co.uk/christians-are-more-likely-be-fat-atheists-1480732

(5) Dr Rafat Amari, Islam in the light of history, 2004, Religion research institute, http://www.amazon.com/Islam-Light-History-Rafat-Amari/dp/0976502402 & http://www.brotherpete.com/index.php?PHPSESSID=f05b251c1a590b48e0f7d5a2b6d54fab&topic=1240.msg4776#msg4776

(6) Immanual Velikovsky, Worlds in Collision, 1950, http://www.truthseekersministries.org/files/Velikovsky-Worlds-in-Collision.pdf

(7) Kenneth J Dillon, Venus, the Ancient Near East, and Islam, Scientia press, http://www.scientiapress.com/venus-the-ancient-near-east-and-islam

(8) Venus Barbata, Wikipedia, https://en.wikipedia.org/wiki/Venus_Barbata

(9) Budha, Wikipedia, https://en.wikipedia.org/wiki/Budha

(10) Edwin Black, The Transfer agreement, Tradeselect LTD 2009, https://books.google.co.th/books?id=QjVxPwAACAAJ&dq=transfer+agreement&hl=en&sa=X&ved=0ahUKEwin_uiuuKPJAhUMk5QKHWBbByYQ6AEIGjAA

(11) Harris, J. (1998), The Israeli Declaration of Independence, The Journal of the Society for Textual Reasoning, Vol. 7.

(12) Declaration of Establishment of State of Israel, Israel Ministry of Foreign Affairs. http://www.mfa.gov.il/mfa/foreignpolicy/peace/guide/pages/declaration%20of%20establishment%20of%20state%20of%20israel.aspx

(13) Mark Weber, Zionist Report, Powerful Speech! "The Challenge of Jewish-Zionist Power", youtube, https://www.youtube.com/watch?v=9hqnV_4JlCQ&t=453s

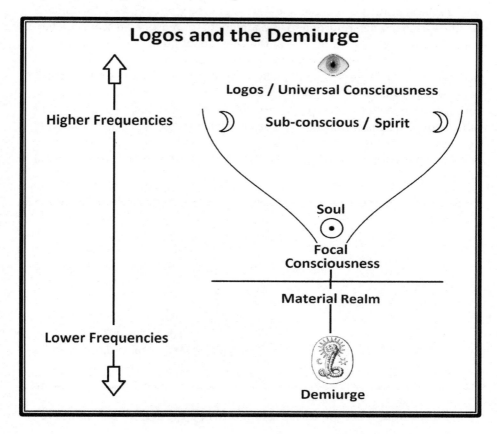

The Logos

"In the beginning was the Word (Logos), and the Word (Logos) was with God, and the Word (Logos) was God." - John 1 : 1 (NIV)

From a metaphysical/astrological perspective the Logos can be viewed as universal consciousness, whereas the physical realm including the planets within our solar system are various expressions of that consciousness. Although the physical material realm has limitations, within the fabric of time and space, the spiritual realm and the Logos do not, they are timeless and limitless, regarded as an endless sea of profound possibility.

Logos comes from the Greek word λόγος which can be translated as word, reason, speech, opinion and discourse. The Greek philosopher Heraclitus (535 - 475BC) used the term Logos to mean order and knowledge. He saw it as the logic behind an argument or persuasive rhetoric. Greek Sophists, who were philosophical orators and public speakers, used the word to mean discourse. Aristotle used it when referring to 'the argument' or reasoned discourse. The common theme regarding the use of the word Logos points to it being used to express higher levels of conscious awareness, even God like with infinite potential of knowledge and wisdom. Stoic philosophers in Athens during the 3rd century BC linked the term Logos to a Divine animating principle which spread throughout the whole universe. In Christianity the Logos is also used as a name or title for Jesus Christ, which makes sense from a metaphysical perspective because Jesus or Jupiter Zeus represents the crescent of spirituality over the cross of materialism. Coincidently, Jupiter has a higher resonant frequency than Saturn.[1]

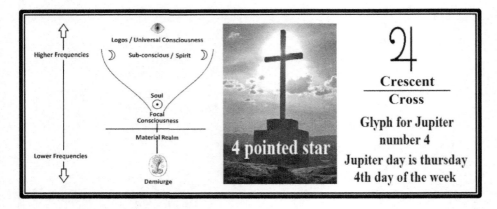

"Jesus answered, "I am the way and the truth and the life. No one comes to the Father except through me."" - John 14 : 6 (NIV)

Aristotle divided any form of rhetoric into three basic components. In his day astrology and metaphysics played a major role as the benchmark for understanding their conscious relationship to the universe together with their view of the triad of consciousness. He described all forms of rhetoric as having the Logos (logical reason), the ethos (character) and the pathos (emotion).

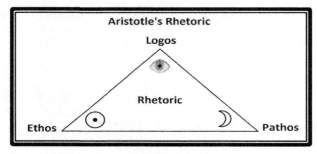

"Philo (c. 20 BC – c. 50 AD), a Hellenized Jew, used the term Logos to mean an intermediary divine being or demiurge. Philo followed the Platonic distinction between imperfect matter and perfect Form, and therefore intermediary beings were necessary to bridge the enormous gap between God and the material world. The Logos was the highest of these intermediary beings, and was called by Philo "the first-born of God". Philo also wrote that "the Logos of the living God is the bond of everything, holding all things together and binding all the parts, and prevents them from being dissolved and separated" - Philo of Alexandria, Hellenistic Judaism[2]

In Sunni Islam the Logos was viewed as 'the intellect', 'the universal man', 'the word of God' and 'the Mahammadan light'.[2] In Islamic mysticism, known as Sufism, both Jesus and Mohammed are seen as the personification of the Logos.

From an astrological perspective, the Logos consciousness interacts with both our physical biology, through the soul, and our subconscious through the spirit. Consequently, the planets within the solar system, express various aspects of that Logos energy through their own triad of consciousness, influencing us on multiple levels as they move majestically throughout their orbits, interacting with one another while transiting the Earth.

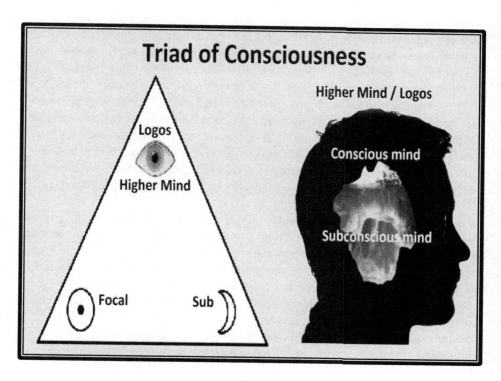

Demiurge

A lion-faced serpent found on a Gnostic gem in Bernard de Montfaucon's 1922, *L'antiquité expliquée et représentée en figures* may be the Demiurge.

When analysing the lion faced serpent picture of the Demiurge, it holds many esoteric secrets. The lion in front of the Sun could represent the focal consciousness or soul, placed on top of a serpent's body. As nocturnal feeders serpents have for thousands of years been used to represent the spiritual aspect of consciousness. So here we have the Soul taking precedence over the spirit, an inversion of the human relationship with the Logos or the Christ, where the spirit has priority over the material realm and the soul. Another way to view it would be to say the smaller material mind, of focal awareness, takes precedence over the larger emotional and spiritual subconscious, limiting interaction with Divine potential. On the serpent's left hand side we see a six pointed star, which could represent the planet Saturn. On the right side is the symbol for the Moon (Sin).

In many schools of philosophy the Demiurge is viewed as a craftsman or artisan like character, responsible for fashioning and maintaining the physical/material universe. The Demiurge is seen as a separate entity from the Logos or the creator. In many Gnostic traditions the material universe is considered as evil, overseen by a malevolent Demiurge, whereas the non-material or spiritual world is considered as good. The Demiurge is thought to act as a channel for the Logos consciousness as a mechanism to devolve pure spirit into matter, the consequence of which is thought to manifest imperfections as the Logos consciousness interacts with the human collective, both on a focal and subconscious level.

Marcionism, which was an early form of Christianity, believed that the God of the Old Testament was a tyrant or a demiurge, a lower entity than the God of the New Testament. Consequently, they rejected the Old Testament all together.

"According to the Gnostics, the Demiurge was able to endow man only with psyche, sensuous soul; only the True God could add the pneuma, or the rational soul. This is the "feminine aspect of the Spirit" – the Greek term pneuma, often associated with the Holy Spirit of the New Testament. The Gnostics identified the Demiurge with the Jehovah of the Hebrews. In philosophy, the term is used to denote a Divine Being that is the builder of the universe rather than its creator." - Columbia Encyclopedia, Sixth Edition

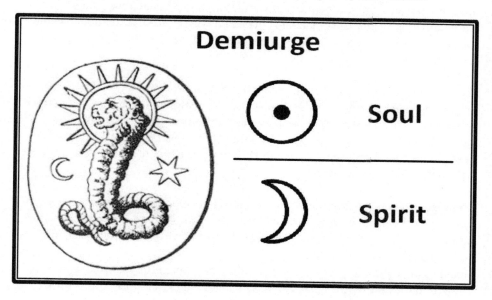

In Psalms 82 : 1, in the (NET) Bible, it talks about God meeting with an assembly of other Gods.

"God stands in the assembly of El; in the midst of the gods he renders judgment." - Psalms 82 : 1 (NET)

El is the Hebrew name for the God of Israel (The theological position of the Tanakh is that the names Ēl and 'Ĕlōhîm, when used in the singular to mean the supreme god, refer to Yahweh, beside whom other gods are supposed to be either non-existent or insignificant).[3] In Psalms 82 it suggests that God stands in the assembly of the God of Israel. Could this mean that the Logos has an assembly with the Demiurge in the midst of other Gods? And could those Gods be aspects of planetary consciousness within our own solar system?

The above picture of the Demiurge stands between the Moon and a six pointed star, often representing the planet Saturn. Is it the case that the influence of the Demiurge is felt most strongly through some form of connection with the energetic characteristics of Saturn and the Moon, both planets which play leading roles in the religion of Judaism?

Nag Hammadi codices

At the end of World War II, in 1945, thirteen ancient Gnostic books, thought to be from the 3rd or 4th century AD, were discovered, in caves, near the city of Nag Hammadi, in Upper Egypt. The leather bound papyrus books, found by local farmers, became one of the most important archaeological finds concerning early Christianity and Gnostic beliefs ever to be discovered. Also known as the Gnostic Gospel, the books include : *The Gospel of Thomas, The Secret Book (Apocryphon) of John* and *The Gospel of Truth.*

Early Gnosticism morphed out of ancient Judaism, with Jewish Gnosticism beginning years before Christian Gnosticism. Gnostics believed that the material realm was evil, ruled by a Demiurge, while the spiritual realm was all good, ruled by a Divine cosmic consciousness. The important aspect of the Nag Hammadi texts is the creation of man story, which was altered by Christianity to fit their new post Gnostic perspective.

The texts explain the creation story as follows : Life originated from the core of our galaxy, a central core of pure light, which was the home of Divine spiritual consciousness, 26,500 light years away from the Earth. A number which also resembles the Great Year of astrological precession of the equinoxes. The Gnostics believed the galactic centre, which they called the Pleroma, was alive. They thought that matter, like stars and planets, did not exist in the central core. A core inhabited by pure spiritual beings, like torrents of energy, which they called Aeons (Gnostic word for Gods). They saw it as a balanced core of both male and female Aeons, whirling around like serpents in an ocean of conscious light, similar to the yin and yang symbolic expression of balanced dualistic-monism. From this central core the galaxy spiralled outwards forming four galactic arms of progressively denser matter. Our Solar System is situated 26,500 light years out on the 3rd galactic arm. These galactic limbs provide almost infinite opportunity for galactic consciousness to express itself, in a variety of material forms. When the Aeons within the Pleroma had a thought, which they wanted to manifest into matter, they would send out an extension of plasmatic light, outward from the centre, to a suitable place along one of many galactic arms.

"And God said, "Let there be light," and there was light." - Genesis 1:1 (NIV)

The Gnostics concluded that thoughts from the core which manifested along the galactic arms were left to their own devices, to evolve like a divine cosmic experiment, without the day to day control of the Aeons. The Gospel of Philip says the world was created as a mistake or anomaly.

"The world came about through a mistake. For he who created it wanted to create it imperishable and immortal. He fell short of attaining his desire." - Gospel of Philip, the Nag Hammadi Library.[4]

The fall of Sophia

The Gnostic creation story suggests that the Earth came into existence through the independent actions of the Aeon Sophia, a name which means wisdom in Greek. It suggests she wanted to manifest an expression of herself without the approval or consent of her male counterpart the father God.

"It happened that Sophia began to think for herself, She wanted to reveal an image from herself. She did this without the consent, approval, thoughtful assistance or knowledge of her masculine counterpart. Because she had unconquerable power her thought was not unproductive. So she brought it into being. Something imperfect came out of her, different in appearance from her, a misshapen being unlike herself. When Sophia saw what her desire had produced, it changed into a dragon with a lion's head, and its eyes flashed bolts of lightning. Disturbed by this she cast him outside of the realm of the immortal beings so they could not see what she had created." - Paraphrased from The Secret Book of John[5]

Sophia named him Yaldabaoth, and he became the chief ruler with great power, inherited from his mother. Believing he was the only true God of the material realm, he moved away and created other realms with subservient Archons for company. He was described as an artificial non-organic life form with machine like qualities.

"He is blasphemous through his thoughtlessness. He said "I am God, and there is no God but me!" - "He made the first seven rulers to reign in the seven spheres of heaven." - Secret Book of John[5]

Yaldabaoth and the Demiurge appear to be the same being. In some ancient texts Yaldaboth is also linked in with Satan, Chronos or the planet Saturn.[6][7] This all begins to tie together when you consider that Saturn is the planet associated with the cross of materialism over the crescent of spirituality. It is the furthest planet to the naked eye from the Sun. So if the Demiurge was cast out, by Sophia, far from the Earth and the spiritual purity of her intended creation, this would be the logical place to go, manifesting his perverted consciousness out in the dark regions of our solar system. Many scholars and theologians speculate that the God of the Old Testament is indeed the non organic Demiurge, while the God of the New Testament is the spiritual Father at the centre of the Pleroma.

The Gnostics believed that Sophia's consciousness came from the Pleroma to manifest out here in the material realm. Fascinated with the human genome and the development of our species she left the galactic core and took on a physical form to become the living Earth or Gaia, this is known as the 'fall of Sophia'. Saturn or Chronos, on the other hand, known as Old Father Time, the slowest moving planet in ancient astrology, could be the home of the Demiurge, a non-biological entity with elements of galactic power given to it by its mother Sophia.

"When Sophia realized that her miscarriage was so imperfect, she repented and wept. The divinity within the pleroma heard her prayer and poured the Holy Spirit over her, brought forth from the whole full realm. She was elevated above her son, but she was not restored to her own original realm. She would remain in the ninth sphere until she was fully restored." - Secret book of John[5]

The Demiurge or Lord of the material realm continued to create new Archons together with other non organic realms. This could possibly included the other planets within our solar system.

"But Yaldabaoth had a multitude of faces, more than all of them. He shared his fire with them; therefore he became lord over them. Because of the power of the glory he possessed of his mother's light, he called himself God. And he did

not obey the place from which he came. And he united the seven powers in his thought with the authorities which were with him." - The Gnostic God Yaldabaoth[7]

When he gazed upon his creation surrounding him He said to his host of demons. The ones who had come forth out of him: "I am a jealous God and there is no God but me!". - Secret book of John[5]

It could well be the case that the God of the Old Testament is indeed the Demiurge. Early Gnostic Christians regarded Jesus as the Masculine twin or counterpart to Sophia the Divine feminine. Consequently, Jesus came from the galactic centre to resolve the imbalance of Divine energy, bringing forth the spirit in order to balance this realm towards dualistic monism with Logos consciousness.

Marcionism, an early form of Christianity believed that Jesus was our saviour, sent by the true God and that the wrathful God of the Hebrew Bible was a separate God, a lower entity of low vibrations.[8]

"He is called Yaldabaoth, which means "child, pass through to here" or the name Samael, the Blind god or "the God of the Blind. This type of "blindness" corresponds with the Spiritual Mysteries hidden within each of us. This Godform was the arrogant creator-god of the Old Testament. In his arrogance, he spoke of no other Gods – due to His ignorance, He does not even recognise his own Mother Sophia." - "The Gnostics identified the Demiurge with the Jehovah of the Hebrews. In philosophy, the term is used to denote a Divine Being that is the builder of the universe rather than its creator." - Demiurge: The Vengeful Old Testament God[9]

"And the Lord said unto Moses, Make thee a fiery serpent, and set it upon a pole: and it shall come to pass, that every one that is bitten, when he looketh upon it, shall live." - Numbers 21 : 8 (KJV)

Archons

Archon is from the ancient Greek word ἄρχοντες, which means principalities or rulers. The term was used to describe any number of servants of the Demiurge, who was regarded as Lord over the Archons. Directly beneath this Archonic Lord are beings described as Hebdomad , worldly Archonic beings. Below these Hebdomads are thought to be various devilish powers. An early Gnostic Christian teacher, by the name of Basilides, who most likely attended the Great Library in Alexandra, taught about a great and powerful Archon who presided over 365 lower Archons. What is interesting here, is that we have 7 worldly creating Archons and seven planets in ancient astrology. It is even more remarkable to find 365 lesser Archons, the same number of days in a modern calendar, or a full cycle of zodiacal days. Could this be an esoteric explanation reflecting the physical dimensions of time and space, falling under the dominion and rulership of the Archons. Influenced by transiting planets on our biological composition here on Earth, as they gracefully orbit the solar system and the Earth throughout all 365 days of the year?

There was another early form of Christian Gnosticism known as Ophites, who appeared around the 2nd century AD. They related the 7 major Archons to the 7 visible planets.[10]

- Yaldabaoth - Saturn
- Iao - Jupiter
- Sabaoth - Mars
- Astaphanos - Venus
- Elaios - Mercury
- Horaios - Moon
- Adonaios - Sun

Some Gnostics believed that while aspects of the Divine galactic spirit, within the Pleroma, descends into matter through various levels of galactic density before reaching the Earth, the opposite was the case, regarding our souls, as we ascend out from this dense material realm back into spirit form. It is thought our souls undergo some form of fragmentation as our consciousness leaves this physical reality and returns back into pure spirit. It could be the case that the Gods and Archons of this material realm extract or receive our discarded soul energy as we undertake our journey back towards the pleroma.

Although some of the Archons could be personifications of the planets and celestial bodies, the lower Archons are said to take on either a reptilian appearance or an emotionless synthetic or trans-human like quality. Some ancient descriptions talk about thin small grey creatures, with baby like skin and big black motionless eyes similar to that of an insect. Very similar to the grey alien description, which we hear about today. The Gnostics tell us that the Archons are jealous of our Divine connection to the Logos, and for this reason they go out of their way to interfere in our world by creating chaos. They say the Archons are masters at deception, having the ability to manipulate our perception of reality by turning the truth 180 degrees around. They envy our Divine spark, along with our creative potential, a spark which we were given from the Plaroma through the wisdom of Gaia/Sophia. Throughout human history the Archons have frustrated and fed off our Earthly experience and emotions, trying to interface and control our species. As non-biological entities they are unable to exist for long periods of time in our atmosphere, which appears to be toxic to them. However, it is thought that they can interface with our consciousness using various methods of suggestion and deception, in an attempt to pull us down into lower frequencies, in tune with their own disposition. Steering humanity away from the Divine spark which enables us to reach higher levels of awareness, with the added potential of bringing forth inspiration, art and genius. It has been suggested that they use technology and artificial intelligence to interface with other biological life forms, creating opportunities and openings for them to take full control over other forms of life. The Archons target the subconscious, with perverted suggestions, promoting distorted perspectives of reality, together with a variety of other perversions which pave the way for more Archonic control and manipulation.

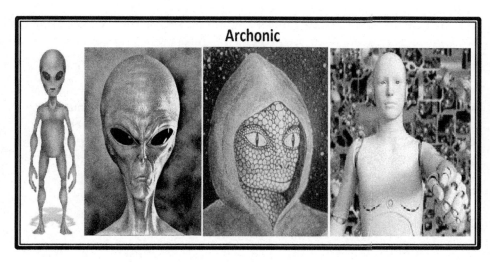

Archonic

Gnostic Adam and Eve perspective

The Gnostics also believed that part of the human being was produced by the Demiurge, the creator of the flesh, this would essentially be the soul. Another part was produced by the light of the true God, at the galactic center, which would be the spirit. After the Demiurge created the first humans he placed Adam under a spell of ignorance before putting him to sleep. The Demiurge then placed Eve next to Adam, giving her the instruction to wake him. When Adam awoke he believed that Eve was his creator. The Demiurge wanted Adam and Eve to serve him forever, so he placed them in the Garden of Eden keeping them under a spell of ignorance. As long as they believed he was the only God they would continue to worship him always. He gave them specific instructions, that they could eat from any tree in the garden but not from the tree of knowledge. In Gnosticism the serpent came from the true God within the Pleroma, speaking to Adam and Eve, to try and break their spell of ignorance. It told them that the Demiurge is not the true God of the universe but only the creator of their imperfect material world, and through ignorance the false god holds them in perpetual servitude. They believed that the only way to salvation was to illuminate one's self and connect with the spirit or Divine spark through a process of gnosis (knowledge). But not all humans have this Divine spark or the capacity to connect with it, some are earthly bound with a materialistic nature. The Gnostics saw Jesus as a saviour, who came from the galactic centre, sent by the true God of the universe to save humanity from ignorance not sin. The Gnostics believed that at the end of a person's life, if they had not reached a satisfactory level of gnosis then their soul would take on a new body for another life cycle in an attempt at achieving a sufficient level of knowledge.

Is it the case that some people throughout history, who lacked the Divine spark, were blood descendants of those Archons who mixed with the daughters of men, mentioned in the Bible?

**"When people had spread all over the world, and daughters were being born, some of the heavenly beings saw that these young women were beautiful, so they took the ones they liked. Then the Lord said, "I will not allow people to live forever; they are mortal. From now on they will live no longer than 120 years. In those days, and even later, there were giants on the earth who were descendants of human women and the heavenly beings. They were the great heroes and famous men of long ago." - Genesis 6:1-4 (GNTA)

The persecution of the Gnostics

During the 1st, 2nd and 3rd centuries both mainstream Christians and Gnostics would go to church along side each other. In the 2nd century, Valentinus, one of the greatest Gnostic teachers of that period, was almost elected as the Christian Bishop of Rome (precursor to the position of pope). Because Christianity had not yet consolidated itself within rigid parameters of defined scriptural canon, it was acceptable, at that time, to have a Gnostical view of Christianity. However, once the Christian church organised itself as being the true holy doctrine, convinced they had the only credible lineage of trained commissioned men who's line originated from the first Apostles, arguments began to erupt concerning the direction of the church, and which texts should be used along with an official understanding of the nature of Jesus himself. In 367 CE, under the orders of Bishop Athanasius of Alexandria, the Christians set out to create a list of authentic holy writings, and to discard those which they considered to be unworthy, having no legitimate authentic Divine message. At this point most of the Gnostic writings were rejected and became a target for destruction. It is thought that around this time a Pachomian monk, fearing the confiscation of their Gnostic writings, hid them in a cave in the desert near the town of Nag Hammadi, only to be found almost 1600 years later. Once the Church had formally defined its textual and theological position it was then poised to eradicate all forms of competition, labelling them as heresy. When Theodosius I (379 - 395) came to power he made Nicene Christianity the official state religion of the Roman Empire. At the same time he banned all non Christian religious customs, broke up pagan associations and dismantled the old style Roman/Greek Hellenistic practices, which had once dominated the region. As all these tyrannical policies were being implemented he described all other Christians as "foolish madmen", and was determined to promote his authority on the matter. As the Roman Catholic Church evolved, becoming ever more authoritarian and powerful, it sometimes imposed ruthless tactics in order to eradicate competition, a line in which the Gnostics felt the full force of the Church's brutality. The reason why the Nag Hammadi texts were so important, in terms of a Gnostic record, is because the Catholic Church had destroyed, not only the Gnostic writings, but also the Gnostics themselves.

During the early 13th century, at the time of the initial crusades into the Holy Land, Pope Innocent III, initiated a 20 year military campaign against the Cathars, known as the Albigensian Crusades. Scholars today consider them to be of a Gnostic orientation, because of this they were targeted for eradication by the Pope. The Pope offered the land belonging to the Cathars to any French noblemen who were willing to take up arms and defeat them. On 21 July 1209 an army of crusaders turned up at the small village of Beziers, near the coast of southern France. The crusaders called for all the Catholics to come out from the village so they could identify the Cathars from the Catholics. When no one came out, the Papal commander Arnaud Amalric, eventually gave the order to kill every man, woman and child in the village. In a letter to the Pope he later wrote :[11]

"While discussions were still going on with the barons about the release of those in the city who were deemed to be Catholics, the servants and other persons of low rank and unarmed attacked the city without waiting for orders from their leaders. To our amazement, crying "to arms, to arms!", within the space of two or three hours they crossed the ditches and the walls and Béziers was taken. Our men spared no one, irrespective of rank, sex or age, and put to the sword almost 20,000 people. After this great slaughter the whole city was despoiled and burnt." - Arnaud Amalric 1209

Massacre at Beziers 1209

Hagia Sophia

In 537 AD the Byzantium Emperor Justinian I ordered the construction of a new church, to replace the old one which had been destroyed during the Nika Revolt of 532. Riots, which only lasted a week, were the bloodiest and most destructive in Constantinople's long history. Thousands of people were killed and half the city was destroyed. The new church was to be an engineering marvel, taking the title of the world's largest building for almost 1000 years. The Church was known as Hagia Sophia, an Eastern Orthodox Cathedral, which translates from the Greek as 'holy wisdom'. It is interesting to note, although the Christians made a conscious effort to eradicate Gnostic literature, culture and its followers, some important references to Sophia were maintained. From 1204 to 1261, during the crusades, the Romans took over the church and converted it into a Roman Catholic Cathedral. When Constantinople fell to the Muslim Turks in 1453, after an 8 week siege, it was again converted, this time into a mosque. It stayed this way, under the rule of the Ottoman Empire, until the end of WW1, when, in 1935, it was secularised, and opened to the public as a museum.

Hagia Sophia (Holy Wisdom)

Under Islamic cultural tradition, it is regarded as a legitimate right for one conquering culture to take over the religious buildings of the defeated culture, adopting and altering them for their own use. However, this policy could backfire on the Muslims in Israel regarding their own mosque built on the old Temple Mount. Both the Al Aqsa Mosque and Dome of the rock may be under threat from the conquering Zionists, who may want to build a new Temple to Solomon in the same place. Furthermore, if the Muslims in Istanbul regard their transformation of Hagia Sophia as legitimate, then the Zionists could proceed unchallenged on those same moral standards.

The fall of Sophia was in essence the first example of the left hand path. Because the feminine aspect of the galactic consciousness decided to go it alone, its deviation down the left hand path resulted in the creation of the Demiurge, the Archons and a great deal of human suffering.

Notes for chapter 2

(1) Star sounds orchestra, cosmic octave.
http://www.starsounds.de/octave/jupiter/

(2) Philo of Alexandria, Hellenistic Judaism, Logos, wikipedia,
https://en.wikipedia.org/wiki/Logos

(3) El Deity, Hebrew Bible, https://en.wikipedia.org/wiki/El_(deity)

(4) Gospel of Philip, Nag Hammadi Library, The Gnostic Society Library,
http://gnosis.org/naghamm/gop.html

(5) The crisis that became the world, The Secret Book of John, The Apocryphon of John Collection. The Gnostic Society Library, translated by Stevan Davies.
http://gnosis.org/naghamm/apocjn-davies.html

(6) Maclugash the Priest, The fall of Sophia, Nov 2017.
https://joshualightningwarrior.wordpress.com/2017/11/15/the-fallen-sophia

(7) Moe, The Gnostic God Yaldabaoth, Gnostic Warrior,
https://gnosticwarrior.com/yaldabaoth.html

(8) Marcionism, wikipedia, https://en.wikipedia.org/wiki/Marcionism

(9) Demiurge, the vengeful Old Testemant God. Christian Wicca,
https://christianwicca.org/demiurge-the-vengeful-old-testament-god/

(10) Archon Gnostasism, Wikipedia,
https://en.wikipedia.org/wiki/Archon_(Gnosticism)

(11) Arnaud Amalric, Massacre at Beziers,
https://en.wikipedia.org/wiki/Arnaud_Amalric

Chapter 3. The Saturnisation of Christianity

As Saturn is the planet of order, restriction and control those who align themselves with its energetic characteristics become submerged and resonate those Saturnian values in almost every aspect of their lives. This includes division, abolition and control of other monotheistic groups. Throughout history many divisions have occurred within the initial root religions, leading to some extreme and perverted offshoots promoting division throughout various communities.

Some of the first Gnostic Christians were known as 'people of the way'. They appreciated the ancient wisdom of astrology/astronomy which was handed down to them from previous cultures such as the Sumerians and Babylonians. The Way refers to a balanced consciousness in tune with nature's rhythms and cycles, connected with the Logos. This includes a polytheistic or pantheistic view of the heavens, with an understanding of planetary ruler-ships which influenced particular epochs or Ages of time.

Jesus was born into a Jewish culture, his mother was Jewish and he lived in a predominantly Jewish area. He worshipped in Jewish temples and preached from Jewish scripts. He was a Jew who was at the forefront of the new Age of Pisces, teaching the world about the optimistic energies associated with Jupiter/Zeus. He transformed himself from a Saturnian Jew into a Jupitarian Christian, essentially going from Jew to Zeus, Jew-zeus. The story of Jewzeus is an astrological one, the Age of Aries (the ram) ruled by Mars was coming to an end, and the significant characters of that Age, like Abraham (Abram), Moses (Marses), Tuthmoses and Ramesses needed a replacement, someone who would reflect the metaphysical characteristics of the new Age of Pisces, while shaking off any association with Aries, Mars and rams. The new Messiah had to represent the optimistic, goodwill aspects of Jupiter in Pisces, throughout the Age of belief and the two fish. Jewzeus became the chosen figurehead who would represent this. Jewish leaders aware they had to wait another 2160 years for their Messiah, Saturn, to take precedence and rule the heavens in the Age of Aquarius, did not see Jewzeus as their Messiah or king of the Jews, to them he was just another rebellious false claimant. They did not want the optimistic expansive energy of Jupiter interfering with their restrictive controlling saturnian traditions.

During the initial phase of the Piscean Age Roman military rule dominated many Mediterranean countries and much of Europe. But when military rule became unsustainable Rome adopted Christianity as their official religion and promoted themselves as a Holy Empire, taking control of the physical realm through the programming of the subconscious with its own version of Jupiter worshipping monotheism. Although Constantine had made Christianity the state religion, it was not formalised until 391 AD when Emperor Theodosius outlawed all forms of heresy and closed all Pagan temples, essentially closing down the competition. As the Roman Empire in the west began to decline, Christian intellectuals within the empire sought to create a government within the church and a body of belief which all Christians could accept, essentially the church would now take over from the old Roman military rule. This was also the time when monks (moonks) appeared on the scene. Early Christians serious about worship came together to form communities, they were able to support each other in what became known as monasteries. St Benedict (480 – 543) of Italy was one of the first and most famous early organisers of the monastic movement, expanding his particular brand of monasteries throughout Europe. These organised communities, pockets of self-sufficient civilisations, attracted some of the most literate and learned people around at the time. As the world outside drifted into decline, following on from the empires collapse, everyday life inside the monasteries was relatively good.[1]

The metaphysical nature of Jupiter and Saturn means that they have always opposed each other in a perpetual conflict stretching the fabric of time and space, like sparring partners they battle it out seeking to draw their followers into a particular tapestry of energetic frequencies. These opposing energies are reflected in the glyphs used to symbolize these two planets.

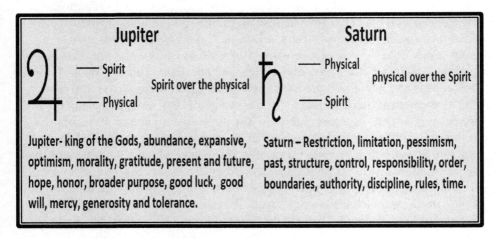

Jupiter is also known as Jove, which is where the expression jovial comes from, as we can see, the energies associated with Jupiter are positive compared with those of Saturn. Christianity has aligned itself with Jupiter and all its optimistic expressions, resulting in a religion offering belief, faith, hope and a positive future. Being the largest and most expansive planet in our solar system it is therefore no coincidence to see Christianity as the largest and most expansive of all man's religions.

Prior to the first Jewish/Roman war which led to the destruction of the 2nd Temple in 70AD, both Jews and early Christians would worship together in synagogues. The identity and ideologies of this new Christianity and Rabbinic Judaism became noticeably different and incompatible after the first war of 66AD. As the centuries past the optimistic good will of Jupitarian Christianity became more opposed to the restrictive nature of Judaic Saturn worship. During the 2nd Century these divisions became apparent when Marcionism (early Christians) rejected all Jewish influence on Christianity, believing that the wrathful Hebrew God was an entity of lower vibration, separate from the all forgiving God of the New Testament. Marcion of Sinop also believed that the God of the Old Testament was a tyrant or demiurge.

In ancient Platonic and neoplatonic schools of philosophy the demiurge is viewed as an artisan or craftsman figure, who created the physical, material universe, separate from the Logos. Some early Gnostic thinkers considered the material realm as evil, and the demiurge as a malevolent figure, while viewing the non material/spiritual realm as good.[2]

Gnosticism comes from ancient Greek meaning 'to have knowledge'. The early Gnostics originated from the Jewish Christians of the 1st and 2nd centuries and flourished throughout the Mediterranean. Believing the material world was created by a lower God, known as the Demiurge, a world where the Divine spark within humanity became trapped, the Gnostics thought that only way to liberate this Divine spark was through spiritual knowledge (gnosis). Basic Gnostic teachings include the following :[3]

- All physical matter is evil, and the non-material/spirit-realm is good.
- There is an unknowable God, who gave rise to many lesser spirit beings called Aeons.
- The creator of the material universe is not the supreme God (Logos), but an inferior spirit or Demiurge.
- Gnosticism does not deal with 'sin', it deals only with ignorance.
- To achieve salvation, one needs gnosis (knowledge).

On this rock I shall build my church

The Nebataeans were nomadic Bedouins, who, from the 4th century BC developed an empire which included parts of Jordan, Egypt, Israel, Syria and Saudi Arabia. It became a successful and wealthy trading society situating its capitol at Petra (the rock) in Jordan. Like many cultures at that time, the Nebataeans were polytheistic and influenced by the movements of the planets and the stars. Some of their artwork and architecture displayed astrological images and zodiacs. The famous temple at Petra built into the rock around the 1st century AD, was originally a mausoleum and crypt, but was later named Al-Khazneh (The treasury), as locals believed it contained treasure. The Nabataeans were eventually overrun by the Romans in 106AD, becoming another annex of Rome.

Peter and Saturn

The twelve disciples who followed Jesus represent the twelve houses of the zodiac, Peter who was initially called Simon represents Saturn in Aquarius. As Simon, he was a fisherman with many Saturnian qualities to his character. Jesus seeing the potential in Simon offered to teach and guide him towards self mastery over his afflicting Saturnine disposition. In those days it was common to change a person's name to reflect their new circumstances or philosophy. Jesus chose to call Simon 'Cephas' which means 'rock' in Aramaic, this translates into Petros in Greek giving us the name Peter, rocks and stones are under the domain and ruler-ship of the planet Saturn.

He brought him to Jesus. Jesus looked at him and said, "You are Simon the son of John; you shall be called Cephas" John 1:42

"And I tell you that you are Peter, and on this rock I will build my church, and the gates of Hades will not overcome it." Matthew 16:18

When Simon had doubted Jesus' optimistic request about going fishing after one of his sermons, a sermon in which Simon witnessed a large haul of fish being caught; realising the power of Jupitarian optimism, fell to his knees in front of Jesus.

When Simon/Peter saw this, he fell at Jesus' knees and said, "Go away from me, Lord; I am a sinful man!" - Luke 5:8

"Then Peter got down out of the boat, walked on the water and came toward Jesus. But when he saw the wind, he was afraid and, beginning to sink, cried out, "Lord, save me!" Immediately Jesus reached out his hand and caught him."You of little faith," he said, "why did you doubt?"- Matthew 14:30

When Jesus began to teach the apostles the truth about his mission and that he must suffer many things along the way before finally be killed, Peter on hearing these prophecies began to cast doubt.

"Peter took him aside and began to rebuke him. "Never, Lord!" he said. "This shall never happen to you!" Matthew 16:22

"Jesus turned and said to Peter, "Get behind me, Satan! You are a stumbling block to me; you do not have in mind the concerns of God, but merely human concerns." Matthew 16:23

Peter was regarded as the spokesman for the group, the leading apostle. The smoking gun which connects him to Saturn is in his own crucifixion. Just as the glyphs for Jupiter and Saturn are inversions of one another, Peter's death became an inversion of Christ's death, by insisting they crucified him upside down.

The Roman name for Zeus was Jupiter, a perfect reflection of the metaphysical aspects to Jupiter's astrological glyph. Ju-Peter, the crescent of Ju and the cross of Peter (the earthly rock). Juju or Ju-ju is defined as a spiritual belief system.[4]

Some of the early Christian writers, around the time of the destruction of the 2nd Temple in 420 AD, were known as Apologists, and in their efforts to justify the new Christian ideology they would vilify the Jews and condemn the old Israel as sinful. When the New Testament was written, it clearly identifies both Christian and Jewish opposition towards one another.

"Then Jesus said to the crowds and to his disciples: "The teachers of the law and the Pharisees sit in Moses' seat. So you must be careful to do everything they tell you. But do not do what they do, for they do not practice what they preach. They tie up heavy, cumbersome loads and put them on other people's shoulders, but they themselves are not willing to lift a finger to move them."" - Matthew 23: 1-4 (NIV)

"Woe to you, teachers of the law and Pharisees, you hypocrites! You travel over land and sea to win a single convert, and when you have succeeded, you make them twice as much a child of hell as you are." - Matthew 23: 15 (NIV)

"Abraham is our father," they answered. "If you were Abraham's children," said Jesus, "then you would do what Abraham did. As it is, you are looking for a way to kill me, a man who has told you the truth that I heard from God. Abraham did not do such things. You are doing the works of your own father." "We are not illegitimate children," they protested. "The only Father we have is God himself." Jesus said to them, "If God were your Father, you would love me, for I have come here from God. I have not come on my own; God sent me. Why is my language not clear to you? Because you are unable to hear what I say. You belong to your father, the devil, and you want to carry out your father's desires. He was a murderer from the beginning, not holding to the truth, for there is no truth in him. When he lies, he speaks his native language, for he is a liar and the father of lies. Yet because I tell the truth, you do not believe me! Can any of you prove me guilty of sin? If I am telling the truth, why don't you believe me? Whoever belongs to God hears what God says. The reason you do not hear is that you do not belong to God." John 8 : 39-47 (NIV)

Christian anti-Semitism

Because Christians blamed the Jews for the death of Christ, Jews became the subject of a great deal of contempt, along with, what we would now call, anti-Semitism. Consequently, Jewish people suffered terrible persecution as Christianity spread all over the Mediterranean and throughout the known world. In 1213 Pope Innocent III, during the Fourth Council of Lateran, produced a Papal Bull requiring all Jews to wear something which would distinguish them from everyone else. At this time the Jews were accused of drinking the blood of Christian children as a mockery to the Holy Communion.[5] Even the Apostle Paul admits to his zealous opposition to the new Christian Church in his early days as a practising Jew.

"For you have heard of my previous way of life in Judaism, how intensely I persecuted the church of God and tried to destroy it. I was advancing in Judaism beyond many of my own age among my people and was extremely zealous for the traditions of my fathers." - Galatians 1 : 13-14 (NIV)

After Christianity was formalized into the state religion by Emperor Theodosius in 391 AD, The Holy Roman Empire began to grow, along with its contempt for the Jews. Consequently, by the time the Middle Ages approached, and with the slaughter of many Jews by the First Crusade, the Catholic Church thought it necessary to formally protect the basic rights of the Jewish people throughout the whole of Christendom, with a papal bull entitled 'Sicut Judaeis (Constitution for the Jews)'. Signed into effect in 1120 by Calixtus II, it protected basic rights of the Jews by forbidding Christians from harming them, taking their property, interfering with their festivals and also forbade Christians from forcing Jews to convert to Christianity.[6]

During and after the Crusades, antagonism towards the Jews continued to increase, even with the Sicut Judaeis being reaffirmed by successive Popes. Some Christians believed that Jews were deliberately poisoning wells in order to promote plagues, together with blood libels and host desecration (a form of sacrilege in Christianity). Periodic expulsions occurred all over Europe, culminating in King Edward I expelling all the Jews from England in 1290. The king accused the Jews of undermining loyalty to his dynasty through the practice of usury. Two centuries later, during the reunification of Spain, all Jews and Muslims, who would not convert to Christianity were made to leave.

Relations between Christians and Jews steadily deteriorated prompting Pope Paul IV to issue the papal bull, Cum nimis absurdum in 1555.[7] This revoked all previous rights held by Jews, placing tough economic and religious restrictions on their behaviour and freedoms, affecting all Papal States. The result of this saw most Jews hoarded into small ghettos and restricted them to one synagogue per city. Consecutive popes, like Pius IV, added to this by creating more ghettos, and restricting Jewish freedoms even further.

The Roman Catholic Church was the most dominant business/religious enterprise on the planet, spreading its influence all over the world. This monopolistic position to Christianity changed in the 16th century with the reformation and the birth of the Protestant movement (Christians Protesting against Catholicism). The Lutherans, led by Martin Luther, initially invited the Jews into the arms of the Protestant movement, suspecting that the oppressive evil nature of the Catholic Church was the main reason for their refusal to convert over to Christianity. But once he realised they had no intentions of converting, he became openly hostile towards them. In 1543 Martin Luther published a book entitled '*On the Jews and their lies'*.[8] In the book he argued that Jewish synagogues and schools should be set on fire, along with all their possessions confiscated. He also wrote the following:

- **"These poisonous envenomed worms should be expelled for all time."**

- **"We are at fault for not slaying them."**

- **"They are base, whoring people, that is, no people of God, and their boast of lineage, circumcision, and law must be accounted as filth."**

- **"Full of the Devil's feces. Which they wallow in like swine."**

- **"The Jewish synagogue is an incorrigible whore and an evil slut."**

Martin Luther's attitude towards the Jews epitomised the attitude of many Christians at that time. However, just before he died he held out the olive branch by saying the Jews should be treated with love and prayer, hoping that one day they would see the error of their ways and convert over to Christ.

After the Partition of Poland in the 18th century, many Jews found themselves under the rule of the Russian Orthodox Church. Its discrimination policy towards Jews resulted in them being restricted from entering the Russian interior, isolating them within their small town settlements, known as the Pale.

At this point the Roman Catholic Church was trying to clarify its position towards anti-Judaism, as a religion on religious and ideological grounds, known as 'good anti-Semitism', as opposed to raw racial discrimination, known as 'bad anti-Semitism'. They were fully aware of the influence and implications of promoting Saturn's energetic characteristics within a culture or religious philosophy. And as Jupitarians, were very much 180 degrees opposed to Saturnian values. They viewed Saturnian characteristics of control, order, austerity and restrictions as possible problems for the future expansion of optimistic Christendom, and as Judaism aligned itself with Saturn, they wanted to avoid the possibility of falling under the shackles of Satanic control. Much of Europe prohibited Jews from certain occupations. However, they were welcome within Freemasonry due to their opposition towards Catholicism, this new intellectual army was uniting Christians and Jews against Rome. There is a great deal of Jewish symbolism within Freemasonry and generally a greater ratio of Jews inside lodges as opposed to outside. The Masons and the Catholic Church both drew their underlying principle influences from ancient Egypt. This is why you find obelisks, planets, stars and astrological symbolism in both Catholic and Masonic circles, keeping much of the important knowledge at the high levels.

When Napoleon rose to power, after the French revolution, he gave the Jews the same rights, equal to that of the Frenchman. This policy of emancipation was also implemented in all conquered territories, giving the Jews new freedoms. However, after Napoleon's defeat at Waterloo, in 1815, many of these new rights granted to the Jews were overturned with the restoration of the Catholic Church's prestige and power under Pope Pius VII, reverting back to some of the old discriminatory measures which were in place before the revolution broke out. It has never been firmly established whether Napoleon himself was a Freemason, but many believe he was, or at least sympathetic to their cause. Napoleon's older brother Joseph certainly was, he became the Grand Master of the Grand Orient of France (1804 – 1815), managing its growth and reputation throughout Napoleon's Empire.

In the mid 19th century the French Catholic Journalist Louis Veuillot argued against what he called the Jewish financial aristocracy. He believed the Jews to be a 'deicidal people' (people who kill God), and are driven by hatred to enslave Christians.[9]

The Christians were initially against usury but as the international financial cartel became more sophisticated they would seduced Christian monarchs with easy access to huge sums of money. This promoted some Christians and Jews to work together, bolstering each others ambitions for growth. This was clearly the case with the British Empire's alliance with Judaic international finance, everywhere the British Empire went a new Rothschild controlled private central bank would spring up in its wake.

In the 1880s many French Catholic priests published books blaming the Jews for France's economical and political problems, concluding that they should be either executed, kicked out the country or permanently assigned to Ghettos.[10]

Papal attitudes and quotes towards the Jews

Pope Pius VII (1800 - 1823) : Under Napoleon many of the Jewish ghettos were abolished, giving similar rights to the Jews which equalled that of the Frenchman. After Napoleon's defeat Pope Pius VII brought back the old rules confining Jews to ghettos, where they were to be locked inside at night.

Pope Leo XII (1823 - 1829) : Passed laws forbidding Jews from owning property, and the property they did have was to be sold within a unreasonably short space of time. Many Roman Jews fled the country to Tuscany, Triest or Lombardy.

Pope Gregory XVI (1831 - 1846) : ordered an inquiry into reports that Christians were being employed in Jewish ghettos. In a statement Pope Gregory clarified the Catholic Churches policy towards the Jews.[11]

Pope Gregory XVI attitude towards the Jews

† Gregory XVI. in 1843, in connexion with the Holy Inquisition of Rome, published a cruel edict against the persecuted Jews. In this decree. they were forbidden to receive Catholic masses, or to engage Christians in their service. The conclusion of this intolerant decree, conceived in the true spirit of Popery, is as follows : " No Israelite shall sleep out of his Ghetto, nor induce a Christian to sleep in that accursed enclosure, nor carry on friendly relations with the faithful, nor trade in sacred ornaments, nor books of any kind, under a penalty of five hundred crowns, and of seven years' imprisonment. The Israelites, in interring their dead, shall not make use of any ceremony, nor shall they use torches, under penalty of confiscation. Those who shall violate our edicts *shall incur the penalties of the Holy Inquisition.* The present measure shall be communicated in the Ghetto, to be published in the synagogue. Dated from ' *The Chancellary of the Holy Inquisition. June 24th.* 1843.'

Source : https://messianicjewishhistory.wordpress.com

When Pope Gregory was pressed on this issue from the Chief Minister of the Austrian Empire, appealing for tolerance towards the Jews. The Pope replied:

"The Jews are forbidden such ownership (property) by the sacred canons as a nation of deicides (the killing of God) and blasphemers of Christ". Pope Gregory XVI

Pope Pius IX (1846 - 1878) : At the start of his papacy Pius IX began with a liberal approach towards the Jews by opening up the ghettos in Rome, and repealing some laws relating to their restrictions. However, after his overthrow in 1849, by the Roman Republic movement, led by Giuseppe Mazzini and Carlo Armellini, his attitude towards the Jews changed. He reversed many of those early repeals and re-instituted the ghettos. Later in his life he made a speech concerning certain Jews who he suspected as influencing his loss of authority.

"Of these dogs, there are too many of them at present in Rome, and we hear them howling in the streets, and they are disturbing us in all places." - Pope Pius IX (1846-1878), In a speech in 1871 - after losing temporal authority over Rome - he said of certain Jews of Rome.[12]

Pope Leo XIII (1878 - 1903) : With regard to the Catholic Church's position on marriage between Christians and Jews, Pope Leo XIII clarifies the Church's position.

"For this reason We must commend those Catholic men who, when the legislative assembly of Hungary was asked two years ago whether it would consider the marriage of Christians with Jews valid, rejected the proposal unanimously and freely and succeeded in having the old marriage law retained. Their vote received the approval of the vast majority of people from all parts of Hungary, proving with admirable testimony that the people thought and felt as they did. May there be Like consent and similar constancy whenever the Catholic cause is in controversy, for then victory will be at hand." - Pope Leo XIII.[13]

Pope Pius X (1903-1914) : A few months before Theodore Herzl (the father of Zionism) died, he had a 25 minute meeting with Pope Pius X. His mission was to ask for the Catholic Church's help towards the Zionist project, relocating the Jews into Palestine. The answer he received from the new pope was clear.

"We cannot give approval to this movement. We cannot prevent the Jews from going to Jerusalem – but we could never sanction it. The soil of Jerusalem, if it was not always sacred, has been sanctified by the life of Jesus Christ. As the head of the Church I cannot tell you anything different. The Jews have not recognized our Lord, therefore we cannot recognize the Jewish people." - "And so, if you come to Palestine and settle your people there, we shall have churches and priests ready to baptize all of you." - "Gerusalemme, he said, must not get into the hands of the Jews." - Pope Pius X.[14]

Although Pope Pius X died of a heart attack at the age of 79. The timing of his death is interesting. It took place almost one month after the start of WW1. It was rumoured that the news of the war sent the old pope into a sorry state of melancholy, which seems to have hastened his death. World War 1 was a turning point for the Jews, in the sense that the Balfour Declaration, a promise made by the British Government to hand over Palestine to the Jewish Zionists, was formalised. From that moment on, the political attitude towards the Jewish question appeared to change.

Pope Benedict XV (1914-1922) : In 1916 Pope Benedict XV made a statement opposing anti-Semitism. On May 6th 1917 Nahum Sokolow, a Zionist leader, author, translator and Hebrew journalist was given a 45 minute meeting with Pope Benedict XV, concerning the plight of the Jews, and their resettlement into Palestine. 45 minutes with the Pope is more than most heads of state are normally given.

"The Pope declared that Jewish efforts to establish a national home in Palestine were viewed by him sympathetically and he expressed his best wishes for the realisation of the Zionist programme." - Century Island report on

Pope Benedict XV's meeting with Nahum Sokolow.[15]

Pope Pius XI (1922-1939) : In 1926 an organisation called the Clerical Association of Friends of Israel was created within the Catholic Church. Its main purpose was to promote a positive attitude towards the Jews, with the overriding intention of converting them to Christianity. The organisation requested that changes be made to the wording of some traditional Catholic ceremonies regarding the phrase 'perfidious (deceitful/untrustworthy) Jews' in their Good Friday public service. Pope Pius XI was in favour of the changes. However, the Roman Curia, or central body of the Catholic Church reacted negatively towards this proposal, stating that any change made to old liturgy would inevitably lead to more changes.

"The official publication La Civiltà Cattolica explained the action in a story headlined *The Judaic Danger and the "Friends of Israel."* Its author drew a distinction between race-based anti-Semitism, which it condemned, and the need for Catholics to maintain a "healthy perception of danger coming from the Jews" - Opus sacerdotale Amici Israel, Pope Pius XI and Judaism.[16]

Consequently, The Clerical Association of Friends of Israel was dissolved in 1928.

"Mark well that in the Catholic Mass, Abraham is our Patriarch and forefather. Anti-Semitism is incompatible with the lofty thought which that fact expresses. It is a movement with which we Christians can have nothing to do. No, no I say to you it is impossible for a Christian to take part in anti-Semitism. It is inadmissible. Through Christ and in Christ we are the spiritual progeny of Abraham. Spiritually we are all Semites." - Purported speech by Pope Pius XI to Belgium Pilgrims in 1938.

After the horrors of World War II, there was a great deal of sympathy generated for the Jews, resulting from the way they had been diabolically treated throughout the conflict. Their new victim status opened up many avenues of opportunity, which before were out of reach. The victors of the war, together with the United Nations, made a concerted effort towards sorting the problem of anti-Semitism out once and for all. In 1947 the Seelisberg Conference, or the International Emergency Conference on anti-Semitism took place at Seelisberg, Switzerland, attended by Jules Isaac, a French Jewish scholar. It was the second conference of the International Council of Christians and Jews with the following objectives being proposed:[17]

- An assessment of anti-Semitism throughout Europe with reasons for its continuation after the war.

- The formulation of practical measures to combat anti-Semitism at all levels of society.
- The healing of Jewish-Christian relations was to begin.

Pope Pius XII (1939-1958) : Before Giovanni Paccelli became Pope Pius XII he was instrumental in many pro Zionist activities. He used his influence to arrange Nahum Sokolow's meeting with Pope Benedict XV in 1917. In 1926, Paccelli encouraged German Catholics to join the Committee Pro Palestina, which supported the Zionist cause of relocating Jews to Palestine. In 1940 Pope Pius XIII was reported to have rejected anti-Semitism, stating that within the Catholic Church there is **"neither Gentile nor Jew, circumcision nor uncircumcision."**

"Let us pray also for the faithless Jews: that almighty God may remove the veil from their hearts; so that they too may acknowledge Jesus Christ our Lord. Let us pray. Let us kneel. [pause for silent prayer] Arise. Almighty and eternal God, who dost not exclude from thy mercy even Jewish faithlessness: hear our prayers, which we offer for the blindness of that people; that acknowledging the light of thy Truth, which is Christ, they may be delivered from their darkness. Through the same our Lord Jesus Christ, who liveth and reigneth with thee in the unity of the Holy Spirit, God, for ever and ever. Amen." - Pope Pius XIII prayer for the Jews 1955.

Pope John XXIII (1958-1963) : Although Pope John XXIII was only pontiff for four and a half years, he became one of the best loved popes of the 20th century. His reputation essentially came from his underlining character as a good natured human being, which later resulted in him being know as the 'good pope' or the 'incomparable pope'. He initiated a policy of Jewish/Christian reconciliation, developing a special relationship with the Jews. In March 2014, Rabbi David G Dalin, gave a lecture on his years of research into Pope John XXIII in which he said the following :

"In the Jewish community he has been recognized and revered, together with Pope John Paul II, as one of the 20th century's greatest papal friends and supporters of the Jewish people. Catholics are anticipating the day of their shared canonization. I think that's being anticipated with a great deal of reverence, happiness, and gratitude by the Jewish community as well." - Rabbi David G Dalin[18]

In 1959 Pope John XXIII gave the order to remove the Latin word 'perfidis' from the age old Good Friday prayer liturgy, wording which offended the Jews and had been a contentious issue within the church for many years.

On January 25th 1959 Pope John XXIII, seeing a need to modernise and bring the Catholic Church up to date, began the process of initiating the Second Vatican Council, or commonly known as 'Vatican II'. He could see that change was necessary but didn't want to be the one seen to be dictating those changes throughout Christendom.

In 1960 over 100 Jews from the United Jewish Appeal Group were invited to meet with the Pope on their tour of European countries. During the meeting the Pope made a simple statement summing up the Catholic Church's new position.

"We are all sons of the same Heavenly Father. Among us there must ever be the brightness of love and its practice. I am Joseph your brother." - Pope John XXIII, 1960

"You are of the Old Testament and I of the New Testament, but I hope and pray that we will come closer to the brotherhood of humanity... It gives me great pain and sorrow to see these recent events which not only violate a natural right of human beings but destroy the understanding between brothers under God..." - Pope John XXIII at a meeting with B'nai B'rith in 1960.

On 13th June 1960 Pope John XXIII met with the French Jewish Scholar, Jules Isaac, where they exchanged ideas concerning the approach necessary in resolving the Jewish problem. Isaac proposed that a commission be established to study the relations between the church and the Jewish people in order to properly understand the difficulties ahead and to work towards a solution.

On 11th October 1962 Pope John XXIII began the Second Vatican Council by inviting over 2000 Bishops to the Vatican, from all over the world, to discuss and debate with one another over the changes needed for the future direction of the Church. It was a brilliant idea, a parliament of Bishops freely voicing their concerns, on a myriad of issues, as they tried to pull the antiquated Roman Catholic Church from its medieval traditions into an integral part of the modern post World War II period. Some traditionalists saw it as a council of crisis whereas the vast majority saw it as a council of hope.

Over the next three years the council set about outlining their objectives, it was a long process, but the overall mood was positive. The main areas of concern were as follows :

- Decentralisation of Papal authority, to make the church more efficient.
- Modernise church ceremonies.
- Religious liberty for all.

- Elimination of anti-Semitism.
- Reconsider birth control.

As part of this reconciliation process towards religious liberty for all, the Council invited observers from many Christian denominations which had split from the Catholic Church throughout its long history. There were Orthodox Christians, Anglicans and many forms of Protestants, all were invited to observe and possibly offer their views and opinions on the various topics under discussion. Finally, after three years the Council identified three main areas which needed modernising :

- Liturgy (public worship performed by religious groups)
- Laity (lay people, distinct from the clergy)
- Ecumenism (promoting unity among the world's Christian churches)

On 28th October 1965, two years after the death of Pope John XXIII, the final document of the Second Vatican Council was made public. It was known as 'Nostra Aetate' (Latin 'in our time'). It was the first official document of its kind to focus on the relationship between the Catholic Church and the Jews.

"The Church examines more closely her relationship to non-Christian religions. In her task of promoting unity and love among men, indeed among nations." - "The Church, therefore, urges its sons and daughters to enter with prudence and charity into discussion and collaboration with members of other religions." - "This sacred council remembers the spiritual ties which link the people of the new covenant to the stock of Abraham." - "On this account the church cannot forget that it received the revelation of the Old Testament by way of that people with whom God in his inexpressible mercy established the ancient covenant." - "The church believes that Christ who is our peace has through his cross reconciled Jews and Gentiles and made them one in himself." - "Jews for the most part did not accept the Gospel; on the contrary, many opposed its spread." - " Since Christians and Jews have such a common spiritual heritage, this sacred council wishes to encourage and further mutual understanding and appreciation." - " Even though the Jewish authorities and those who followed their lead pressed for the death of Christ, neither all Jews indiscriminately at that time, nor Jews today, can be charged with the crimes committed during his passion." - " It deplores all hatreds, persecutions, displays of anti-semitism directed against the Jews at any time or from any source." - Parts of Nostra Aetate[19]

The whole notion of bringing Jews closer into the heart of the Catholic Church, with the establishment of the Vatican II, was seen by some traditional Catholics as a trap set up by the Jews to compromise the old Jupitarian traditions over to a perverted and diluted entanglement with Satanic Judaic values. Many were not happy and saw it as the beginning of the end or the saturnisation of Christianity.

One such traditionalist was the French Archbishop Marcel Lefebvre. He refused to implement the Council's reforms and resigned his leadership of the Holy Ghost Fathers in 1968. He later went on to say :

"The Church, in the course of the 1960's, thus during the Council, acquired values that have come from outside the Church, from the liberal culture - due secoli – from two centuries of liberal culture. It is clear: these are the "rights" of man, it is religious freedom, it is ecumenism. It is Satanic." (Marcel Lefebvre, Conference, December 13, 1984)

"They (traditional Catholics) **view interfaith dialogue with Jews as unnecessary and potentially leading to a "watering-down" of the Catholic faith." -** Traditional Catholics, Catholic Church and Judaism (Wikipedia)

Pope Paul VI (1963-1978) : During the three years of the Second Vatican Council, Pope John XXIII died, which temporarily put a halt to the proceedings. It was important for the Vatican to choose a successor who would continue with the reforms initiated by John and the Council. When Giovanni Montini was selected to become Pope Paul VI, the Council resumed under a totally different style of leadership, but the reforms went ahead. Pope Paul VI transformed the papacy in many ways, he removed much of the traditional regal splendour and simplified many ceremonial functions. He was the last pope to be crowned with the three tier papal tiara, after which it was sold to be displayed in the basement of the Basilica of the National Shrine of the Immaculate Conception in Washington DC. He also abolished the military units of both the Palatian Guard and the Noble Guard, leaving only the Swiss Guard to defend the Vatican. It is interesting to note that the Swiss flag is a white cross on a red background. The cross is an astrological symbol for the earthly or material realm. Pope Paul VI was the first Pope ever to visit Jerusalem in Israel, which took place, during the Second Vatican Council, in January 1964.

Although the attempt of the Second Vatican Council appears to be honourable and humanitarian in spirit, the result essentially diluted the underlining concept of the Church's basic monotheistic foundation, that of Jupiter worship. The Jupitarian crescent of spirituality which takes precedence over the cross of materialism has been replaced by a more pantheistic approach to religion, bringing in other faiths and thus other planets into the mix. Whether they knew what they were doing from a metaphysical perspective or not, the consequence of Vatican II, in many ways, brings its followers one step closer to a balanced appreciation of all the planets/Elohim, and therefore a more balanced consciousness. This meant leaving behind the restrictions and eccentricities associated with monotheism, which isolates one group of worshippers by focusing on one specific planet.

Anti-Semitism should not be confused with anti-Saturnism. And those who oppose the negative energetic characteristics of the planet Saturn should not be labelled as anti-Semites. The initial concept of Catholic Christianity was built upon the optimistic hope and good fortune associated with the Jupitarian crescent of spirituality over the cross of materialism. However, this concept has now been dissolved, in favour of the cross of materialism. An astrological explanation for this can be found within the cycles of the Great Year, in the precession of the Ages. We are now moving into the Age of Aquarius, where the old ruler of Pisces, Jupiter, will be replaced by the new ruler of the Aquarian Age, which happens to be Saturn. Vatican II has essentially morphed from Piscean Jupiter worship into the foundation of a new church which will need to align itself to the new ruling planet, Saturn.

"Therefore go and make disciples of all nations, baptizing them in the name of the Father and of the Son and of the Holy Spirit, and teaching them to obey everything I have commanded you. And surely I am with you always, to the very end of the Age."
Matthew 28 : 19-20 (NIV)

Both popes who oversaw the Second Vatican Council were later canonised (made into Saints) by Pope Francis. St John XXIII in 2014 and St Paul VI in 2018.

Pope John Paul I (26th August 1978 - 28th September 1978) : Following on from both his reforming predecessors, chose a name which would suitably reflect, not only his admiration for the two previous popes, but I suspect the name also intentionally displayed the characteristics and direction of the new church.

Bearing in mind we are looking for any symbolic signatures which may metaphysically show the church's new expression of cosmic consciousness. As Saturn is the new ruler for the Age, anything which places materialism before spirituality could be seen as a symbolic reflection of that energy. For a pope to adopt two names is unusual, and the order in which those names appear is significant. According to official history, the name John comes from the Hebrew 'yochanan' meaning 'YAHWEH is gracious'. Furthermore, it can also be viewed as a composite of the symbols of Capricorn and Saturn, Saturn being the ruler of Capricorn and the cardinal sign following the winter solstice. St John's day is December 27th. The crest or emblem for the Apostle St John is a chalice with a snake inside, essentially representing poison. It is believed that, at one time, St John drank a cup of poison and lived.

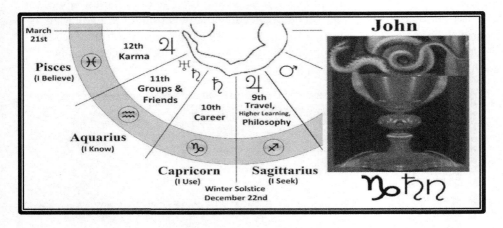

In contrast, within the history of Christianity, St Paul the Apostle is often considered to be the most important person after Jesus, a religion which put the crescent of spirituality before the cross of materialism. Consequently, to choose the name John Paul, in that order, could be viewed as an attempt to esoterically express the 180 degree shift in the Church's new direction.

John Paul I was pope for only 33 days. The Vatican's official explanation of his sudden death was put down to a heart attack, while he was lying in bed reading. However, there is some speculation surrounds his death due to inconsistencies in the stories. Although the law in Italy states embalming can only take place after 24 hours has elapsed a rush was made to embalm his body only six hours after death. This left no time for an autopsy to identify the Pope's actual cause of death, adding suspicion and more speculation. Over the years these puzzling facts have led to some investigators concluding he was murdered through the use of poison because he was about to order an investigation into the affairs of the Vatican Bank. In David Yallop's book, *In God's Name*,[20] he identifies a link between Freemasons within the Vatican, and the death or murder of the new Pope. These Freemasons within the Vatican are known as P2 (propaganda due), the Grand Orient Masonic Lodge of Italy, founded in 1805 during the Napoleonic kingdom of Italy. Interestingly, one of the P2 Masons suspected of being involved, Gian Roberto Calvini, linked to the Vatican Bank, was found hanging from scaffolding under Blackfriars Bridge in London's banking district in June 1982. His death had all the hallmarks of a masonic ritual killing.

Pope John Paul II (1978 - 2005) : Another pope with the double name of John Paul, reflecting his pro reform position of the Second Vatican Council, became known as 'Pope John Paul the Great' due to many aspects of his papacy. He was the first pope ever to visit both a synagogue and a mosque, as part of the Vatican II's attempt at bringing all the religions closer together. His long service gave him the opportunity to visit more countries than nearly all the other Popes put together. He was also another recent pope to be canonised, which took place on 27th April 2014.

"John Paul II significantly improved the Catholic Church's relations with Judaism, Islam, the Eastern Orthodox Church, and the Anglican Communion." - Wikipedia on John Paul II

"He also became the first pope known to have made an official papal visit to a synagogue, when he visited the Great Synagogue of Rome on 13 April 1986. The Pope has said that Jews are "our elder brothers."" - Pope John Paul II and Judaism, Wikipedia.

Pope Benedict XVI (2005 - 2013) : Joseph Ratzinger was born in Germany in 1927. On his 14th birthday he was conscripted into the Hitler Youth by the German National Socialists. In 1943 he was drafted into the German Liftwaffenhelfer in the anti aircraft corp, then later moved to be trained as an infantryman. In 1945, as the Allies closed in on Germany, he deserted his hopeless position and made his way back home to his family. On his arrival he surprisingly discovered that the US military had set up headquarters in their family home. Dressed in German uniform, he was arrested and immediately interned in a prison camp. In May 1945 he was released, and finally returned home. During his papacy he reintroduces some of the traditional papal garments which had been previously phased out. After 8 years as pope he made the decision to resign.

"I have had to recognize my incapacity to adequately fulfil the ministry entrusted to me" - Pope Benedict XVI resignation statement

The resignation of Pope Benedict XVI is an extraordinary event; it is not something the Catholic Church takes lightly. The last Pope to resign, prior to

Benedict, was Pope Gregory XII back in 1415. Some people see this as a clear indication that we are now in the Age of Aquarius. The significance of the Pope's timing comes into focus later that day. His resignation of the throne of Peter (Jupiter) was announced at 11:30 am. At 5:59 pm when the planet Jupiter was overhead, almost on the mid-heaven, a lightning bolt came from the sky and struck the very top of the Vatican's roof, not once but twice. However, this event could very well be just a remarkable coincidence.[21]

Christian covenant with God

The fist covenant mentioned in the Bible was between God and Noah.

"Then God said to Noah and to his sons with him: "I now establish my covenant with you and with your descendants after you and with every living creature that was with you—the birds, the livestock and all the wild animals, all those that came out of the ark with you—every living creature on earth. I establish my covenant with you: Never again will all life be destroyed by the waters of a flood; never again will there be a flood to destroy the earth." - Genesis 9 : 8-11 (NIV)

The next covenant was between God and Abraham.

"When the sun had set and darkness had fallen, a smoking fire-pot with a blazing torch appeared and passed between the pieces. On that day the Lord made a covenant with Abram and said, "To your descendants I give this land, from the Wadi of Egypt to the great river, the Euphrates— the land of the Kenites, Kenizzites, Kadmonites, Hittites, Perizzites, Rephaites, Amorites, Canaanites, Girgashites and Jebusites." - Genesis 15 : 17-21 (NIV)

"When Abram was ninety-nine years old, the Lord appeared to him and said, "I am God Almighty; walk before me faithfully and be blameless. Then I will make my covenant between me and you and will greatly increase your numbers." Abram fell face down, and God said to him, "As for me, this is my covenant with you: You will be the father of many nations. No longer will you be called Abram; your name will be Abraham, for I have made you a father of many nations. I will make you very fruitful; I will make nations of you, and kings will come from you. I will establish my covenant as an everlasting covenant between me and you and your descendants after you for the generations to come, to be your God and the God of your descendants after you. The whole land of Canaan, where you now reside as a foreigner, I will give as an everlasting possession to you and your descendants after you; and I will be their God." Then God said to Abraham, "As for you, you must keep my covenant, you and your descendants after you for the generations to come. This is my covenant with you and your descendants after you, the covenant you are to keep: Every male among you shall be circumcised. You are to undergo circumcision, and it will be the sign of the covenant between me and you. For the generations to come every male among you who is eight days old must be circumcised, including those born in your household or bought with money from a foreigner—those who are not your offspring. Whether born in your household or bought with your money, they must be circumcised. My covenant in your flesh is to be an everlasting covenant. Any uncircumcised male, who has not been circumcised in the flesh, will be cut off from his people; he has broken my covenant." - Genesis 17 1-14 (NIV)

Although the Jews were God's chosen people, prior to the Age of Pisces, when Jesus arrived, they would not accept him as the new Messiah, preferring to stay with their traditions. They chose to wait for their Messiah to come, some time in the future, a person who would represent the energetic characteristics of Saturn during the future Age of Aquarius.

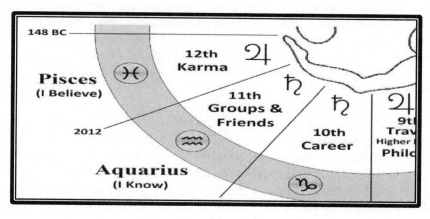

Christians believe that the Bible comes from God, that it is the word of God, inspired through the Holy Spirit. For this reason, every detail is sanctified, and must not be removed or tampered with.

"I warn everyone who hears the words of the prophecy of this book: if anyone adds to them, God will add to him the plagues described in this book, and if anyone takes away from the words of the book of this prophecy, God will take away his share in the tree of life and in the holy city, which are described in this book." - Revelation 22:18-19 (ESV)

Christians believe that a new covenant with God was initiated during the Last Supper, through the blood of Christ.

"Then he took a cup, and when he had given thanks, he gave it to them, saying, "drink from it, all of you. This is my blood of the covenant, which is poured out for many for the forgiveness of sins. I tell you, I will not drink from this fruit of the vine from now on until that day when I drink it new with you in my Father's kingdom."" - Matthew 26 : 27-29 (NIV)

The High Priest of a New Covenant (Hebrews 8 (NIV))

"Now the main point of what we are saying is this: We do have such a high priest, who sat down at the right hand of the throne of the Majesty in heaven, and who serves in the sanctuary, the true tabernacle set up by the Lord, not by a mere human being. Every high priest is appointed to offer both gifts and sacrifices, and so it was necessary for this one also to have something to offer. If he were on earth, he would not be a priest, for there are already priests who offer the gifts prescribed by the law. They serve at a sanctuary that is a copy and shadow of what is in heaven. This is why Moses was warned when he was about to build the tabernacle: "See to it that you make everything according to the pattern shown you on the mountain." But in fact the ministry Jesus has received is as superior to theirs as the covenant of which he is mediator is superior to the old one, since the new covenant is established on better promises. For if there had been nothing wrong with that first covenant, no place would have been sought for another. But God found fault with the people and said:

"The days are coming, declares the Lord, when I will make a new covenant with the people of Israel and with the people of Judah. It will not be like the covenant I made with their ancestors when I took them by the hand to lead them out of Egypt, because they did not remain faithful to my covenant, and I turned away from them, declares the Lord. This is the covenant I will establish with the people of Israel after that time, declares the Lord. I will put my laws in

their minds and write them on their hearts. I will be their God, and they will be my people. No longer will they teach their neighbour, or say to one another, 'Know the Lord,' because they will all know me, from the least of them to the greatest. For I will forgive their wickedness and will remember their sins no more." By calling this covenant "new," he has made the first one obsolete; and what is obsolete and outdated will soon disappear." - Hebrews 8 : 1-13 (NIV)

Jewish theologians have always held the position that Jesus did not fulfil the requirements necessary to be their Messiah, therefore they rejected him.

"He said to them, "Go into all the world and preach the gospel to all creation. Whoever believes and is baptised will be saved, but whoever does not believe will be condemned."" - Mark 16 : 15-16 (NIV)

"Therefore I tell you that the kingdom of God will be taken away from you and given to a people who will produce its fruit." - Matthew 21 : 42 (NIV)

"Who is a liar but he that denieth that Jesus is the Christ? He is antichrist, that denieth the Father and the Son." - 1 John 2 : 22 (KJV)

Christian theologians prior to the Second Vatican Council concluded that because of the Jewish formal rejection of the Messiah the old covenant between God and the Jews had lost its status as God's kingdom on earth. They consider that Jesus Christ superseded the old covenant with a new one. Therefore, Vatican II and its document of Nostra Aetate is out of step with two millennia of traditional Catholic teaching.

In 1985 notes concerning the relationship between Catholics and Jews were released with the approval of Pope John Paul II. Notes which talk about the preparation for a new Messiah.

"Attentive to the same God who has spoken, hanging on the same word, we have to witness to one same memory and one common hope in Him who is the master of history. We must also accept our responsibility to prepare the world for the coming of the Messiah by working together for social justice, respect for the rights of persons and nations and for social and international reconciliation... To this we are driven, Jews and Christians, by the command to love our neighbour, by a common hope for the Kingdom of God and by the great heritage of the Prophets. Transmitted soon enough by catechesis, such a conception would teach young Christians in a practical way to cooperate with Jews, going beyond simple dialogue." - Vatican text 1985[22]

Michel Munir, a Syrian Catholic historian, suggests in his new book, *A synagogue within the church*, that Pope John Paul II is the architect of a conspiracy to place the Catholic Church under Jewish rule.

"Ever since his election ... John Paul II has not spared any effort to strengthen the Jewish faction within the Catholic church," - Michel Munir (*A Synagogue Within the Church*.[23]

Another top historian from Syria, Soheil Zakar, suggested that the Vatican came under enormous pressure during the last years of the Second Vatican Council, from various Zionist organisations, to absolve the Jews for the death of Christ.

"It is like a pope who comes along and says, 'I don't care about the historical side of Christianity and I am only concerned with the creation of a new Christianity for a new world," - Soheil Zakar[23]

"Pope Francis told the Italian newspaper *La Repubblica* that the United States of America has "a distorted vision of the world" and Americans must be ruled by a world government, as soon as possible, "for their own good." - Phrophecy in the news[24]

Notes for chapter 3.

(1) Steven Kreis, Christianity as a cultural revolution, 2001, the history guide, http://www.historyguide.org/ancient/lecture15b.html

(2) Demiurge, Wikipedia. https://en.wikipedia.org/wiki/Demiurge

(3) Gnosticism, Wikipedia. https://en.wikipedia.org/wiki/Gnosticism

(4) Ju-ju, https://en.wikipedia.org/wiki/Juju

(5) Ritual murder in Russia, Eastern Europe, and beyond : new histories of an old accusation. Avrutin, Eugene M.,, Dekel-Chen, Jonathan L.,, Weinberg, Robert,. Bloomington, Indiana. pp. 39–40. ISBN 9780253026576. OCLC 972200793.

(6) Sicut Judaeis, https://en.wikipedia.org/wiki/Sicut_Judaeis

(7) David B Green, 1555 Pope Paul IV Orders Jews to Live in a Ghetto, Jewish World, Haaretz. https://www.haaretz.com/jewish/1555-roman-jews-banished-to-ghetto-1.5295240

(8) Martin Luther, On the Jews and their lies, Wikipedia, https://en.wikipedia.org/wiki/On_the_Jews_and_Their_Lies

(9) Graetz, Michael (1996). The Jews in Nineteenth-century France: From the French Revolution to the Alliance Israélite Universelle. Stanford University Press. p. 208.

(10) Michael, Robert (2008). A History of Catholic Antisemitism: The Dark Side of the Church. Springer. pp. 128–129.

(11) Pope Gregory XVI Orders Inquiry on Jews Employing Christians in the Ghetto, On This Day In Messianic Jewish History, Sept 2015, https://messianicjewishhistory.wordpress.com/2015/09/29/29-september-1843-pope-gregory-xvi-orders-inquiry-on-jews-employing-christians-in-the-ghetto-otdimjh/

(12) Pope Pius IX and Judaism, https://en.wikipedia.org/wiki/Pope_Pius_IX_and_Judaism

(13) Pope Leo XIII continues to forbid Catholic-Jewish marriage, On This Day In Messianic Jewish History, August 2015, https://messianicjewishhistory.wordpress.com/2015/08/22/22-august-1866-

pope-leo-xiii-continues-to-forbid-catholic-jewish-marriage-otdimjh/

(14) Benjamin Glatt, The Jerusalem Post, TODAY IN HISTORY: POPE PIUS REFUSED TO SUPPORT A JEWISH JERUSALEM, Jan 2016. https://www.jpost.com/Christian-News/Today-in-History-Pope-Pius-refused-to-support-a-Jewish-Jerusalem-442696

(15) Pope voices sympathy for Jewish state in Palestine, Century Island, RTE. https://www.rte.ie/centuryireland/index.php/articles/pope-voices-sympathy-for-jewish-state-in-palestine

(16) Pope Pius XV and Judaism. https://en.wikipedia.org/wiki/Pope_Pius_XI_and_Judaism

(17) Seelisberg Conference 1947. https://en.wikipedia.org/wiki/Seelisberg_Conference

(18) Thomas Mcdonald, John XXIII and the Jews, The Catholic World Report. 2014. https://www.catholicworldreport.com/2014/04/03/john-xxiii-and-the-jews/

(19) Nostra Aetate, PDF, https://www.urbandharma.org/pdf/NostraAetate.pdf

(20) David Yallop, In Gods Name, Basic Books 2007, http://www.goodreads.com/book/show/733940.In_God_s_Name

(21) Brian O'Reilly, Lightning strikes Vatican city just hours after Pope's resignation. 2013. https://www.independent.ie/world-news/lightning-strikes-vatican-city-just-hours-after-popes-resignation-29065168.html

(22) Judaism & the Church: before & after Vatican II, Society of Saint Pius X, 2013, http://sspx.org/en/news-events/news/judaism-church-after-vatican-ii-1342

(23) Associated Press, Fox News, Vatican Controlled by Jews, Say Syrian Academics. 2001, https://www.foxnews.com/story/vatican-controlled-by-jews-say-syrian-academics

(24) Pope Francis quote, Prophecy in the news, January 2019, https://prophecyinthenews.com/world_news/pope-francis-world-government-must-rule-u-s-for-their-own-good/

For 1400 years Islam has influenced the lives of millions of people. It is a religion based around the energies and characteristics of the planet Venus, a planet associated with aspects of love, pleasure and liking. Its astrological glyph is a circle or the soul over the cross of the physical material world.

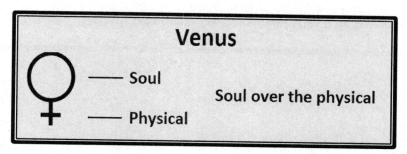

Due to Venus' metaphysical orientation it is predominantly concerned with the soul's relationship towards the material world. A monotheistic society aligned mainly with energies associated with Venus are more likely to manifest those characteristics within the fabric of their societies' behaviour as a whole.

When assigning Moonday or monoday as the first day of the week, Friday or Venus day becomes the 5th day, friday is also Islam's holy day. Venus produces an interesting geometric pattern as it orbits both the Sun and the Earth. During its orbit it will produce five conjunctions with the Sun, this is one of the reasons why the number 5 has been associated with Venus for thousands of years.

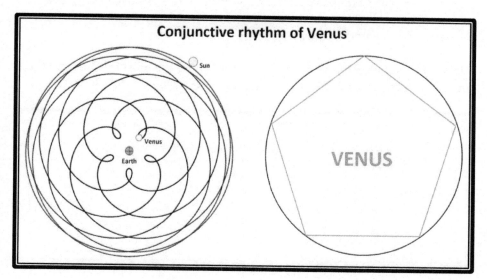

When we look at the two signs of the zodiac ruled by Venus, Taurus and Libra, we discover that they make up the second and seventh houses, 2&7 or 7&2. This is interesting because each angle of a pentagram is 72 degrees, the same number of virgins waiting for those good Muslims who finally make their way into paradise. With the glyph for Venus being a circle (focal consciousness) over the cross (physical), it reflects the conscious mind's dilemma of balancing what part of the physical realm it chooses to focus on, this is essentially a metaphysical reflection of Libra (I balance/complement) and Taurus (I have).

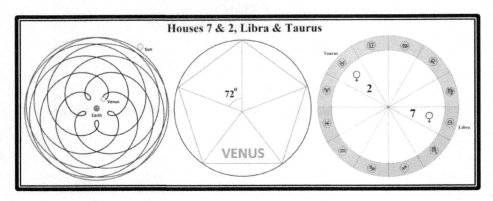

Muslims pray five times a day, and follow the five pillars of Islam. Their first pre-dawn prayer meeting, known as the Fajr, takes place when Venus appears on the horizon at Mecca in Saudi Arabia.

Positive characteristics of Venus energy (the morning star) are all the pleasurable aspects of love and liking, whereas the inversion of this positive energy gives rise to the negative or undesirable side of Venus, this could be the true basis behind the personified character known as Lucifer (the light bringer).

"How art thou fallen from heaven, O Lucifer, son of the morning! how art thou cut down to the ground, which didst weaken the nations!" - Isaiah 14:12 (KJV)

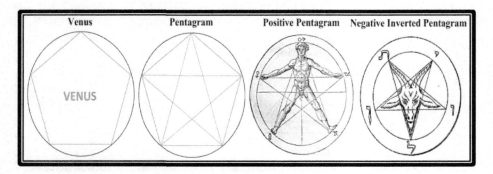

The giant black cube at Mecca, known as the Kaaba, was thought to have started life as a pre-islamic observatory, a place where stars and solstices could easily be viewed and calculated. In Islamic tradition the Kaaba (Arabic for cube) was believed to have been built by Abraham, at a time when pagan religious practices were conducted at its altar. A metaphysical explanation for the black cube as a temple, can be found when considering that the black cube is not a natural phenomena, it is not something which is commonly found throughout nature. Consequently, it is a shape which reflects those artificial and machine like qualities associated with the Archons, qualities which oppose Sophia/Gaia's expression of divinity and spiritual beauty. Therefore, it is possible that the Kaaba's initial pre-Islamic role was as an altar to the Demiurge and his 365 lower Archonic creations.

Muhammad ibn was born in Mecca in 570 AD. His father Abdullah ibn, was a member of the Banu Hashim clan, but tragically died a few months before Muhammad was born. When Muhammad was 6 his mother Amina, on a trip to Medina also died, leaving him in the care of his grandfather Abd al-Muttalib, who would also die just 2 years later. He eventually found himself under the care of his uncle Abu Talib, who would become his protector as well as a great influence for him throughout his life. When Muhammad became a young adult he began working as a simple shepherd, but later he accompanied his uncle on merchant caravan excursions into Syria and other cities around the Middle East. His time as a merchant was successful, due to his good and trustworthy reputation which he had developed along the way. When Muhammad was 25 he was invited to help a distinguished Quraysh merchant lady by the name of Khadijah, a widow 15 years his senior. They eventually fell in love and were married.

Living in and around Mecca, Muhammad would occasionally go up to the rocky hills on the outskirts of the town to relax and meditate. One night he had a profound vision, a revelation, in which the one true God revealed himself to Muhammad. Over the next few years Muhammad withdrew from his life as a merchant and spent more time contemplating in the caves outside Mecca. Muslims believe that Muhammad was the final messenger of God, who from 610 AD received direct verbal revelations from the All Mighty. All these revelations were eventually compiled in their holy book, the Quran, together with the Hadith, a comprehensive record of Muhammad's words and actions. The Muslims also believe that the arrival of Muhammad was foretold in the Bible.

"But when the Comforter is come, whom I will send unto you from the Father, even the Spirit of truth, which proceedeth from the Father, he shall testify of me." John 15 : 26 (KJV)

If we look at the time Muhammad was born, 570 AD, as a segment of time within the Piscean epoch, we find not only was that year in Leo the lion, ruled by the Sun (focal consciousness) on the outer wheel, but also, Muhammad dies and becomes King of Kings to the Muslims in Leo on the inner wheel. This is a double Leo/Sun, in the expansive Age or epoch of Jupiter, highlighting such a significant time within the zodiacal time-frame. If astrology has any validity it seems inevitable that someone of significance would appear at that time. From Muhammad's death in 632 CE there were two Caliphates, expressing the strong will of the double lion as it expanded in the Piscean Age of Jupiter. The first Rashidun Caliphate was from 632 – 661 CE, followed by the Umayyad Caliphate which ended in 750, coinciding with the move from Leo into Virgo on the outer wheel. I regard this as more than just a coincidence.

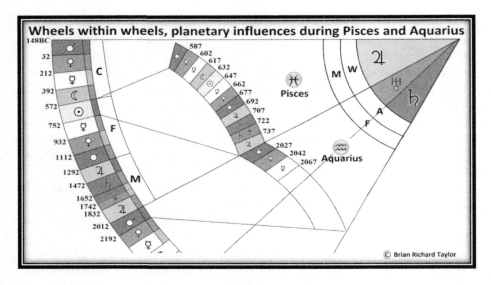

As Muhammad's revelations increased, together with the number of followers, the Quraysh tribe, who, at that time, ruled Mecca, saw Muhammad's teachings as a threat to their traditional way of life and their well established trading arrangements. During that time the Kaaba was a polytheistic pagan religious focal point for various tribes to congregate and pay homage to their chosen gods. Weapons were not allowed in the vicinity, and as a result a large market grew around this relatively safe environment. The Quraysh saw Muhammad's monotheistic, one god, approach as a destabilising ideology which could undermine their business interests. Consequently, the leaders of the Quraysh began to apply pressure on Muhammad, in an attempt to bring him back in line with their procedures. They eventually placed a complete ban on the city from conducting any form of trade with Muhammad, including preventing him and his supporters from buying food. When this failed, they escalated into violence, killing a number of Muhammad's followers who were vulnerable. By 622 the situation in Mecca had become too dangerous for Muhammad and his followers. Consequently, they abandoned their home and city of birth to begin a new life in the northern town of Yathrib, which, at that time was an oasis town of belligerent Pagan and Jewish tribes. With a reputation for fairness and trustworthiness, Muhammad was asked, by Yathrib's various tribes, to help mediate with their internal squabbles. With nothing to lose, he offered his assistance, which gave him the opportunity to make his mark within the new city. The result of Muhammad's involvement led to the creation of the Constitution of Medina, a contract between Muslims, Jews and non-Muslims, concerning their relationship towards one another. It was the first constitution of its kind in the region, promoting mutual respect for the lives, property and places of worship for all involved, essentially regulating the rights and obligations between all the city's descendants of Abraham.

With a new constitution the city of Yathrib became a more peaceful place, attracting trade and improving the overall lives of its citizens. At this point Muhammad received a new revelation persuading him that he must prepare to fight back against his enemies.

"Fight in the way of Allah those who fight you but do not transgress. Indeed, Allah does not like transgressors." "And kill them wherever you overtake them and expel them from wherever they have expelled you, and fitnah is worse than killing. And do not fight them at al-Masjid al- Haram until they fight you there. But if they fight you, then kill them. Such is the recompense of the disbelievers." "And if they cease, then indeed, Allah is Forgiving and Merciful." - Quran 2 : 190-192

In 624 a large Quraysh trading caravan was returning from Syria back to Mecca. Muhammad and the Muslims decided they would go on the offensive by capturing the caravan in the desert. Anticipating this, the Quraysh diverted the caravan and sent a small army into Yathrib to attack the Muslims. Muhammad and his forces met the Meccan army at a watering hole on the outskirts of the city called Badr. A skirmish erupted which ended in the Meccan army retreating. Once the news of this victory spread, the credibility and status of Muhammad and his followers grew among the common Arabs. Consequently, more recruits joined the Muslims growing the religious order together with its army.

At this point Muhammad had another revelation, a message telling him, from now on all Muslims must pray facing the direction of Mecca.

"So from wherever you go out [for prayer, O Muhammad] turn your face toward al- Masjid al-Haram, and indeed, it is the truth from your Lord. And Allah is not unaware of what you do." - Quran 2 : 149

Before this new revelation it was considered normal practice to point towards the holy city of Jerusalem. When the Muslims began facing Mecca to pray, it was seen, by the Jews, as a insult to their tradition, which antagonised and offended many traditional Jewish tribal leaders. It also symbolised the progressive deterioration of Jewish/Muslim relations. Furthermore, just as they had done with Jesus 600 years before, the Jews also rejected Muhammad's Divine connection and would not accept him as an Apostle of God. The more successful and powerful Muhammad and his followers became the greater was the deterioration in relations with the Jews, leading to secret meetings and negotiations between the Jewish tribe of Banu Nadir in Yathrib and Muhammad's enemies in Mecca. This eventually erupted in a showdown, where Muhammad felt compelled to act against the underhand actions of those Jewish tribes who, he felt, had compromised the Constitution of Medina/Yathrib, by planning to attack him. As a result, his army surrounded the Jewish villages for a two week siege, before finally banished them from the city, sparing all their lives.

One year after the battle of Badr, the Quarysh sent an army three times larger than Muhammad's, in an attempt to crush him. Although the Muslim army was outnumbered, the battle resulted in a stalemate, giving Muhammad time to bolster his position. On his return to Yathrib, Muhammad discovered that some of the remaining Jewish tribes on the outskirts of the city were actively helping his enemies defeat him.

In 627 AD, the Quraysh of Mecca returned with help from the Jewish tribes, with an army of 10,000 warriors, more than three times the size of Muhammad's 3,000 men. However, Muhammad gained the initiative by digging a massive trench to the north of the city, making it extremely difficult for the enemy's cavalry to cross. In an attempt to break the deadlock, the Quraysh secretly negotiated with a Jewish tribe in Yathrib known as the Banu Qurayza, asking them to attack Muhammad from the south. When this failed to gain any serious momentum the Quraysh gave up and retreated back to Mecca, leaving the Banu Qurayza Jews to the mercy of the Muslims. Once again Muhammed felt betrayed by the Jews, who had dishonourably reneged on the Constitution of Medina/Yathrib. He sent his army to their village, and after a 25 day siege, the Jews surrendered. This time Muhammad had a problem, he knew if he banished them from the city, like he had done with the previous Jewish tribes, they may join with his enemies and come back later to attack him. He decided to hand over judgement to an independent mediator, who found the tribe guilty of treason and sentenced all the men to death. The women and children were spared only to become slaves to the Muslims. All 800 men were eventually put to the sword. Although the deaths of these Jews was not based on race or religious grounds, the knock on effects created deep divisions within Muslim/Jewish relations, which, it could be argued, has never recovered.

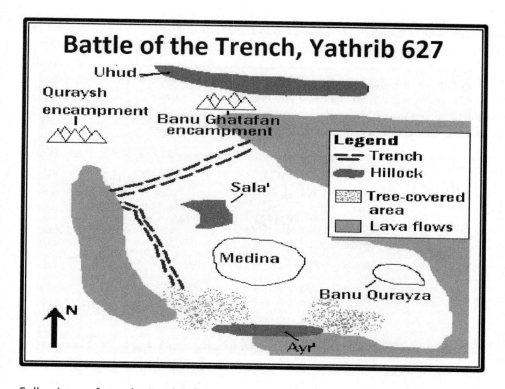

Battle of the Trench, Yathrib 627

Uhud

Quraysh encampment

Banu Ghatafan encampment

Sala'

Medina

Banu Qurayza

Ayr

N

Legend
- ═══ Trench
- ▬▬ Hillock
- ░░ Tree-covered area
- ▬ Lava flows

Following on from the Battle of the Trench, a truce was declared between the two opposing sides. However, in 629 the Quraysh broke this truce by attacking one of Muhammad's allies. This set in motion the beginning of the end for the Quraysh. A few months later, in 630, Muhammad gathered an army of 10,000 Muslims and headed south for Mecca. Although the Meccan army put up fierce resistance, fighting for a whole month, they were eventually defeated by Muhammad and his army, who entered the city in triumph. Instead of putting his enemies to the sword, Muhammad, true to Allah's command, declared a merciful amnesty and forgave all those who fought against him. When the city was safe, he made his way to the Kaaba, walked around it seven times before removing all 360 idols which represented various pagan gods of the time, leaving only the black stone, which is still there to this day. At this point, he declared that there is only one true God 'Allah'.

In the ancient pagan world of star worship, many idols represented planets, stars and constellations. It is an interesting coincidence that there were 360 idols in the Kaaba, the same number of degrees in the Zodiac. And the act of circulating the Kaaba seven times before removing the idols could have some metaphysical significance to the seven planets of the ancient world or, as we shall discover later, the seventh Sefirot of victory on the kabbalistic Tree of Life.

By 631, the last pagan stronghold fell to the Muslims giving them complete rule over all of Arabia.[1][2] The only stone left in the Kabba was the meteorite which could have fallen to Earth as Venus moved into its new orbit around the time of Abraham. From the early days of Islam to today, the Kabba is the focal point of the Muslim religion, just as the glyph for Venus is the circle of focal consciousness over the cross of the physical material realm, the act of circling the black cube at Mecca reflects these metaphysical principles.

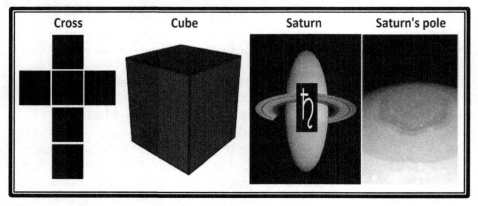

Muhammad had now done all he had set out to achieve. In his final sermon to his followers, the very next year, he commented on how he had abolished usury from the land that now belonged to the Muslims.

"Verily your blood, your property are as sacred and inviolable as the sacredness of this day of yours, in this month of yours, in this town of yours. Behold! Everything pertaining to the Days of Ignorance is under my feet completely abolished. Abolished are also the blood-revenges of the Days of Ignorance. The first claim of ours on blood-revenge which I abolish is that of the son of Rabi'a b.

al-Harith, who was nursed among the tribe of Sa'd and killed by Hudhail. And the usury of the pre-Islamic period is abolished, and the first of our usury I abolish is that of 'Abbas b. 'Abd al-Muttalib, for it is all abolished." - extract from Muhammad's final sermon. Sahih Muslim Book 15, Hadith 159

Prior to the Muslims, Arabia was once ruled by a significant power, known as the Jewish Kingdom of Himyar. According to the Institute of Advanced Studies, few scholars have been made aware of this aspect of history.[3] The Himyarite Kingdom was established around 110 BC in the area of south west Arabia, where Yemen is today. It initially spread its influence through trade, between the Roman Empire, Africa, Arabia and the spice trade with India, growing as a formidable fighting force along the way.

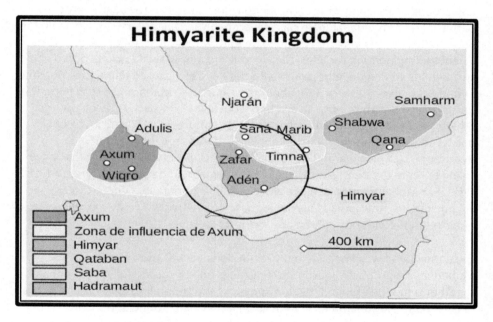

The ruling kings of the Himyar Empire appear to have abandoned paganism in favour of Judaism, around the year 380 AD. Over the next 150 years the Abyssinians and Romans began military campaigns towards Yemen, in an attempt to control the population and trade through the influence of Christianity. Around 518 the Jewish king Yosef Nu'as (Dhū Nuwās) became angry at the ingress of Christianity towards his own empire and sphere of influence, as a consequence he sent an army to attack the northern city of Najran. After taking control of the city, he burned the Christian churches and put to death any Christian who would not convert to Judaism. The number of victims vary depending upon accounts, but it is believed that around 1000 were either put to the sword or burnt to death.[4]

"We can now say that an entire nation of ethnic Arabs in southwestern Arabia had converted to Judaism and imposed it as the state religion." - Glen Bowersock, Institute for Advanced Studies.[3]

Once the word of the massacre reached Byzantium and the Christian kingdom of Ethiopia, forces were amassed from both kingdoms and sent into Himyar, with the aim of putting an end to king Yosef's plans of conquest. The King of Ethiopia, not only wanted revenge for the slaughter of the Christians in Najran, but he also wanted back the territory which his kingdom had held during the 3rd century. From the Byzantium perspective, the Jews, at that time, were allies of Persia, and Persia was a rival of the Byzantium Empire, so a victory over the Jews in Himyar would also be a tactical blow for the Persians. The traditional Arab tribes living in and around Mecca and Yathrib throughout this period were caught in the middle of these great Christian/Judaic clashes, probably leaving them with a disdain for both. In 525 Yosef's kingdom came to an end, when Christian forces took over his kingdom, fragmenting the Jews throughout most of Arabia. Pockets of Judaic strongholds sprang up, who, allied with the Persians, caused damage to Christian ambitions of expansion. In 570, about the same time Muhammad was born, the Persians, allied with the Jews, took back control of Himyar, by driving out the Ethiopians from the Arabian peninsula. Furthermore, in 614, Persian forces, bolstered by Jewish tribal warriors took over Jerusalem, during the Byzantium/Susanian war (602-628).[5] Under this backdrop, it is clear that anyone trying to unite the people of Arabia was under a great deal of pressure from all sides. For Muhammad to achieve what he did, is remarkable under the circumstances. However, as his power base grew, it would come at the expense of his relations with both Christians and Jews alike.

Once the Quran was finalised and written down, it was used to promote Muhammad's prophetic words and teachings and to successfully bring people together under one unified religion known as the Ummah (community). For the first 13 years of Muhammad's preaching he only had around 150 followers, but once they took up arms, to defend themselves against warring tribes, they found they were able to repel their enemies even when outnumbered. Each successful campaign would bring forth more recruits and followers, swelling the numbers to almost 100,000 at the time of Muhammad's death in 632 AD. Each time a warring enemy tribe was successfully defeated, the Muslims gained more credibility along with the spoils from each conflict, bringing in a great deal of wealth and prestige. Because the Muslims forbad usury, they freed themselves from the shackles of debt and were beholden to no other source for their money or wealth. Consequently, within a very short time, of only 200 years, the Muslims had gone from strength to strength, becoming one of the largest and greatest empires the world has ever seen.

With the strict abolition of usury, it became relatively easy for the Muslims to increase their standard of living at a steady rate, without the parasitical influence of money lenders sucking their wealth away.

Diabolos

The devil was known as "DIABOLOS" in ancient Greek, a name derived from two words divide and abolish. Satan or Saturn is the accuser, it has divisive qualities which abolish an individual's ability to live and embrace the now by trapping their cognitive rhetoric in a deceptive spiralling cycle of negative pessimism concerning past events, loss and frustration. The Persian word for Saturn was Satan, a planet associated with Judaic religious ideology.

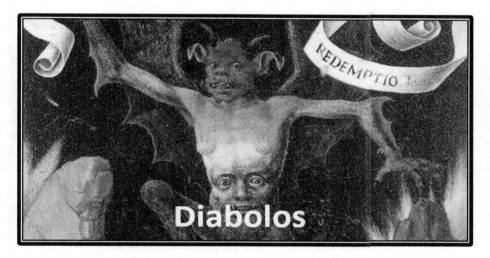

So what went wrong with Islam? How did Satan get its way, dividing and abolishing a religion which almost united the whole world?

When Muhammad died, in June 632, divisions began almost immediately. The problem was, who would take over from Muhammad as successor. His followers were divided, many wanted to elect a new leader on merit, while others regarded his family lineage as natural heirs. Muhammad only had one surviving daughter, Fatimah who was married to Ali ibn, a cousin of Muhammad, and for this reason, many considered Ali as the logical successor. However, the father of Muhammad's third and youngest wife Abu Bakr also had a claim to the position, with many followers supporting him. This led to the split which we now call Sunni and Shia. Shia Muslims regard Ali as the first and only legitimate Caliph (leader of the Muslims). But the majority voted for Abu Bakr, who was eventually chosen to be the first Caliph.

First four Caliphs

1. Abu Bakr - A.H. 11–13 / A.D. 632–634
2. 'Umar ibn al-Khattab - A.H. 13–23 / A.D. 634–644
3. 'Uthman ibn 'Affan - A.H. 23–35 / A.D. 644–656
4. 'Ali ibn Abi-Talib - A.H. 35–40 / A.D. 656–661

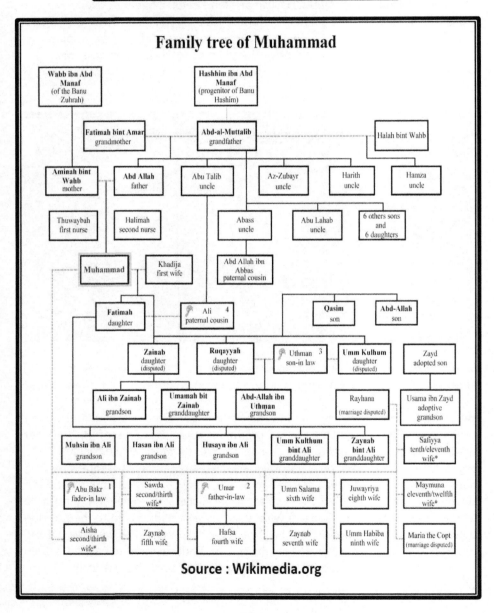

Family tree of Muhammad

Source : Wikimedia.org

After the death of Muhammad, Abu Bakr, the first Caliph, began the process of compiling the material for the Quran. It was eventually written down in a standardised version under the 3rd Caliph Uthman ibn Affan (579 - 656). Over the next 200 years the Muslims spread their influence at an impressive rate, with two major Caliphates they took control of the Middle East, North Africa and even Spain. Later, through trade routes, they became a major influence in various parts of South East Asia.

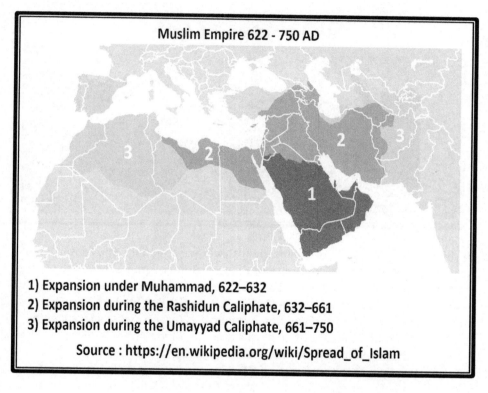

Muslim Empire 622 - 750 AD

1) Expansion under Muhammad, 622–632
2) Expansion during the Rashidun Caliphate, 632–661
3) Expansion during the Umayyad Caliphate, 661–750

Source : https://en.wikipedia.org/wiki/Spread_of_Islam

After the 2nd Caliphate, the 5th Caliph of the Abbasid Caliphate, Harun al Rashid, initiated, what many call, the Golden Age of Islam. While most of northern Europe was heading into the Dark Ages, the Muslims were entering an era of great success. In Baghdad, Rashid set up 'The House of Wisdom', where he brought scholars from all over the world to work on translating the best classical knowledge known at that time into Arabic. It was a time of incredible progress, where some of the world's greatest Islamic buildings were created along with many advancements and discoveries in science and mathematics.

While most of Europe was struggling to feed itself, the Islamic Spanish city of Córdoba was installing street lighting for its citizens. The city's Mosque which was built in 786 was an architectural masterpiece, with a capacity to hold 5,000 worshippers, becoming the envy of people from all over the world. In the 10th century, after hearing about the wonderful city of Cordoba, the Saxon nun and poet Hroswitha wrote:

"The brilliant ornament of the world shone in the west, a noble city …. Cordoba was its name and it was wealthy and famous and known for its pleasures and resplendent in all things …." - Nun Hroswitha 10th century

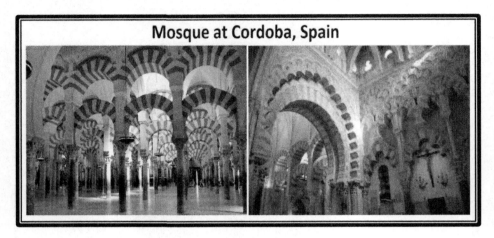

Mosque at Cordoba, Spain

With its military capacity, discipline and usury free economics, the Muslims became a threat to the very survival of the Holy Roman Empire, especially in the trading cross roads of the Middle East. Consequently, the Pope began to militarise the Catholic's position with the order of the Knights Templar. The crusades began in 1095, and went on for almost 200 years, steadily weakening the Muslims in the Holy Land. Also at this time the Mongols, under Genghis Khan, were spreading their unique brand of fear and barbarity, sacking Baghdad in 1258, putting an end to the 'House of Wisdom', destroying their vast libraries along the way. They executed the Caliph, Al-Musta'sim Billah, along with many of his men. This is generally considered as the end of the Golden Age of Islam. Weakened by attacks from all sides, Islam, as it evolved, branched off in various directions. Just as a tree grows branches, which deviate from the root, some offshoots became extreme interpretations of the original foundations of Islam, far removed from the initial teachings and spirit of Muhammad. The older the tree grows the further and more numerous the branches become. The most extreme sect of Islam began with the preacher and activist Muhammad ibn Abd al-Wahhab (1703-1792), commonly known as Wahhabism. He began his reform movement in the region of Najd, central Saudi Arabia, in the middle of the 18th century. This version of Islam evolved into a far right, ultra conservative and fundamental offshoot of Sunni Islam. Muhammad ibn Abd al-Wahhab eventually joined up with a local leader to create a politico-religious alliance which later became the 'House of Saud', then the Kingdom of Saud in 1932. Today Wahhabism is the official state sponsored form of Sunni Islam in the country, gaining power and influence from the wealth generated from their natural resource of oil. It is estimated that there are around 5 million practising Wahhabists in the Persian Gulf region alone. However, the majority of Sunni and Shia Muslims disagree with many of their interpretations concerning Islam, regularly denouncing the Wahhabists as a 'vile sect' or even as a 'Satanic faith'.[6]

"The US State Department has estimated that over the past four decades concerns in Riyadh have directed at least $10bn (£6bn) to select charitable foundations toward the subversion of mainstream Sunni Islam by the harsh intolerance of Wahhabism." - Telegraph 2017[7]

The dark side of Saudi Arabian Wahhabism

"We have to frankly say that; Al-Wahabi's superficial and false teachings, and grasping on to the shell is the main obstacle standing in the way of Muslims' goal to unite, and the biggest cause of the killing, dispersing, and breaking up of Muslims." - Intelligence Colonel Sa'id Mahrnud Najrn Al-'Arniri (The Birth of Al-Wahabi Movement And it's Historic Roots)[8]

In 2008 a top secret report was released from the U.S. Defence Intelligence Agency. A report written by Iraqi Intelligence Colonel Sa'id Mahrnud Najrn Al-'Arniri on the birth of Wahhabism. The report suggests that the British Empire, during the 19th century, infested the Middle East with its agents, looking for a way to undermine the Muslims in an attempt to weaken the Ottoman Empire, and to lay the foundations for a Jewish state in Palestine. In 1973 the autobiography of the British Middle Eastern spy Hempher was translated. In the book he includes British plans to dominate Muslim countries.[9] Because Muslim men have a strict tradition of discipline and adherence to their daily practices and principles in regard to Islam, the British colonials were finding it difficult to corrupt them through simple, traditional means, which had been successful throughout the world and in other cultures.

"The British Colonies' Ministry sent the trained spy Mr. Hempher to the city of Baghdad in Iraq in order to create disorder between the Sunni and Shiites and find the weak point of Muslims so he can penetrate its body to defuse the unity of Islam. Also, his mission in this trip was to identify the conflicts among Muslims and create an atmosphere of disagreement, expiation, and mistrust among them as well as make up different faiths and form fake colonial religions to enable the colonizer to reach its objectives in creating division." - Intelligence Colonel Sa'id Mahrnud Najrn Al-'Arniri (The Birth of Al-Wahabi Movement And it's Historic Roots)[8]

According to Hempher, British agents were sent all over Arabia with orders to create extreme differences among the four main groups of Sunni Islam. The agents went out all over Arabia promoting fake and extreme ideologies in an attempt to divide the Muslims and get them to kill each other. This is when they came across Muhammad Abd-al-Wahab.

"The British found in Muhammad Abd-al-Wahab many attributes such as the love of glory, immorality, and extreme views so; they came to realize that he is the right person to establish the group they wanted." - "Both groups; Al-Wahabi and Al-Shaykhiyyah are established on wrong views therefore they brought about disorder, blood shedding, and killing." - Intelligence Colonel Sa'id Mahrnud Najrn Al-'Arniri (The Birth of Al-Wahabi Movement And it's Historic Roots)[8]

In 1745 Muhammad Abd-al-Wahab met with Muhammad bin Saud, in a meeting where they both agreed to support one another. An alliance where Muhammad Abd-al-Wahab would be in control of religious matters and Muhammad bin Saud would control the government. Some Islamic scholars point out that the genuine roots of both Muhammad Bin Saud and Muhammad Abd-al-Wahab were of Jewish descent, with Muhammad Bin Saud being a descendant of a Jewish merchant from Basra by the name of Mardakhai bin Ibrahim bin Mushi,[8] and Muhammad Adb-al-Wahab's grandfather, Tjen Shulman, was also a member of the Jewish community in Basra, Iraq. The Intelligence report also claims that Shulman had been banished from Damascus, Cairo and Mecca for his practice of quackery. In his book *History of al Saud*, the author Nasir al-Said, claims that in 1943 the Saudi Ambassador in Cairo had paid a man by the name of Al-Tamimi 35,000 Jinee, to produce a fake family tree, which would tie both the Saud family and Muhammad Abd-al-Wahab's family to the Prophet Muhammad.[8] Nasir was a Saudi dissident who was reportedly abducted, by Saudi agents, in Beirut, in 1979, put on a plane bound for Saudi Arabia, where it is believed that he was thrown out at an altitude of ten thousand feet. His body was never found.[8a]

To make sense of the situation in the Middle East, especially concerning Saudi Arabia, a basic understanding of British involvement throughout the region is necessary. With a strong sense of unity and stability inherent within traditional Islam, the British Empire sought ways to undermine the Ottoman Empire and fragment Sunni Muslims. Anticipating a major war during the early 20th century, between the major powers in Europe, the British sent a network of agents into Arabia in an attempt to create alliances with various Arabian tribes and factions. Alliances which would come in useful in attacking the Turks once the war began. One of these agents was T E Lawrence (Lawrence of Arabia). Because of his knowledge relating to the area as a historian and archaeologist, he was assigned the position of intelligence officer to the Arabs. His job at the start of WW1 was to see if the Arabs had the will and resources to start a rebellion against the Ottoman Turks, who at that time ruled Arabia.

Prior to WW1 there were three major factions dominating Arabia and the Bedouin tribes. The first was the Hashemite family tribe who ruled over the Hejaz region, led by Hussein ibn Ali al Hashimi, the Sharif of Mecca. He was reported to be the 37th generation descendant of the Prophet Muhammad, regarded as the significant heir and leader of the Sunni Muslim Arabs in the Hejaz region. However, prior to WW1 his kingdom was under the rule of the Ottoman Empire, and also an enemy to the House of Saud in the east.[10]

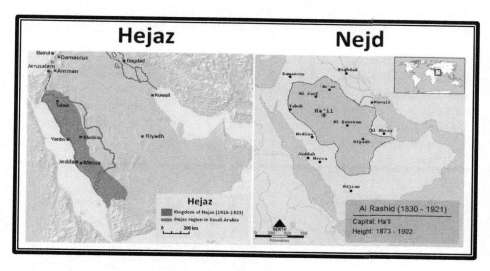

The second significant tribe were the House of Rashid, rulers over the Nejd region, and also formidable enemies to the House of Saud. A rivalry in which they spent years competing with one another for the capital city of Riyadh.

The third tribe was the House of Saud which had joined with the formidable fighting force of the Ikhwan ('the brotherhood' of pro Wahhabi nomadic militias).[11] As a united front they promoted fundamental and radical Islam, viewing all non Wahhabists as infidels, enemies who they felt it necessary to defeat. Because of their ruthlessness and aggressive tenacity, the British thought they could negotiate with their leader Iban Saud / Abdul Aziz, and use him as a counterweight against the efforts of the other Arab tribes who were trying to unite the country. In 1915 the Treaty of Darin was signed between the British and Abdul Aziz, an agreement which made the lands of the House of Saud a protectorate of the British Empire.[12] In return Abdul Aziz agreed not to expand his territory into any other areas under British control. While this was taking place Lawrence of Arabia was negotiating, in the west, with the Sharif of Mecca and his son Faisal bin Hussein, in an attempt to persuade them to unite and liberate themselves from their Turkish overlords. Through Lieutenant Colonel Sir Henry McMahon, and Lord Kitchener, the British high command, sent a guarantee to Hussein ibn Ali, the Sharif of Mecca, which stated that if the Arabs helped the British defeat the Ottoman Turks, the British government, would in return, recognize a united Arabian state under the control of the Arabs.

"Great Britain would, in exchange for support from the Arabs of Hejaz, ...guarantee the independence, rights and privileges of the Sharifate against all foreign external foreign aggression, in particular that of the Ottomans" - Telegram of 1 November 1914 from Lord Kitchener (recently appointed as Secretary of War) to Faisal bin Hussein.[13]

Believing that the western Arabs would not be able to sustain an attack on the Turks for long, the British did not take their agreements with the Arabs seriously. While the western Arabs were being cajoled by the British to help fight the Turks, The Sauds were given instructions to sit and wait, holding onto Riyadh and the area they had seized in 1913 around the port city of Al Hofuf, and not to get involved in the Arabian revolt to the west.

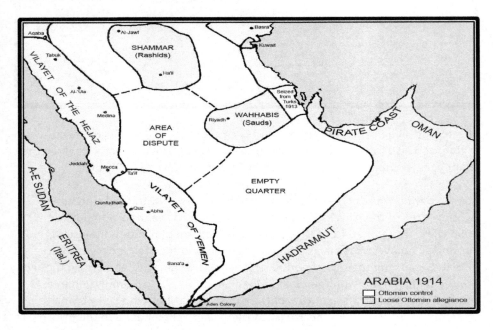

Under the pretext of a new unified Arabia, together with British supplies of hardware and munitions, the Sharif of Mecca, the genuine descendant of the Prophet Muhammad, rallied what Arabs he could and began an offensive against the Ottoman Turks. The first attacks on Medina were unsuccessful, repelled by

Turkish artillery and German aircraft. However, as more munitions poured in, at the request of TE Lawrence, the Arabs gained new momentum. They decided to leave the Turks in Medina isolated and went north towards their ultimate goal of Damascus. The Sharif of Mecca called upon Auda Abu Tayeh, a former warrior for the House of Rashid, to come and help in the Arab revolt. Auda, was regarded as one of the greatest warriors of his day. Furthermore, if the Arabs were to succeed they would need all the help they could get. A plan was put in place to attack the Red Sea port of Aqaba, at the north west tip of the Hejaz. Auda, along with 500 Arab warriors devised a surprise attack on the Turkish garrison on the edge of the city. On 2 July 1917 the Turks fell, with 300 of their soldiers being slaughtered at the expense of a handful of Arabian warriors. The attack was such a success, the British high command started to take the Arab revolt seriously.[13]

With Aqaba now in the hands of the Arabs, British and Allied forces were able to use the port to bring supplies and troops for a further push north, in an attempt to liberate Jerusalem and Damascus from the Ottoman Turks.

While all this fighting was taking place, the British high command, back in England were hatching secret plans of their own. In May 1916, together with the French, the British produced the Sykes-Picot agreement, an arrangement which, in the event of victory, redefined and shared the northerly territories or Arabia between the two major powers, neglecting any legitimate claims made by the Arabs. Also in November 1917 Lord Balfour, as Foreign Secretary, wrote to Lord Rothschild, the head of the international banking cartel, promising the Zionists, in the event of victory, the area of land known as Palestine.[13] Although the Arabs thought they were fighting for their freedom and independence, the European powers had other plans. When Lawrence of Arabia, fighting alongside the Arabs, found out about these secret agreements, he was furious. Realising the magnitude of deceit to which he was caught up in, not only towards the Arabs, but also to him personally, he had no other choice but to keep the information to himself.

"For my work on the Arab front I had determined to accept nothing. The Cabinet raised the Arabs to fight for us by definite promises of self-government afterwards. Arabs believe in persons, not in institutions. They saw in me a free agent of the British Government, and demanded from me an endorsement of its written promises. So I had to join the conspiracy, and, for what my word was worth, assured the men of their reward. In our two years' partnership under fire they grew accustomed to believing me and to think my Government, like myself, sincere. In this hope they performed some fine things, but, of course, instead of being proud of what we did together, I was bitterly ashamed." - T E Lawrence, *Seven Pillars of Wisdom*, P20[14]

In the summer of 1916 there were around 30,000 Arabs, united in the struggle against the Ottoman Empire. By 1918 that number had grown to over 50,000. The overall casualty figure is unknown, but many lost their lives in an effort to bring freedom to their country. Ashamed of his predicament Lawrence, without spilling the beans, told Faisal Hussain if they could get to Damascus before the British, they would be in a strong position to hold onto their Independence.

"It was evident from the beginning that if we won the war these promises would be dead paper, and had I been an honest adviser of the Arabs I would have advised them to go home and not risk their lives fighting for such stuff." - T E Lawrence, *Seven Pillars of Wisdom.*

At the end of 1917 the British forces moved on Jerusalem. After victories against the Ottomans, seizing control of towns along the way, most of the Turks had abandoned the city by the time the British arrived. While the British were strengthening their position in Palestine, the Arabs under Faisal were making plans to reach Damascus. This would take time as there were still many towns and villagers to liberate along the way. By the time the British and Arabs reached Damascus, in October 1918, the Turks, anticipating what was coming, had fled, and the new Emir (ruler) Faisal was chauffeur driven into the city, as the head of the new independent Arabian government. Over the next few weeks, Faisal became aware of the British secret negotiations with the French and the Zionists, through the Sykes - Pecot agreement and the Balfour Declaration. He felt bitterly betrayed by the British, objecting strongly to their deceit and underhand tactics, he walked out on many meetings with the British, who were trying to negotiate a new settlement. At this point Lawrence, already back in England, was invited to Buckingham Palace to be presented a Knighthood by King George V. However, unhappy and ashamed by the whole episode, he turned the King's offer down as a protest for the British betrayal towards the Arabs.

With Emir Faisal's dreams of an independent Arab state, having slowly evaporated, T E Lawrence tried to help him by promoting his cause at the Paris Peace Conference in early 1919. Unfortunately, all they could do was present their case and wait for the results. During the Paris Piece Conference Chaim Weizmann, President of the Zionist movement, approached Emir Faisal to sign an agreement for amicable cooperation between Arab and Jews within the Middle East especially concerning Palestine. This agreement was known as the Faisal - Weizmann agreement. A document which was used by the Zionist delegation at the 1919 Peace Conference, to stress that Zionist plans for Palestine were given prior approval by the Arabs.[18] Faisal believed that by accepting the proposals for a Jewish state, supporting mutual agreements with the allies, he could increase the probability of achieving an Arab statehood for his own people. He wrote :

"Dear Mr. Frankfurter, I want to take this opportunity of my first contact with American Zionists to tell you what I have often been able to say to Dr. Weizmann in Arabia and Europe. We feel that the Arabs and Jews are cousins in having suffered similar oppressions at the hands of powers stronger than themselves, and by a happy coincidence have been able to take the first step towards the attainment of their national ideals together. The Arabs, especially the educated among us, look with the deepest sympathy on the Zionist movement. Our deputation here in Paris is fully acquainted with the proposals submitted yesterday by the Zionist Organisation to the Peace Conference, and we regard them as moderate and proper. We will do our best, in so far as we are concerned, to help them through: we will wish the Jews a most hearty welcome home. With the chiefs of your movement, especially with Dr. Weizmann, we have had and continue to have the closest relations. He has been a great helper of our cause, and I hope the Arabs may soon be in a position to make the Jews some return for their kindness. We are working together for a reformed and revived Near East, and our two movements complete one another. The Jewish movement is national and not imperialist. Our movement is national and not imperialist, and there is room in Syria for us both. Indeed I think that neither can be a real success without the other. People less informed and less responsible than our leaders and yours, ignoring the need for cooperation of the Arabs and Zionists, have been trying to exploit the local difficulties that must necessarily arise in Palestine in the early stages of our movements. Some of them have, I am afraid, misrepresented your aims to the Arab peasantry, and our aims to the Jewish peasantry, with the result that interested parties have been able to make capital out of what they call our differences. I wish to give you my firm conviction that these differences are not on questions of principle, but on matters of detail such as must inevitably occur in every contact of neighbouring peoples, and as are easily adjusted by mutual good will. Indeed nearly all of them will disappear with fuller knowledge. I look forward, and my people with me look forward, to a future in which we will help you and you will help us, so that the countries in which we are mutually interested may once again take their places in the community of civilised peoples of the world. Believe me, Yours sincerely, (Sgd.) Faisal." - Letter from Emir Faisal (Son of Hussen Ibn Ali, Sharif of Mecca) to Felix Frankfurter, associate of Dr. Chaim Weizmann. Paris Peace Conference, March 3, 1919.[15]

While the world waited for the results from the Paris Peace Conference, Emir Faisal was crowned king of the Arab Kingdom of Syria by the Syrian National Congress Government on March 7th 1920. However, in the following month an offshoot meeting to the Paris Peace Conference gave France the mandate over Syrian territory. Consequently, the new King Faisal was asked to step down and leave the country. Outraged by this, Faisal and his followers put up resistance which began the Franco - Syrian war. After nearly three months of fighting, the French took control of the country and kicked out the new king by installing their own puppet government. With no kingdom and nowhere to go, Faisal went to live in the UK, hoping to negotiate with the British on their own soil. The following year, in an attempt to resolve the Arab issue, Winston Churchill, acting as Colonial Secretary, asked T E Lawrence to join him at the Cairo Conference of 1921. Because of the violent backlash caused by the Sykes - Picot agreement and Balfour Declaration the British arranged a series of meetings in an attempt at defusing the escalating violence. As a result, the British asked Faisal to be monarch of the newly created British mandate of Iraq; an area in which most of the inhabitants had no clue as to who he was. Furthermore, the majority of the Arabs living in Iraq were Shiite, and because the Heshemites of Hejaz were Sunni Muslims, the Iraqs had not played a significant role in the Great Arab Revolt against the Turks. Even so, Faisal, seeing very little choice in his predicament, accepted the offer and became King Faisal I of Iraq on 23rd August 1921.

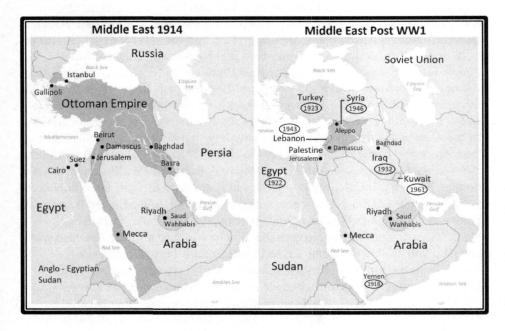

As a result of the Paris Peace Conference, the hopes and aspirations of the Arabs, towards an independent nation, were brushed aside, in favour of the major victorious powers of WW1 and their Rothschild Zionist sponsors. Consequently, the Sykes - Picot agreement was comprehensively enforced together with the initiation and promotion of Zionist aspirations towards a national homeland of their own in Palestine. The old policy of divide and rule (Diabolos) was playing out yet again, in favour of the British Empire's move towards global governance.

Syria was placed in the hands of the French, as a mandate, while the British were given control of the lands south of Syria, from Palestine in the west to Basra in the east. This area was now to be called Iraq, with Faisal Ist as its new king.

Sharif Hussein ibn Ali al - Hashimi, 37th generation descendant of the Prophet Muhammad, and King of the Hejaz.

Faisal I bin Hussein bin Ali al - Hashemi. Son of Sharif Hussein. King of Syria (1920). King of Iraq (1921 - 33).

Abdullah I bin Al - Hussein. Son of Sharif Hussein. Emir of Transjordan (1921-46). King of Jordan (1946-51).

Abdulaziz or Ibn Saud. King of the Nejd & Hejaz (1926-32). King of Saudi Arabia (1932-53).

Unleash the hounds

The British had the Arab descendants of the Prophet Muhammad fragmented, exhausted and disillusioned from years of fighting for a nation state, which, due to greater powers than themselves, would never be allowed. Throughout the war years, and the partitioning process; with all the efforts made and the lives lost; Ibn Saud and the Wahhabists were sitting patiently, biding their time, waiting for the right moment to begin their next move. Backed and protected by the British under the Treaty of Darin (1915), the House of Saud was now given the green light to initiate the clean up operation, by unleashing the Ikhwan Wahabbiests on the Sunni Arabs to the north and west.

Faisal had written to the Zionists, during the Paris Peace Conference, giving them his best wishes in their endeavours over Palestine. After the British reneged on their initial promise for an Arab independent nation state, stretching from Palestine to the Gulf, Sharif Hussein of Mecca was in no mood to accept either the Balfour Declaration or the new borders drawn up by the French and British victors. No matter how much the British tried to cajole him around to their new post war reality, he would not budge.

"The Sharif let it be known that he will never sell out Palestine to the Empire's Balfour Declaration; he will never acquiescence to the establishment of Zionism in Palestine or accept the new random borders drawn across Arabia by British and French imperialists. For their part the British began referring to him as an 'obstructionist', a 'nuisance' and of having a 'recalcitrant' attitude. The British let it be known to the Sharif that they were prepared to take drastic measures

to bring about his approval of the new reality regardless of the service that he had rendered them during the War. After the Cairo Conference in March 1921, where the new Colonial Secretary Winston Churchill met with all the British operatives in the Middle East, T.E. Lawrence (i.e. of Arabia) was dispatched to meet the Sharif to bribe and bully him to accept Britain's Zionist colonial project in Palestine. Initially, Lawrence and the Empire offered 80,000 rupees. The Sharif rejected it outright. Lawrence then offered him an annual payment of £100,000. The Sharif refused to compromise and sell Palestine to British Zionism." - How Zionism helped create the Kingdom of Saudi Arabia[16]

When Lawrence could see that no amount of bribery was working on Sharif Hussein of Mecca, he changed tact and threatened him with an Ibn Saud takeover. Churchill had previously spoke to the Sharif's son, the Emir of Transjordan, Abdullah bin Al - Hussein, during the Cairo Conference in 1921. Churchill made it clear to Abdullah that he must make an effort to persuade his father into accepting the new proposals. If he did not :

"The British would unleash Ibn Saud against Hijas" - *The creation of Saudi Arabia* P107.[17]

Ibn Rashid of the House of Rashid and ruler over the Kingdom of Najd, who throughout 1920 had expanded his territory north towards the borders of Palestine, also rejected these new proposals offered by the British. As a consequence, the British were worried about another Arab alliance making trouble for them in the future. By December 1920 the British were sending Ibn Saud a monthly allowance of £10,000 in gold bullion, which is the equivalent of half a million in today's money. This also came with thousands of rifles, field guns and ammunition supplies.[16] Because of Sharif Hussein's refusal to compromise or consent to new British demands, Ibn Saud and his Wahhabi warriors, in September 1921, were unleashed on the town of Hail, central Arabia. A show of force designed to persuade Sharif Hussein one last time. Following this victory Ibn Saud declared himself the Sultan of Nejd. On top of this show of force, with Ibn Saud on his doorstep, the British asked Sharif Hussein to seriously reconsider the British offer. The proposals that were put in writing and sent to the Sharif were not even looked at. The Sharif tore them up and drafted his own rejection statement. After three more rounds of negotiations had failed, a message was sent to Ibn Saud, in the summer of 1924, stating that the British Empire had terminated all discussions with the Sharif. Within weeks of this telegram an attack into the Hijaz took place by Ibn Saud and his Wahhabi forces. Following the attacks, telegrams were sent to both Hussein's sons, Abdulla in Transjordan and Faisal in Iraq, telling them both to stay put and not to give any assistance to their father in the Hijaz.[16]

By October Sharif Hussain was forced to abdicate. He fled Mecca for the port town of Akaba, the same port seven years earlier which he had liberated from the Turks in aid of the British war effort. He was eventually pushed out finding exile in Cyprus. Reports of this takeover were portrayed, in the media, as an internal religious conflict, no mention was made of British Geo-political objectives. A tactic still in use today, as the rest of the area is decimated and divided, allowing no future union or expansion of traditional Islam, a religious tradition which once created the Islamic Golden Age of enlightenment.

By the end of 1925 the Hejaz had been conquered by Ibn Saud and his band of fanatical warriors. On the 10th January he declared himself to be King of the Hejaz. The following year he also announced himself as the King of the Nejd. Both kingdoms were now firmly under his control.

Ikhwan revolt

Because Wahhabism is such an extreme and perverted version of Islam, traditional moderate ways of living, which had been enjoyed for over a thousand years, came to an abrupt end. The Wahhabist's ruthless fundamental and conservative approach to life made them a feared force among the people who had just been conquered. A number of the extreme fundamental elements at the top of the Ikhwan movement were becoming increasingly unhappy with Ibn Saud's close relationship with the British Empire, and saw it as collusion with the enemy or the infidel. Consequently, a revolt erupted in 1927, rebelling against the authority of Ibn Saud himself. Over the next three years clashes would erupt between forces loyal to Ibn Saud and the 10,000 strong Ikhwan warriors. Without the help of the British and Kuwaiti forces, Ibn Saud and his new Kingdom could have been overrun by an even more ruthless enemy. By 1930 the revolt had been quashed and by 1932 the two kingdoms of Nejd and Hejaz had been brought together under the one kingdom now known as Saudi Arabia.[19]

King Abdulaziz / Ibn Saud

A few years after the Cairo Conference TE Lawrence lost interest in his military career and took early retirement. As a huge national hero, Lawrence had influence over those who respected and admired him. In 1935 he died in a mysterious motorbike accident, which many of his friends and admirers believed to be an assassination. During this period he was aligning himself with Oswald Moseley, the leader of the British Fascist movement. On the day of the accident he was on his way to see his friend Henry Williamson, a Hawthonden prize winner (British literary award), who was negotiating a future meeting between Adolf Hitler and Lawrence. Churchill attended the funeral.[20]

Cairo Conference 1921

T E Lawrence, middle. Churchill, bottom left.

Looking back, at the divisions and fragmentation imposed on traditional Islam, over the centuries, one can't help but suspect, that outside influences, of a sinister nature, have played a major part in the slow decline of a once powerful religious ideology. As a competitor to the expansion and hegemony of other religions such as Christianity and Judaism, it could be argued that some versions of Islam, we see today, have been undermined, deviating so far from their initial roots that even the Prophet Muhammad would have difficulty recognising them. Because of its once glorious, formidable united past, Islam has been targeted by satanic forces for a slow, incremental, divisive demise.

The Wahhabists have throughout the years developed a reputation for merciless brutality, with a desire, not only to kill people, but to destroy artefacts and relics of our ancient history. This is all very contradictory to the activities of the Muslims during the Islamic Golden Age, where they went out of their way to bring together ancient history, philosophy and science, in order to preserve it. This ruthless fighting machine of Wahhabiest warriors, which we are up against today, could be of use to any malicious or sinister organisations who wish to pervert the course of history by erasing elements of our true past from the record.

It is my belief that the globalisation project is still funding and utilising extreme elements of Islam to this day, not only as a mechanism of division in a physical sense, but also as a tool that sow seeds of mistrust and Islamophobia in the minds of non-Muslims throughout the world. These extreme factions, which do not represent traditional Islam, are being groomed and used by Satanic organisations to undermine the old system of sovereign nation states, in an effort to create the chaos necessary to promote the globalist's new system of global governance.

Modern relations between Zionist Israel and Saudi Arabia.

As the decades unfolded, and with the descendants of Prophet Muhammad dethroned and out the way, the Rothschild Zionist Kingdom of Israel was now positioned to dominate the Middle East. Using Judaism as a cover for their Geo-political and financial endeavours, the Zionist movement has used everything in their arsenal to advance their agenda. While publicly distancing themselves from the House of Saud and the Wahhabiests, behind the scenes, both powers appear to be singing from the same hymn sheet regarding specific issues. Over the years both the House of Saud and Israel have received huge financial support from the UK and the United States. For this reason they share a common foreign policy towards the rest of the Middle East, the same policy as their financial sponsors. They both see Iran, Hamas and Hezbollah as a common enemy. Even before the creation and recognition of the State of Israel, back in 1948, the UK/Zionist project for the Middle East was financing Ibn Saud and his warriors. Many credible sources, over the years, have disclosed the Jewish ancestral lineage of the Saudi family, which underpins the genuine close relationship between the House of Saud and the Jews as a whole. On 17th September 1969 King Faisal Al-Saud stated in the Washington Post :

"We, the Saudi family, are cousins of the Jews: we entirely disagree with any Arab or Muslim Authority which shows any antagonism to the Jews; but we must live together with them in peace. Our country (ARABIA) is the fountain head from where the first Jew sprang, and his descendants spread out all over the world." - King Faisal Al-Saud, Washington Post 1969

It appears, to the average observer, that over the past few decades, those Islamic countries showing prosperity, strength and unity have been targeted for either sanctions, regime change or destruction by certain elements within the west. A continuation of the old British Empire's divide and rule policy, to destabilise Islamic countries even further. Although diplomatic relations between Israel and Saudi Arabia, on an official level, appear to be non existent. Suspicion regarding a secret relationship or alliance has been suspected for years.

"On 19 November 2017, Energy Minister Yuval Steinitz said that Israel has had covert contacts with Saudi Arabia amid common concerns over Iran. This is the first public admission of cooperation between the two countries by a senior Israeli official." - Israel - Saudi Arabia relations, Wikipedia.[21]

"In November 2017, Israeli Channel 10 news published a leaked diplomatic cable that had been sent to all Israeli ambassadors from the Israeli Ministry of Foreign Affairs after the resignation of the Lebanese prime minister Saad Hariri. Written in Hebrew, the cable confirmed co-operation between Israel and Saudi Arabia in escalating the situation in the middle-east. The cable called for Israeli diplomats to "do everything possible to ramp up diplomatic pressure against Hezbollah and Iran."" - Israel - Saudi Arabia relations, Wikipedia.[21]

Tartarians

To complicate this issue even further, there are a race of people known as Tartarians, which many historians know little about. Some speculate that they were once a great and sophisticated empire, stretching from the Caspian Sea all the way to the Pacific. Old maps clearly identify Tartary or Great Tartary as a huge land mass. Its people were described as Turkic, an ethno-linguistic culture found throughout Asia, North Africa and parts of Europe. Tartary had its own flag, their own kings and their own language. Because Tartary was so big it was often divided into manageable sections with a prefix denoting the ruling power for that area, creating Russian Tartary, Cathay or Chinese Tartary, Central Tartary and East Tartary. According to official history, as the Europeans and eastern cultures of Mongolia and China mixed with the Tartarians the term fell into disuse replaced by what we see today.

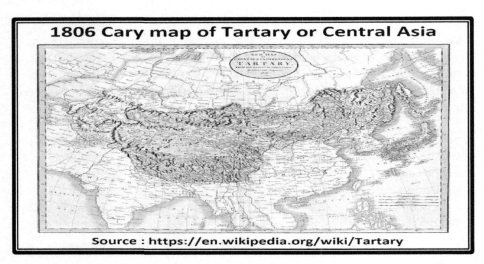

1806 Cary map of Tartary or Central Asia

Source : https://en.wikipedia.org/wiki/Tartary

We even see Marco Polo dressed in a traditional Tartarian costume on his Wikipedia page, standing next to a flag of Tartary.

Marco Polo & Tartary Flag

Empire Tartary　　**Tartary**

Source:https://commons.wikimedia.org/wi ki/File:Naval_flags_of_the_World_1783.jpg

Cathay or Chinese Tartary, which included Xinjiang, Mongolia, Manchuria and Qinghai, most of which were not within the protectional proximity of the Great Wall of China, suggests that the Great Wall was built to keep out some pretty fierce competition, separating ancient China and Tartary.

In the introduction to the book *History of the two Tartar conquerors of China,* published in 1854, it states:[22]

"It embodies the observations of various missionaries in China, together with the highly interesting narratives of two journeys into Tartary in the years 1682 and 1683, made by the famous Jesuit father Ferdinand Verbiest, in the suite of the Chinese emperor. The other, that at a time like the present, when a revolution of the most formidable character has rendered the maintenance of the throne of China by the existing Tartar dynasty a matter of great uncertainty."[22]

Furthermore, it goes on to shed light on the importance of the Tartarian Empire's capability.

"Father Rho dying in 1638, this duty rested solely with Schall, who was engaged upon it during three consecutive reigns, viz., that of the last sovereign of the Ming dynasty, and those of the two first Tartar Chinese emperors. Meanwhile, however, although the Manchu rebels had gained the mastery in the north of China, the south had not yet bowed to the Tartar yoke."[22]

"All hope, however, from such a source was soon put to an end, for in that same year 1651 Chunchi, the youthful heir of the late Tartar conqueror, being declared of age, assumed the reins of government at Pekin ; and the Tartars, impatient of completing their conquest, made a desperate attack upon the southern provinces. Yunlie was vanquished, and both he and his youthful son perished. Helena was led captive to Pekin, and the imperial race of the Ming became extinct."[22]

"The emperor himself was anxious to take lessons off him in mathematics, and at his request Verbiest made himself master of the Tartar language, in order to dispense with an interpreter in communicating his instruction."[22]

"The maintenance of the military character of the Tartars, by which their final establishment on the throne of China was secured, was in a great measure due to the emperor's frequent hunting excursions beyond the Great Wall, thereby exposing them to fatigues and dangers, in many respects analogous to the trials of actual warfare."[22]

According to the Internet Encyclopedia, as Mongolian control in the west weakened throughout the 15th century, the Kazan Khanates took over and its people became known as Tartars. They were eventually conquered in 1552 by Russian forces under the reign of Tsar Ivan IV, becoming the first Muslim subjects within the Tsar's Empire. The internet encyclopedia (Encyclopedia.com) states that after the Bolshevik revolution Tarters were targeted for extermination.

"In the 1920s, most Tatar leaders and intellectuals who wanted independence were eliminated through execution or exile. This policy against the Tatars continued to some extent until the early 1950s." - Encyclopedia.com (Tartars)[23]

It is important to point out, as the victors write the history books, they occasionally try to eliminate important aspects which they see as counter productive to their own importance. In 1999 a CIA document was released into the public domain, written in 1957, suggesting that the Soviet Government set out to erase certain aspects of Tartarian history from the official record, essentially rewriting history to suit their agenda and modern narrative.

"Let us take the matter of history, which, along with religion, language and literature, constitute the core of a people's heritage. Here again the communists have interfered in a shameless manner. For example on 9th August 1944, the Central Committee of the Communist Party, sitting in Moscow, issued a directive ordering the party's Tartar Provincial Committee "to proceed to a scientific revision of the history of Tartaria, to liquidate serious shortcomings and mistakes of a nationalistic character committed by individual writers and

111

historians in dealing with Tartar history." In other words, Tartar history was to be rewritten -- let us be frank, was to be falsified -- in order to eliminate references to great Russian aggression and to hide the facts of the real course of Tartar/Russian relations. And this was no isolated case. In every Muslim area within the USSR historians, on orders from the Communist Party, have rewritten history to distort the facts so that the Russians appear always in a good light. Needless to say, histories which present the facts truthfully have been withdrawn and destroyed, so that the present and future generations of Muslims are forever denied the chance of learning the true facts of their nation's past." - CIA document 1957[24]

When considering that the Bolshevik revolution was partly financed by the international financial cartel, it opens up a whole avenue of historical deceit. Our history really could be, as Napoleon suggested, "a set of lies agreed upon".

Riba (Usury)

"The first claim of ours on blood-revenge which I abolish is that of the son of Rabi'a b. al-Harith, who was nursed among the tribe of Sa'd and killed by Hudhail. And the usury of the pre-Islamic period is abolished, and the first of our usury I abolish is that of 'Abbas b. 'Abd al-Muttalib, for it is all abolished. " - extract from Muhammad's final sermon. Sahih Muslim Book 15, Hadith 159

"Those who consume interest cannot stand [on the Day of Resurrection] except as one stands who is being beaten by Satan into insanity. That is because they say, "Trade is [just] like interest." But Allah has permitted trade and has forbidden interest. So whoever has received an admonition from his Lord and desists may have what is past, and his affair rests with Allah . But whoever returns to [dealing in interest or usury] - those are the companions of the Fire; they will abide eternally therein." - Quran 2.275

When a nation, race or culture frees itself from the parasitical clutches of usury, within a relatively short period of time that union, free from debt, will see the benefits of a honest monetary system by becoming wealthy beyond the scope of perceived normality.

The modern private central banking system, a usurious enterprise, is the foundation which underpins modern globalisation which is dominated by the Rothschild banking family, a dynasty which was founded in the mid 18th century. This banking dynasty is a large Jewish owned financial cartel, which, through debt, influences the present and future prosperity of each nation's economical and political positioning within world commerce. Through government borrowing conditions are placed on loans offered by the IMF and World Bank, which slowly manoeuvre those countries towards political, social and financial parity with one another. This is the main tactic used to steer each country towards their place within the, one size fits all, mono-mechanism of globalisation. For the global financial usurious monetary system to be complete, everyone must be under its control. This is one of the main reasons why Islam is targeted by western powers due to its religious laws forbidding usury. Over the past two centuries the British Empire teamed up with the Rothschild Zionist banking cartel, to promote each other's interests as they expanded their Empires. The banking cartel would supply the money necessary for war and conquest, while the British would make each country under its rule safe for usury to prosper.

Baphomet, the Sabbatic Goat of Capricorn (I use)

10th Career

Capricorn (I Use)

THE DEVIL.

After the fall of Arabia to the House of Saud, resistance to the global financial system, built on usury, diminished. According to Islamic scholar Imran Hosein the modern world of Islam has become impoverished and enslaved by riba.

"Since 1924, however, riba has penetrated the total economic life of Muslims all around the world. The financial imperialism inherent in riba has delivered the entire world of Islam by its very throat into the hands of enemies with sharpened knives. Indeed all of mankind is now trapped in the world of riba." -
"Riba has impoverished the masses in the entire Muslim world. Riba has rendered Muslims powerless to resist financial blackmail. Because of riba Muslims now live a collective life not entirely dissimilar to slavery. He who pays the piper continues to call the tune. Riba has paralyzed us!
" - Imran Hoesin, Islamic scholar[25]

The Quran is quite specific when it comes to the severity of punishment for those involved in usury. The result is no less than war waged by Allah himself.

"O you who believe! Be careful of (your duty to) Allah and relinquish what remains (due) from usury, if you are believers." - "But if you do (it) not, then be apprised of war from Allah and His Apostle; and if you repent, then you shall have your capital; neither shall you make (the debtor) suffer loss, nor shall you be made to suffer loss." - Quran 2.278 - 2.279

Many Muslims see the west as a place of decadence, where the infidel align themselves with satanic energy in a sea of materialism. Iran has publicly referred to the United States, on more than one occasion, as the Great Satan. Not surprising when one understands the nature of usury, together with knowledge of the Federal Reserve being a private central bank, and the heart of the world's reserve currency. The Quran warns its followers about the dangers of associating with certain friends and alliances, and is specific with regard to what to look out for in order to protect the interests of the Muslim people.

"O you who believe! do not take the Jews and the Christians for friends; they are friends of each other; and whoever amongst you takes them for a friend, then surely he is one of them; surely Allah does not guide the unjust people." - Quran 5.51 Shakir

Islamic eschatology

Eschatology is a part of theology which deals with the end times of humanity, it relates to judgement day and the final destiny of the human soul and spirit. In Islam, a close reading of both the Quran and Hadith, can give numerous insights, that offer up an understanding towards gauging a better idea of the coming Yawn ad - Din (day of reckoning). Muslims believe that prior to judgement day the Dajjal (anti-Christ) will appear to deceive the world, by proclaiming to be an apostle of God. He will eventually be followed by the Mahdi (the guided one) / Isa (Jesus), who will banish evil from the world once and for all. The closer we are to the day of reckoning the further modern offshoots of Islam will have deviated from their initial source, those early roots which aligned their basic core ideology with the teachings of Muhammad and the love and liking characteristics of the planet Venus.

"There will come a time upon the people when nothing will remain of Islam except its name and nothing will remain of the Quran except its words. Their mosques will be splendidly furnished but destitute of guidance. Their scholars will be the worst people under the Heaven; strife (fitna) will issue from them and avert to them." (Mishkat al-Masabih 1/91 Hadith 276)

The Minor Signs :

- The coming of fitna (tribulations) and removal of khushoo' (fear of God).
- The coming of Dajjal, declaring himself as an apostle of God.
- A person passing by a grave might say to another: "I wish it was me".
- The loss of honesty, and authority put in the hands of those who do not deserve it.
- The loss of knowledge and the prevalence of religious ignorance.
- Frequent, sudden, and unexpected deaths.
- Increase in pointless killings.
- Time appears to move faster.
- The spread of riba (usury, interest), zina (adultery, fornication), and the drinking of alcohol.
- Pride and competition in the decoration of mosques.
- Women will increase in number and men will decrease in number.
- More earthquakes.
- Frequent occurrences of disgrace, distortion, and defamation.
- When people wish to die because of the severe trials and tribulations that they are suffering.
- Jews fighting Muslims.
- When paying charity becomes a burden.
- Nomads will compete in the construction of very tall buildings.
- Women will appear naked despite their being dressed.
- People will seek knowledge from misguided and straying scholars.
- Liars will be believed, honest people disbelieved, and faithful people called traitors.
- The death of righteous and knowledgeable people.
- The emergence of indecency (obscenity) and enmity among relatives and neighbours.
- The rise of idolatry and polytheists in the community.
- The Euphrates will uncover a mountain of gold.
- The land of the Arabs will return to being a land of rivers and fields.
- People will increasingly earn money by unlawful (Haram) ways.
- There will be much rain but little vegetation.
- Evil people will be expelled from Al-Madinah.
- Lightning and thunder will become more prevalent.
- There will be a special greeting for people of distinction.
- Trade will become so widespread that a woman will help their husbands in business.
- No truly honest man will remain and no one will be trusted.
- Only the worst people will be left; they will not know any good nor forbid

any evil.

- Nations will call each other to destroy Islam by any and every means.
- Islamic knowledge will be passed on, but no one will follow it correctly.
- Muslim rulers will come who do not follow the guidance and tradition of the Sunnah. Some of their men will have the hearts of devils in a human body.
- Stinginess will become more widespread and honorable people will perish.
- A man will obey his wife and disobey his mother, and treat his friend kindly while shunning his father.
- Family ties will be cut.
- There will be attempts to make the desert green.
- A man will leave his home and his thigh or hip will tell him what is happening back home.
- There will be an abundance of food, most of which has no blessing.
- Men will begin to look like women and women like men.
- Men will lie with men and women with women.
- There will be many women of child bearing age who no longer give birth.
- It will become hot in the winter.
- Great distances will be travelled in short time.
- The Jews will gather again to live in Canaan (Palestine).
- Voices will be raised in the mosques.
- The leader of a people will be the worst of them.
- People will treat a man with respect because they fear the evil he could do.
- Much wine will be drunk.
- Muslims shall fight against a nation who wear shoes made of hair and with faces like hammered shields, with red complexions and small eyes.
- The emergence of the Sufyani (a tyrant who will spread corruption and mischief) within the Syria region.
- The truce and joint Roman-Muslim campaign against a common enemy, followed by al-Malhama al-Kubra (Armageddon), a Roman vs. Muslim war.
- The Black Standard will come from Khorasan, nothing shall turn them back until it is planted in Jerusalem.
- Quran will be forgotten and no one will recall its verses.
- All Islamic knowledge will be lost to the extent that people will not say "Lā ilāha illā llāh" (There is no god but Allah), but instead old people will babble without understanding, "God, God".
- People will fornicate in the streets "like donkeys".
- The first trumpet blow will be sounded by Israfil (angel of music), all that is in heaven and earth will be stunned and die except what God wills, and silence will envelop everything for forty undetermined periods of time.
- Mecca will be attacked and the Kaaba will be destroyed.
- A pleasant breeze will blow from the south that shall cause all believers to

die peacefully.
- The Moon will split in two, but non-believers will insist it isn't happening for real.
- There are two groups of ummah whom God will free from the fire: The group that invades India (Ghazwa-e-Hind), and the group that will be with Isa bin Maryam.
- Emergence of an army, from Yemen, that will make Islam dominant.

The Major signs :[26]

- The false messiah—anti-Christ, Masih ad-Dajjal—shall appear with great powers as a one-eyed man with his right eye blind and deformed like a grape. Although believers will not be deceived, he will claim to be God, to hold the keys to heaven and hell, and will lead many astray. In reality, his heaven is hell, and his hell is heaven. The Dajjal will be followed by seventy thousand Jews of Isfahan (city in Iran) wearing Persian shawls.
- The return of Isa (Jesus), from the fourth sky, to kill Dajjal.
- Gog and Magog, a Japhetic tribe of vicious beings who had been imprisoned by Dhul-Qarnayn, will break out. They will ravage the earth, drink all the water of Lake Tiberias, and kill all believers in their way. Isa, Imam Al-Mahdi, and the believers with them will go to the top of a mountain and pray for the destruction of Gog and Magog. God eventually will send disease and worms to wipe them out.
- A huge black cloud of smoke will cover the earth.
- The Dabbat al-ard, or Beast of the Earth, will come out of the ground to talk to people.
- The sun will rise from the west.
- Three sinkings of the earth, one in the east, one in the west, and one in Arabia.
- The second blow of the trumpet will be sounded, the dead will return to life, and, out of Yemen, will come a fire that shall gather all to Mahshar Al Qiy'amah (The Gathering for Judgment).

Notes for chapter 4

(1) Muhammad the Prophet, Wikipedia,
https://en.wikipedia.org/wiki/Muhammad_in_Islam

(2) The life of Muhammad, BBC documentary, narrated by Rageh Omaar, 2011,
https://www.youtube.com/watch?v=EBx-RYW1FjE

(3) Glen W Bowersock, The rise and fall of a Jewish Kingdom in Arabia. Institute for
Advanced Studies. https://www.ias.edu/ideas/2011/bowersock-jewish-arabia

(4) Dhu Nuwas, Wikipedia, https://en.wikipedia.org/wiki/Dhu_Nuwas

(5) Aksumite - Persian wars, Wikipedia,
https://en.wikipedia.org/wiki/Aksumite%E2%80%93Persian_wars

(6) Wahhabism, Wikipedia, https://en.wikipedia.org/wiki/Wahhabism

(7) What is Wahhabism? The reactionary branch of Islam said to be 'the main source
of global terrorism'". The Telegraph, May 2017.
https://www.telegraph.co.uk/news/2016/03/29/what-is-wahhabism-the-
reactionary-branch-of-islam-said-to-be-the/

(8) Intelligence Colonel Sa'id Mahrnud Najrn Al-'Arniri, The Birth of Al-Wahabi
Movement And it's Historic Roots. Top secret report released on March 13, 2008, by
the U.S. Defense Intelligence Agency. https://fas.org/irp/eprint/iraqi/wahhabi.pdf

(8a) Paul Khalifeh, Saudi dissident in Beirut believes he escaped same fate as
Khashoggi, Middle East Eye. January 2019.
https://www.middleeasteye.net/news/saudi-dissident-beirut-believes-he-escaped-
same-fate-khashoggi

(9) Humfer, Confessions of a British Spy. Omnia Veritas LTD.
https://www.amazon.com/Confessions-British-Spy-Mr-Hempher/dp/1910220159

(10) Hussein ibn Ali al Hashimi, Sharif of Mecca, Wikipedia,
https://en.wikipedia.org/wiki/Hussein_bin_Ali,_Sharif_of_Mecca.

(11) Ikhwan, Wikipedia, https://en.wikipedia.org/wiki/Ikhwan

(12) Ibn Saud, Wikipedia, https://en.wikipedia.org/wiki/Ibn_Saud

(13) Arab Revolt, Wikipedia, https://en.wikipedia.org/wiki/Arab_Revolt

(14) T E Lawrence, Seven Pillars of Wisdom. Published 1926. PDF, Limpidsoft.com.

http://www.limpidsoft.com/small/sevenpillars.pdf

(15) Pre-State Israel: Faisal-Frankfurter Correspondence
(March 1919), Jewish Virtual Library. https://www.jewishvirtuallibrary.org/feisal-frankfurter-correspondence-march-1919
(16) Nu'man Abd al-Wahid, How Zionism helped create the Kingdom of Saudi Arabia, Mondoweiss, Jan 2016. https://mondoweiss.net/2016/01/zionism-kingdom-arabia/

(17) ASKAR H. Al-ENAZY, The Creation of Saudi Arabia: Ibn Saud and British Imperial Policy, 1914–1927, Page 107, https://academic.oup.com/jis/article-abstract/23/2/242/681163?redirectedFrom=PDF

(18) Faisal - Weizmann agreement, Wikipedia,
https://en.wikipedia.org/wiki/Faisal%E2%80%93Weizmann_Agreement

(19) Ikhwan revolt, Wikipedia. https://en.wikipedia.org/wiki/Ikhwan_revolt

(20) Tony Hays, The murder of Lawrence of Arabia, 2013,
https://www.criminalelement.com/blogs/2013/04/the-murder-of-lawrence-of-arabia-tony-hays

(21) Israel - Saudi Arabia relations, Wikipedia.
https://en.wikipedia.org/wiki/Israel%E2%80%93Saudi_Arabia_relations#cite_note-5

(22) History of the two Tartar conquerors of China : including the two journeys into Tartary of Father Ferdinand Verhiest, in the suite of the Emperor Kanh-Hi, By the Hakluyt Society. 1854. https://archive.org/details/historyoftwotart17orle/page/n7

(23) Tartars, Encyclopedia.com. https://www.encyclopedia.com/social-sciences-and-law/anthropology-and-archaeology/people/tatars

(24) National Cultural Development under Communism, CIA document released in 1999. https://www.cia.gov/library/readingroom/docs/CIA-RDP78-02771R000200090002-6.pdf

(25) Imran N. Hosein, The Importance of the Prohibition of Riba in Islam. Director of Islamic Studies, Joint Committee of Mulsim Organizations of Greater New York.http://data.quranacademy.com/QA_Publications/ariticles/English/ImranNHosei n/ImportanceofProhibitionofRibaInIslam.pdf

(26) Islam eschatology, Wikipedia, https://en.wikipedia.org/wiki/Islamic_eschatology

(27) Al Khalidi, Islamic signs of the hour and the end times, youtube video, Jan 2011, https://www.youtube.com/watch?v=x_obnjFWY2U

Chapter 5. The satanisation of Judaism

According to official history Judaism is the oldest monotheistic religion in the world, dating back some 4,000 years. Today there are only 14 million Jews, around 0.2% of the world's population. Most of these Jews live in either Israel or the United States. Traditionally a person would only consider themselves a Jew if their mother was Jewish. However, in some circles it is acceptable to become Jewish by publicly declaring oneself as such, together with adopting the Jewish faith and many of their religious practices. In some stricter circles a formal conversion is required, under the guidance and supervision of a respected Rabbi. Jews believe in the one God Yahweh, who first revealed himself to the prophet Abraham, establishing a covenant with Abraham and all his descendants. This agreement led to the Jews believing that they were God's chosen people, who were promised the land of Canaan where, one day, they would build a great nation.

"The Lord had said to Abram, "Go from your country, your people and your father's household to the land I will show you."I will make you into a great nation, and I will bless you; I will make your name great, and you will be a blessing." - Genisis 12 : 1-2 (NIV)

Most Jews do not consider Jesus to be the Messiah. However, they do recognise him as a significant figure with prophetic abilities. The Jews are still waiting for their Messiah to appear, and believe he will come some time in the near future to unite and rule over all Jews in the Kingdom of Israel, after which, there will be peace on Earth.

Another significant figure in the Judaic tradition is Moses. Also a prophet, he was asked by God to lead the Israelites out of Egypt, from where many were being used as slaves by the Egyptians. Fulfilling God's wishes Moses led the Israelites out of Egypt, parting the Red Sea in the process allowing all of his followers to cross over towards the promised land. On the way he stopped at Mount Sinai, where he was given a new set of rules by God, in the form of Ten Commandments. When the Israelites finally reached Canaan they developed communities, which, around 1000 BC, eventually led to the Kingdom of Israel, ruled by three consecutive kings Saul, David and Solomon. The first Jewish Temple was built during the rule of king Solomon, a magnificent temple, which became the focal point for Jewish worship. Around the year 931 BC the kingdom was divided and split, with Israel in the north and Judah to the south, a division which made them more vulnerable to outside aggression. In 722 BC the Assyrians invaded the north and destroyed the northern Kingdom of Israel. The Kingdom of Judah continued until 568 BC, a date which saw the Jews overrun by the Babylonians, who in the attack, destroyed the Temple of Solomon and sent most of the Jews into exile. In 539 BC Cyrus the Great, the King of Persia attacked and took over Babylon. As a result, the Jews were freed from exile and returned to Jerusalem to build the Second Temple. This stood for over 400 years until the Romans arrived, in 70 AD, to quash a rebellion. They sacked the city and smashed the temple into a pile of rubble.

With the Temple gone, the focal point for Jewish religious expression was no longer available. Consequently, the Jews turned to various synagogues as a way of keeping their faith alive. Around the year 200 AD Jewish scholars compiled Jewish oral law into text form, they called this the Mishna. This was followed, a century later, by the Talmud, another book on Jewish law together with Jewish theology. It served many early Jewish communities as a guide for the running of their day to day lives. The Jews also have the Torah, which is a term used to describe the first five books of the Old Testament, which they believe was written by Moses. All theses books are used to encompass the totality of Jewish teachings, whether biblical texts or rabbinic writings, they express Jewish morals, Jewish religious obligations along with their civil laws.

"Then the Lord said to Moses, "Write down these words, for in accordance with these words I have made a covenant with you and with Israel." Moses was there with the Lord forty days and forty nights without eating bread or drinking water. And he wrote on the tablets the words of the covenant—the Ten Commandments." - Genisis 34 27-28 (NIV)

If we analyse the passing of the Ages from an astrological perspective, the names given to many biblical characters have greater significance when the ruling planets of those Ages are taken into consideration. During the Age of Aries, the ram, we see many characters, at that time, with names referring to rams. This epoch was ruled by the planet Mars, which also appears in various significant names.

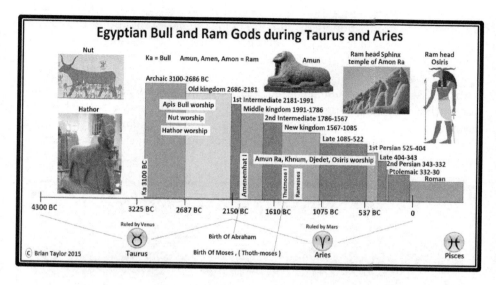

Abraham = Ab-ram. Born at the beginning of the Age of Aries (approx 2000BC).[1]

Moses = Mars-es, the planet of proactive energy and movement, in a specific direction. Moses led the Israelites, in a display of proactive movement in a specific direction, across the Red Sea towards the promised land.

Ramesses = Pharaohs Ramesses I to Ramesses XI. Throughout the New Kingdom period.

Thutmose = Thut-mars I to Thustmose IV. At the beginning of the New Kingdom.

Judaism, being a religion which promotes Saturn's energetic characteristics above all the other planets, leads to unique and specific characteristics being expressed throughout Jewish culture and day to day lives. Saturn is the slowest moving of all the visible planets, and as such is synonymous with time. It is Cronus, Old Father Time and the teacher. Consequently, it is no surprise to see, as a reflection of these energies, Judaism being the oldest monotheistic religion which places great emphasis on tradition, scholarship, self discipline, hard work and career. All characteristics of Saturn.

Although Saturn's personified characters throughout history have conjured up some dark, sinister and frightening images, Saturn's energies are not all bad. By aligning one's cultural identity with Saturn, it will, in time, manifest benefits of a material nature, promoting those under its influence into positions of control within organised structures of authority.

Order, structure and control.
Commands us to get to work and work hard.
Discipline and responsibility.
Limitations, frustrations, loss, restrictions and austerity.
Organising one's time. Governs time from birth to death.
Sense of tradition and conventionality.
Perseverance and withstanding the test of time.
Senior status brings authority.
Pessimism and depression.
The past.

Because Saturn is the cross of materialism over the crescent of spirituality, it promotes all things of a material nature in favour of those of spirituality. This is why some old school Christians considered the Judaic God of the Old Testament to be the Demiurge, the God of the material realm.

The zodiac, as a diagrammatic expression of our conscious connection to the universe, offers insights of a profound nature. Consequently, when we analyse the zodiac signs and houses under the domain of Saturn we find metaphysical correlations between astrology and Judaism.

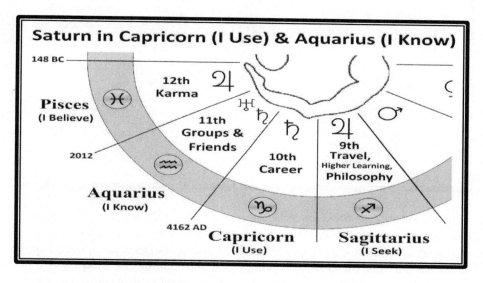

Saturn rules two houses of the zodiac, Aquarius (I know) and Capricorn (I use). Both intelligence and usury are synonymous with Jewish culture and history. The 10th house is concerned with public persona, social reputation, career path and substantial achievements. It is sometimes called the house of world leaders, as it shows us how we fulfil our lifetime's destiny, from hard work and perseverance. It is the house of family tradition, legacy, roots and ancestry. It is a cardinal earth sign which promotes proactive initiation of material matters relating to career, business and our social interaction on the world stage. Consequently, because it is the house of career and hard work, although Jews are only 2-3% of the American population, they make up almost half of the country's billionaires.[2]

With the motto for Capricorn being 'I use', usury comes into the picture, the most powerful of all forms of control, dominated by offshoots of the Jewish establishment. Aligned with the energetic characteristics of Saturn, through the practice of traditional Judaism, some Jews naturally excel in areas of control, restriction, organisation and materialism, culminating throughout the modern

124

practice of fractional reserve banking. When the Piscean Age is divided up into another twelve houses of the zodiac, it can be seen that between the years of 1472 – 1742, when Saturn ruled the outer wheel, many prominent Jewish families (e.g. Rothschilds) excelled in the areas of banking and business.

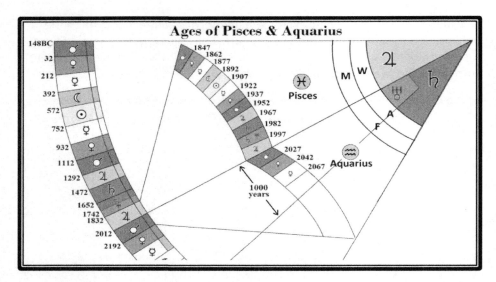

After the Lutheran Protestant movement in the 15th century had rejected the Holy Roman Empire, it subsequently paved the way for the expansion of usury, especially among the aristocracy of Europe and England. Henry VIII, deep in debt, finally allowed usury back into England. Up to this point both Muslims and Roman Catholics had resisted usury, viewing it as one of the greatest sins. The Jewish goldsmiths had limited markets available because of political and social restrictions placed upon them. However, after the Protestants rejected Catholicism, some Jews and Protestants joined forces against their common enemy. Freemasonry sprung up, incorporating both Jews and protestants as a secret intellectual army promoting anti Catholic sentiments underpinned by aspects of Saturn's characteristics. Mammon was to be promoted, materialism over spirituality, the cross was to dominate the crescent in a new joint venture between factions working towards the globalisation or the Saturnisation of humanity.

Throughout this period Saturn's influence propelled many people to get to work and work hard, within the confines of discipline, responsibility, limitations and restrictions. Saturn/Cronus governs time, along with organisations, structure and order. The Commercial Revolution was under way, with expanding trade routes and empires. The most disciplined and structured organisations began to dominate, spreading their influence across all corners of the known world.

Cronus' influence brought forward the mechanical clock. Due to the invention of the escapement mechanism, oscillating timekeeping devices and spring driven clocks began to appear in the 15th century, flourishing over the next 100 years. The whole concept of the clock changed society, governing the day to day lives of the majority of working people, a major tool in commanding the citizens to get to work and to work hard. For commerce to thrive with ease, a fluid mechanism of exchange was necessary, the Judaic Saturnine community were at the spearhead of this business. Their roots as goldsmiths and money lenders facilitated usury, paving the way for new parasitical banking institutions. The first modern private central banks appeared, like the Bank of England (1694), an institution created to enable government and industry to borrow large sums of money with ease. This was the new Age of Jupitarian/Saturnine expansion, joining forces to initiate the Judaic/Christian Empire and globalisation.

Expansion of Saturn with Jupiter

The 11th house of Aquarius (I know) is the house of groups, friends and goals we set ourselves. A house which seeks intellectual security, where collaboration, shared visions and community find ways to express collective objectives. The detachment and individuality associated with Aquarius is here helping to see beyond the familiarity of this known reality. The House of Aquarius is where the mind, and its goals, merge with others, promoting the power of the group, whether that group be a club, network or a professional association.

Groups and Friends of Israel

Aquarius

IX

THE HERMIT.

The Hermit in Tarot represents energies associated with Aquarius. He is the wise hermit (I know), standing on the double wave of Aquarius. Holding a lamp, which illuminates the left hand path with a six pointed star, a star which represents Saturn, the traditional ruling planet of Aquarius.

Just like Christianity and Islam, various forms and offshoots deviated from the basic concept of traditional Judaism. For centuries traditional Judaism mainly focused on admirable and peaceful qualities associated with Saturn, keeping their social and moral structure together, underpinned by the writings contained within the Torah and the commandments. However, over time perverted offshoots began to appear, some of which were so extreme and sinister that even the most liberal Rabbis rejected them as abominations to the faith.

Traditional Orthodox Jews believe that the Jewish exile, which began around 69 AD, was an edict, a decree from God which scattered the Jews out among the nations. They were not to return, en masse, to form any kind of sovereign nation until God, with a new decree, allowed them to do so. God also promised that the Jews would have his protection whilst they lived out among non Jewish nations. God strictly forbad Jews from returning, in large numbers, before their time was right. It is believed, by non-Zionist Jews, that if they forced the redemption too soon and rebelled against God's wishes, all attempts and efforts would ultimately be doomed to failure. It is for this reason, why many Orthodox Jews do not support the concept and actions of the Zionist movement.

"And the Lord shall scatter you among the nations, and ye shall be left few in number among the heathen, whither the Lord shall lead you." - Deuteronomy 4:27 (KJV)

"The Biblical book Song of Songs says: "I adjure you, O daughters of Jerusalem, by the gazelles or the deer of the field, not to arouse or awaken the love before it is desired." This oath occurs three times in the Song of Songs (2:7, 3:5 and 8:4). The Talmud interprets this metaphorical language to mean as follows: the

speaker here is God, and the "daughters of Jerusalem" are the Jewish people and the nations of the world. During the Jewish exile, which began with the destruction of the Temple in the year 69 CE, God placed three oaths upon the world, two upon the Jewish people and one upon the nations. The Jewish people were foresworn not to immigrate as a wall (i.e. en masse) to the Holy Land, and not to rebel against the other nations. The nations were foresworn not to afflict the Jews too much." - Tractate Kesubos 111a[3]

Many Orthodox Jews, like Rabbi Yisroel Dovid Weiss hold the opinion that most practising Jews, who are faithful to the Torah, do not support the concept and actions of the Zionist movement. They believe Zionism, by its nature, of forcing the redemption issue, are antagonistic to the wishes and edicts of All Mighty God, and by forcing the resettlement of Jews back to Israel will ultimately bring about their own end through the wrath of God.[4]

"Zionism is a new movement, a transformation from the religious into a base, materialistic, nationalistic movement. To have a piece of land which is forbidden for the Jews." - Rabbi Yisroel Dovid Weiss[4]

One theory which ties Ashkenazi Jews to the Khazars, is a theory which has many critics among mainstream academia. It suggests that the Ashkenazi Jews originated from the medieval Khazarian Empire, giving them a different genealogy to the Semitic Jews altogether. Although this theory has been widely attacked it is still considered credible by some circles.[4a] During the 8th century AD, King Bulan of the Khazarian Empire had a dilemma. He was surrounded by expanding enemies on all sides. Christians to the west and the north, and Muslims to the south. He concluded that if his people converted to Christianity, they would be targeted by the Muslims from the south. Conversely, if they converted to Islam he would be attacked by the Christians from the north and west. Eager to stay in power and continue being a significant trading hub, he decided the best option would be to convert, en masse, to Judaism. This would allow the king to stay relatively neutral, while keeping his kingdom and trading options open. These Jews became known as Ashkenazi Jews, and seen as a different sub-race to the Semitic Jews of Canaan within the Middle East. Over the centuries, as the Khazarian Empire crumbled many Ashkenazi Jews moved west to Eastern Europe, to places like the Ukraine, Poland and parts of Russia. Although the Ashkenazi Jews had accepted the faith of Judaism, and practised its rituals and ceremonies, they were considered, by the Semitic Jews, as second rate and not part of the 12 tribes of Israel. Because of this, throughout most of history, the Semitic Jews would not allow intermarriage between the two groups. However, over the past 150 years this has become more accepted. The main difference between the Ashkenazi and Semitic Jews, apart from biological lineage, was their attitude towards the Judaic faith. According to the Scholar of Jewish history Muhammad Rafeeq,[5] the Semitic Jews centred their faith around the Torah (Old Testament) using the Talmud as a side commentary. Whereas, the Ashkenazi Jews centred their faith around the Talmud and Zoha (mystical teachings known as Kabbalah) while pushing the Torah to one side. This created two very different ideologies especially concerning the Messiah and a return to the land of Israel. While the Semitic Jews had no desire to relocate themselves back to the Promised Land, without God giving them a signal to do so, with the arrival of a new Messiah. The Ashkenazi Jews were happy to initiate the return to Israel before the Messiah appeared, believing that a return to Israel would promote his appearance in the process.

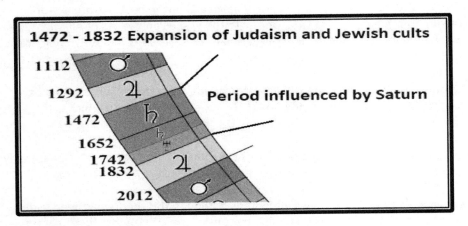

Between 1534 and 1572, Isaac Ben Solomon Luria, known in Jewish circles as Ha'ARI' the lion, was developing his own version of Kabbalism. He lived in the small town of Safed, in upper Galilee. After the expulsion of the Sephardic Jews, from Spain, in 1492, a time when a Jewish mystical renaissance was taking hold, Lurianic Kabbalims became the new foundation of the Judaic Zoha. During this time an urgency was felt among many kabbalistic Jews towards hastening a Messianic redemption.[4] Consequently, new rituals where developed with a communal messianic focus. From this new Lurianic Kabbalistic approach to mystical Judaism some interesting, yet sinister, ideologies emerged.

"This calls for wisdom. Let the person who has insight calculate the number of the beast, for it is the number of a man. That number is 666." - Revelations 13 : 18 (NIV)

Sabbatai Zevi

In 1626, Sabbatai Zevi was born into a Jewish family, in the city of Smyrna, on the east coast of present day Turkey. As a student he was fascinated with mysticism and Kabbalah. It was rumoured that the followers of Lurianic Kabbalism could communicate with God and his angels, predict the future and perform magic and miracles. From his fascination with mysticism he became a well known ordained Rabbi and Lurianic Kabbalist throughout the Ottoman Empire. In 1648, at the age of 22, Sabbatai Zevi, riding on an international wave of messianic anticipation, suggested to his small group of followers that he was the long awaited Messiah. To prove himself he would pronounce the biblical name of God, a practice prohibited to all except the most high priests. He also told his followers that he could fly, but would not do so in public to people unworthy of his display of magic. On top of this he claimed that he had regular visions of God, confirming his Messianic claim. Because he was only 22 at the time, older Rabbis did not take him seriously, and saw him as a mischievous upstart. A few years later, now in his early 30s, he was banished from Smyrna for his outrageous claims, only to appear in Constantinople in 1658. It was around this time Sabbatai Zevi met a preacher named Abraham Yachini, who was believed to have forged a document, in ancient characters, legitimising Sabbatai's claim as the new Messiah.

"I, Abraham, was confined in a cave for forty years, and I wondered greatly that the time of miracles did not arrive. Then was heard a voice proclaiming, 'A son will be born in the Hebrew year 5386 [the year 1626 CE] to Mordecai Zevi; and he will be called Shabbethai. He will humble the great dragon; ... he, the true Messiah, will sit upon My throne." - The great wisdom of Solomon. Purported to have been written by Abraham Yachini.[7]

Around 1659 he moved to Salonica. At that time it was the centre of Kabbalistic studies among Jewish scholars. After spending some time putting on mystical events, in an effort to increase his following, his antics drew the attention of senior Rabbis, who once more banished him from the city. After travelling for a while he eventually settled in Cairo, staying for approximately two years. Here he met Raphael Joseph, a wealth Jewish tax revenue manager working for the Ottoman Empire. Although extremely wealthy and charitable Joseph preferred a life of abstinence and fasting. After a short period of time he became drawn into Sabbatai's messianic claims, and from then on would help support Sabbatai Zevi's projects. After Cairo Sabbatai went to Jerusalem, where he continued to promote his Messianic claims, bolstered by regular episodes of fasting. At this point he gained prestige among the elders of the city due to his close friendship with Raphael Joseph, who from time to time would help with the heavy tax levies imposed on Jerusalem by the Ottoman Government.

On a trip to Gaza Sabbatai Zevi met Nathan Benjamin Levi, an active supporter of Zevi's messianic claims. They became great friends and eventually Nathan would become Zevi's right hand man. In 1665 Nathan announced that the Messianic Age was almost upon them, and would peak in the following year. Furthermore, the new Messiah would conquer the world, without bloodshed, and lead the ten lost tribes of Israel back to the Holy Land. Although Sabbatai Zevi was respected for his relationship with wealthy backers, his messianic claims began to arouse suspicion among the high levels of Rabbis within the city. They told him that Jerusalem was not the city where he should be unveiling his prestige, and threatened him with excommunication. Consequently, he left disappointed and headed back to his home town of Smyrna. At this point Nathan suggested Gaza, not Jerusalem, would be a better place to reveal his Messianic claim to the world. As a result, Sabbatai Zevi and his followers descended on Gaza. Here, in the city of Aleppo, they received a great welcome. By the end of the year he found himself back in his home town of Smyrna, where, at the celebrations for the Jewish new year, he publicly announced himself as the new Messiah. This announcement was followed by trumpet playing and shouts of "Long live the king, our Messiah." It was clear at this stage that he was generating a great deal of interest, whether he had the credentials or not, seemed irrelevant to many of his followers, he was fulfilling their eager anticipation and expectation for the coming year of 1666. It ultimately became a self fulfilling prophecy, with Zevi and Nathan delivering the goods.

1666 became an important year for the Messianic movement, Zevi became leader of Smyrna, deposing the previous Rabbi, placing his own followers in top positions. As the word spread more and more Jews, eagerly wanting their own Messiah, began to believe in him. Throughout Europe Sabbatean Jewish centres opened, dedicated to Zevi's Messianic cause, eventually attracting around 1 million followers. Zevi's secretary compiled a statement which was to be sent out to all Jews.

"The first-begotten Son of God, Shabbethai Tebi, Messiah and Redeemer of the people of Israel, to all the sons of Israel, Peace! Since ye have been deemed worthy to behold the great day and the fulfilment of God's word by the Prophets, your lament and sorrow must be changed into joy, and your fasting into merriment; for ye shall weep no more. Rejoice with song and melody, and change the day formerly spent in sadness and sorrow into a day of jubilee, because I have appeared." - Samuel Primo, Sabbatai's secretary 1666[7]

Sometime in early 1666 Zevi left on a trip to Constantinople. Believing in his own propaganda and importance, he was under the illusion that the Sultan of Constantinople would welcome him with open arms. However, when he arrived, the Sultan had already sent out the order for his immediate arrest, which materialised on his arrival in the city. While Zevi languished in prison, his close circle of followers disseminated reports of a contrary nature, spreading rumours, out into the Jewish diaspora, telling of how Sabbatai's wonderful and miraculous deeds were being received in Constantinople. Unconcerned at the gravity of his predicament, both Sabbatai and his followers believed, with God's help, their new Messiah would prevail. At this point, especially being an important date within Judaism, many powerful onlookers were becoming increasingly anxious towards its spreading popularity, and potential disruption to the established status quo. For this reason the Sultan gave Sabbatai three choices.

- Subject himself to a volley of arrows. If the archers missed his divinity would be proven.
- Be impaled.
- Convert to Islam.

The very next day, after pondering on his options, Sabbatai Zevi, the self proclaimed Jewish Messiah, was taken to stand before the Sultan, where he proceeded to take off his Jewish clothes and place a Turkish turban on his head, an act which confirmed his conversion to Islam. Delighted at the spectacle, the Sultan accepted Zevi's conversion and gave him the new name of Mahmed Effendi. Following the conversion the Sultan was more than happy to inform Sabbatai's followers together with the greater Jewish diaspora of the happy news. While both Christians and Muslims fell over each other laughing, throughout Jewish circles it was taken very badly as a tremendously bitter disappointment. However, 300 of Sabbatai Zevi's close followers, along with their families, suspecting that the conversion was insincere, also converted to Islam, as a show of allegiance to their Messiah. These Jewish Muslims became known as Donmeh (converts). They based their community in Salonica, where northern Greece is now, and are still there to this day. After a few years of pretending to be a Muslim Zevi was discovered singing psalms with fellow Jews. Consequently, he was banished from Constantinople, and moved to Dulcigno, a small town where

Montenegro is now. Sabbatai Zevi died in 1676 in relative isolation.[7]

According to mainstream consensus regarding Jewish history, the story of Sabbatai Zevi ends with his death. However, this perspective is far from the truth. After his downfall and later death, many of his followers, now called Sabbateans went underground. They formed secret societies and groups, which on the exterior took on the religion of their host country, while in secret still practising Lurianic Kabbalism. The Sabbateans essentially went underground, with the knock on effect leading to some rather dark and sinister cult movements. Movements which are still with us today, surprisingly play a formidable role in the modern globalisation project.

Jacob Frank (1726 - 1791)

Fifty years after the death of Sabbatai Zevi, Jacob Frank was born to a family of Sabbateans, in Buchach, East Poland. Purporting to be the reincarnation of both Sabbatai Zevi and Abraham's grandson Jacob, Frank, on the back of the Sabbatean movement, developed an unusual and perverted form of Judaism, which violated many traditional Jewish laws and customs. By the time Frank came on the scene, some Sabbatean sects had deviated into perverted cults promoting promiscuity and degenerate sexual acts. Wife swapping orgies became a common occurrence, referred to by the Sabbatean priests as 'purification through transgression'. Although sexual immorality was encouraged, severe self discipline which avoided various forms of indulgence was practised in other areas of their lives. From this Sabbatean base, Jacob Frank took his new religion to the next level.

After proclaiming himself the reincarnation of Sabbatai Zevi and a new Messiah in 1751, Frank moved to Podolia, a city in the south western part of the Ukraine. Here he began to preach what he had gained from the Donmeh back in Salonica. After some time Frank's teachings drew the attention of some senior Rabbis, who, after hearing his preaching, found it to be unacceptable and forced him out of the city. Consequently, a Congress of Rabbis held a rabbinical court in the village of Sataniv, in the Ukraine. After hearing about sexual promiscuity within the sect, under the guise of mystical symbolism, the Rabbis concluded that many of Frank's followers and the Sabbateans in general, were breaking fundamental Jewish laws on morality and modesty. In 1756, as a result of the hearings, the Rabbis proclaimed excommunication against all 'impenitent heretics', asking all pious Jews to keep a vigilant look out in order to expose them. This new movement of Jews rejected the traditional Talmud, recognising only the sacred book of Kabbalah (Zoha). At this point Jacob Frank publicly announced that he was the true successor to Sabbatai Zevi, and that God had instructed him, and his followers, to convert to Christianity, whilst all the time concealing their inner identity as Sabbatean Kabbalistic mystics. Most of the Frankists were baptised in the Ukrainian town of Lwow. Frank himself was baptised on the 17th Semptember 1759, and again the very next day, witnessed by Augustus III, who acted as his godfather. Records show that by 1790, 26,000 Polish Jews had officially converted to Christianity by being baptised. Although Frank and his followers had publicly converted to Christianity, senior members of the clergy viewed them with suspicion, which on 6th February 1760 was proven correct. Frank was caught teaching heresy, which led to his arrest and a 13 year imprisonment. Apart from discouraging and deterring his followers, his incarceration gave him the mystique of a martyr, attracting more followers to the town of Czestochowa. After his release in 1772, Frank continued his movement, travelling to many cities across eastern Europe, settling in Morovia and finally Offenbach, Germany, where he died in 1791.[8]

Jacob Frank (1726-1791)

The legacy of Frankism or Zoharism, apart from claiming to be yet another Jewish Messiah, is one which Orthodox Jews discredit as a perversion of traditional Judaism. It was a sect which was accused of sexual immorality and the revival of canard (Jews using Christian blood for Passover rituals).[9]

According to the research of Muhammad Rafeeq,[5] both the Sabbatean and Frankist movements were reversals of Judaic principles. Being messianic movements, they tried to do what was necessary to bring forth the new Messiah. Because the Talmud says the Messiah would appear at a time when everyone is either all good or all bad. As a consequence, these movements concluded that it was far easier to be all bad than all good. Therefore, still fulfilling requirements which would bring about the Messiah, together with a new kingdom and world peace, they believed that by being all bad, they were still doing God's work.

"R. Johanan said: When you see a generation ever dwindling, hope for him [the Messiah], as it is written, And the afflicted people thou wilt save. R. Johanan said: When thou seest a generation overwhelmed by many troubles as by a

river, await him, as it is written, when the enemy shall come in like a flood, the Spirit of the Lord shall lift up a standard against him; which is followed by, And the Redeemer shall come to Zion. R. Johanan also said: The son of David will come only in a generation that is either altogether righteous or altogether wicked. 'in a generation that is altogether righteous,' — as it is written, Thy people also shall be all righteous: they shall inherit the land for ever. 'Or altogether wicked,' — as it is written, And he saw that there was no man, and wondered that there was no intercessor; and it is [elsewhere] written, For mine own sake, even for mine own sake, will I do it." - Talmud, Sanhedrin 98a[10]

Jacob Frank's Kabbalistic movement, taught that the concept of evil is only in the minds of the Gentiles (non Jew), and that in this world there is no such thing as pure evil. They believed that good comes from the right hand of God, and what the gentiles considered as evil comes from God's left hand. Consequently, by performing deeds offered by God's left hand, it was still considered as 'doing God's work. Anyone with this ideology would consider murder, rape, incest, blood drinking and sexual immorality as perfectly acceptable forms of behaviour. Believing that if the whole world participated In this form of behaviour, they would help to hasten and bring forth the new Messiah.

Kabbalists believe that both good and evil exist as expressions of Divine energy, being complementary aspects within universal consciousness. Unlike most religions, where evil exists outside of God, some Kabbalists see evil as an essential part of divinity and the creation, where evil originates at the very core of Divine consciousness. The comprehension of good can only be understood through the exploration of evil, just as we appreciate the beauty of the Sun far more after we have experienced the rain. Through the promotion of evil, misery and tragedy, throughout the world, we should have a better understanding and appreciation of compassion, kindness and all the good things life has to offer.

For the conscious mind to gain a higher and deeper level of understanding it must explore the subconscious, and the underworld, thereby gaining knowledge of those darker aspects of itself. Only when the ego is broken down can the subconscious be allowed in, signalling a deeper and more meaningful spiritual transformation, thereby adding extra dimensions of consciousness through the healing process. Evil derives from the separation of unity. Diabolos divides and abolishes all things united, bringing forth new opportunities out of the chaos created. Through destruction, deconstruction, disintegration and chaos, humanity has the potential to achieve higher degrees of consciousness derived from its understanding and experience of the evil generated.

"A sinner who repents is on a higher level than the saint who has never sinned"
- Jung, *Red Book*.[11]

For Kabbalists to deny evil in the world is to deny God. And through the experience of both good and evil they are able to come closer to God in a reciprocal union of consciousness. By going deep within, in an attempt to embrace our dark side, we might come to terms with our baser desires, where the subconscious can evolve to the next level. To be complete we must include a dark side, only then do we have the potential to refine ourselves within a Divine furnace of subconscious purification.

"There is no light except that which issues from darkness, and no true good except it proceed from evil" - The Zohar, key to kabbalistic text[13]

"From the Kabbalistic point of view, evil brings into the world the possibility of choosing between sin and virtue, which is to say that evil is the very origin of the possibility of the highest good. Freedom of choice is a necessary postulate for responsibility, morality and the creation of values. Evil becomes the condition for free choice, and hence, the condition for the full realization of good." - Paul Levy, The Kabbalah's remarkable idea[12]

"You cant reject evil because evil is the brighter of the light" - **"The evil one is holy"** - God could not create true freedom for humanity without giving us a choice between good and evil" - C Jung, Kabbalah.[12]

"The stirring up of conflict is a Luciferian virtue in the true sense of the word. Conflict engenders fire, the fire of affects and emotions, and like every other fire, it has two aspects, that of combustion and that of creating light." - C Jung,[14]

According to Kabbalists, the greater the impulse for evil the greater the potential for good. Consequently, with this philosophy in mind, if Kabbalists found their way into positions of power, the world would see a great deal of division being promoted in order to foment evil for what Kabbalists believe to be an improvement of overall human consciousness.

"Barry Chamish's articles corroborate Rev. Torell's assertion that the old Marrano families are still with us today and that Jewish infiltrators are strategically placed in political and religious institutions expressly for the purpose of implementing the Illuminist (Judeo-Masonic) agenda." - Mystery Babylon the Great part 3.[15]

"The Frankists' modus operandi, namely, through false conversions and phony renunciations of Judaism, gaining the trust of the ecclesiastical powers which obtained for them the protection of the State to carry out their seditious plans." - Rabbi Antelman / Barry Chamish, Mystery Babylon the Great part 3.[15]

According to the research of Muhammad Rafeeq[5], during the latter part of Frank's life, in the 18th century, he had networked his Kabbalistic version of Judaism which spread throughout the wider community, connecting with wealthy and influential people, including the Rothschild banking dynasty and Adam Weishaupt, the founder of the Bavarian Illuminati. According to Rafeeq, it was Frank who instructed Weishaupt to set up the Illuminati with the help of Rothschild's money. Frank also instructed a number of followers to go to Poland and set up a variety of factories in order to prosper and make great wealth.

In Eliyaha Stern's book *Jewish Materialism, the intellectual revolution of the 1870s*, he suggests, as a backlash to Jewish conditions within the Pale of Settlements, a group of Russian Jews began to reform Judaism and Jewish ideology towards the material aspects of the universe.

"Principally, the ideology defined Judaism and Jewish identity within the "material" aspect of the universe."-"Jews in Russia during this time began to reform Judaism, looking towards its resources, which could shed light on the fair distribution of wealth."-"That would become the start of a whole host of Jewish political movements, including Bundism, Zionism and Territorialism,"- "All of these [ideologies] began with one fundamental idea that Jewish identity is fundamentally rooted in the physical-material world." - Times of Israel[16]

In recent years, the spotlight of scrutiny has descended upon the Armenian massacres, which took place prior to WW1. It is claimed that it was not the Turks, but the Sabbateans who planned and implemented the deportation and mass slaughter of most of the Ottoman Armenian population. Prior to the overthrow of the Caliph, the Donmeh, based in Silonica, established three masonic lodges in Turkey. Through these networks they were able to destabilise and overthrow the Caliph, promoting the Young Turks as an antidote to Muslim rule.

"It was this core group of Dönmeh, which organized the secret Young Turks, also known as the Committee of Union and Progress, the secularists who deposed Ottoman Sultan Abdulhamid II in the 1908 revolution, proclaimed the post-Ottoman Republic of Turkey after World War I, and who instituted a campaign that stripped Turkey of much of its Islamic identity after the fall of the Ottomans." - "Historians like Ahmed Refik, who served as an intelligence officer in the Ottoman army, averred that it was the aim of the Young Turks to destroy the Armenians, who were mostly Christian. The Young Turks, under Ataturk's direction, also expelled Greek Christians from Turkish cities and attempted to commit a smaller-scale genocide of the Assyrians, who were also mainly Christian." - Wayne Madsen, The Donmeh : The Middle East's most whispered secret (part1).[17]

Notes for chapter 5.

(1) Margaret Hunter, Bible timeline 1996 BC birth of Abraham. 2013.
https://amazingbibletimeline.com/blog/bible_timeline_chronology/

(2) Mark Weber, Zionist Report, Powerful Speech! "The Challenge of Jewish-Zionist Power", youtube,
https://www.youtube.com/watch?v=9hqnV_4JICQ&t=453s

(3) Where in the Torah does it say Jews can't have a state?, Torah Jews,
https://www.truetorahjews.org/qanda/source1

(4) Rabbi Yisroel Dovid Weiss, Zionism has created rivers of blood. Aljazeera interview. 2017. https://www.youtube.com/watch?v=2qJwKYH7wvk

(4a) Khazar hypothesis of Ashkenazi ancestry. Wikipedia.
https://en.wikipedia.org/wiki/Khazar_hypothesis_of_Ashkenazi_ancestry

(5) Daryl Bradford Smith, French Connection Radio, interview with Muhammad Rafeeq. Sabbatai Zevi, the satanic Jewish Messiah of 1666.
https://www.youtube.com/watch?v=ESgVIhg1Zjs

(6) Lurianic Kabbalah, Wikipedia,
https://en.wikipedia.org/wiki/Lurianic_Kabbalah

(7) Sabbatai Zevi, Wikipedia, https://en.wikipedia.org/wiki/Sabbatai_Zevi

(8) Jacob Frank, Jewish virtual library, a project of AICE.
https://www.jewishvirtuallibrary.org/jacob-frank

(9) Jacob Frank, Encyclopedia Britannica.
https://www.britannica.com/biography/Jacob-Frank

(10) Sanhedrin 98a, Talmud. http://www.come-and-hear.com/sanhedrin/sanhedrin_98.html

(11) Jung, Red Book, p. 229.

(12) Paul Levy, The Kabbalah's remarkable idea. Awaken in the dream.
https://www.awakeninthedream.com/articles/the-kabbalahs-remarkable-idea

(13) Zohar II, 184a; Sperling and Simon, The Zohar, Vol. IV, p. 125.

(14) Jung, CW 9i, The Archetypes and the Collective Unconscious, par. 179.

(15) Babrara Aho, Mystery Babylon the Great, Part 3,
https://www.bibliotecapleyades.net/cienciareal/babylon03.htm

(16) JP O'Malley, How the stereotype of Jews and money goes beyond the Pale
(of Settlement). Times of Israel, 2018. https://www.timesofisrael.com/how-the-
stereotype-of-jews-and-money-goes-beyond-the-pale-of-settlement/

(17) Wayne Madsen, The Donmeh: The Middle East's most whispered Secret.
(Part1). Strategic Culture Foundation. https://www.strategic-
culture.org/news/2011/10/25/the-doenmeh-the-middle-easts-most-whispered-
secret-part-i/

Chapter 6. Kabbalah

Although Jewish mysticism claim that the origins of Kabbalah stem from Adam, Abraham and Moses, the truth is uncertain, and its origins are unclear. It is likely that Kabbalah evolved from ancient pagan star worship, a form of astro magic, and was the result of our ancestor's understanding and interpretation of their conscious relationship to the Creator. Kabbalism is not a religion but a way to comprehend our relationship with that Creator. It is possible that this profound ancient wisdom could have come from a sophisticated antediluvian civilisation with a developed understanding of their relationship to the macrocosm. Many forms of occult knowledge have some connection to Kabbalah. It is a sophisticated, poetical diagrammatic representation of how the Logos/Creator manifested aspects of Divine consciousness here in the material realm. It also maps out our conscious relationship to the creator within various levels of differentiating Divine manifestation, throughout all levels of this known physical reality.

The diagrammatic Kabbalah represents the tree of knowledge or the Tree of Life; the same tree found in the Garden of Eden. Although the Bible mentions two trees in the garden, a Tree of Life and a tree of the knowledge of good and evil. In reality, and in Kabbalism, the Tree of Life is the tree of the knowledge of good, whereas the Tree of Death is the knowledge of evil. While the Tree of Life offers pathways towards union with the creator, the Tree of Death offers the opposite; a path away from Divine consciousness towards spiritual emptiness, disunity and division, towards a material reality devoid of spiritual content and Divine light, a place sometimes referred to as hell.

The basic concept of Kabbalah begins with Divine consciousness deciding to have a physical experience within the constraints of this earthly realm's limitations of space and time. It is thought that Divine light, offering unlimited potential, within the galactic centre, filled a container with the Creator's consciousness. This vessel ultimately shattered under the pressure of Divine brilliance, spreading small pieces of divinity throughout the galaxy. As the fragments of light travelled further away from the pleroma or galactic centre, its density increased allowing Divine consciousness to manifest in physical form, creating various levels and dimensions of physical reality. As the shattered light entered our solar system it differentiated, manifesting into pockets of cosmic consciousness, producing planets and luminaries of varying shapes and sizes. Eventually, here on Earth, numerous expressions of Divine consciousness materialised in a variety of life forms, with the human genome being the closest of all life forms to the Creator.

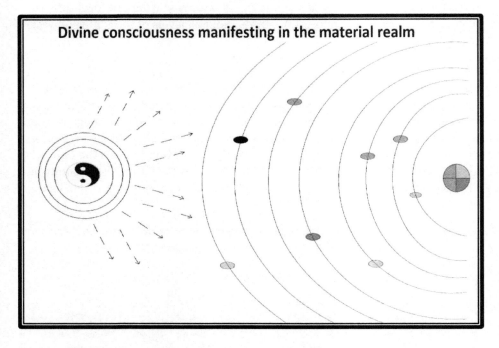

Divine consciousness manifesting in the material realm

To understand Kabbalah's interpretation towards our relationship to the Creator, one must first accept that the Creator/Logos is the unlimited potential of all possibility, the alpha and omega, the beginning and the end; a consciousness beyond our ability to comprehend, existing outside the physical constraints of space and time, a rigid paradigm which traps us in a progressive lineal approach to matter in this physical reality. According to Kabbalah the Creator made the creature (man) with the intention of bestowing, upon that creature, all his wants, needs and pleasures to enjoy, in a divinely created paradise of bliss and plenty.

Made in the image of God, the creature was given full dominion over his environment with freewill to choose whether to ascend the Tree of Life, in an attempt to seek union with his Creator, or descend down the Tree of Death, to become detached and alone, in an empty husk like reality, devoid of light, love and bounty offered by the Creator. Adam and Eve were told they could eat from any tree in the garden but not from the tree of knowledge, which in real terms is the Kabbalistic Tree of Death. This is the left hand path.

Kabbalah expresses the nature of Divine light as it defuses and fragments its way through the solar system, it is the physics and metaphysics of the spiritual realm. As the Divine light/consciousness enters the solar system it leaves, in its wake, 10 energy centres known as Sefirot with a number of conceptual connecting pathways as it descends into material form. The Sefirot represent the planets and luminaries orbiting the Sun.

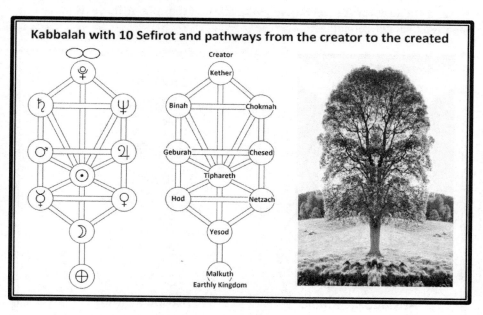

Kabbalah with 10 Sefirot and pathways from the creator to the created

In traditional Kabbalism the objective of the creature was to receive all that the Creator wanted to bestow upon him. However, the only difference between a person who receives in abundance and those who do not, is in the individual's willingness to receive, based entirely on their perceived relationship with the Creator. As the creature matures he finds a need, coming from within, to be like, and know, the Creator. However, in order to do this he must learn how to bestow like the Creator, instead of being one dimensional and only experiencing reality as a receptive vessel. Becoming like the Creator was considered ascending the Tree of Life, a spiritual journey which brought one back in union with the

Creator, essentially fulfilling man's ultimate destiny. Wherever a person finds themselves, at any point in their lives, there are kabbalistic pathways leading up the Tree of Life or down towards the Tree of Death. The choice is ultimately yours. We either take the righteous path, a spiritual journey towards union with the Creator, or we take the left hand path, towards a cold lifeless world of Godlessness, preoccupied by material matters alone.

"Religion assumes that the Creator changes His attitude to the person depending on the person's actions. The science of Kabbalah however states that the Upper Force is invariable, and the actions of a person can in no way affect it. Instead, the person's actions can change himself. He will be able to perceive the Upper Governance differently, if his own changes are aimed toward greater resemblance. He will be able to perceive the Creator as kind and good. By increasing the difference between his properties (reception) and those of the Creator (bestowal), he will feel the Creator's attitude as more negative." - Rav Michael Laitman[1]

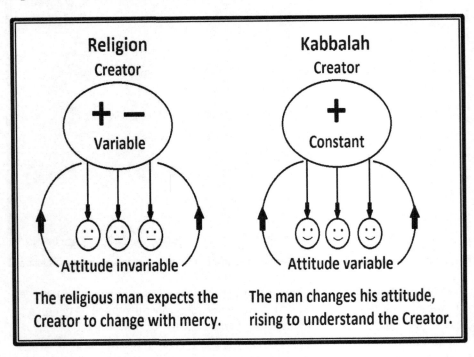

According to Kabbalah, if we are unable to feel the Divine good emanating from the Creator, the problem lies with us and not the Creator, as the Creator is constant in his bestowal. The ultimate goal of Kabbalah is to develop a 6th sense, a second nature, opposing duality and division, all those aspects which are synonymous with the left hand path and the Tree of Death. The term 6th sense is slightly misleading because we are not actually developing another sense but a new perception of reality, promoting the desire to see others as yourself and to understand the whole collective soul consciousness. With this approach we develop a closeness with Divine consciousness towards equilibrium of form, allowing us to perceive things we would not normally perceive, as though we are viewing the human experience through the eyes of the Creator. The only thing limiting a person, in this earthly incarnation, is their desire to receive. Correcting this perception is how we ascend the Tree of Life. We are all pieces of the initial soul, the Adam ha-Rishon, created in the upper worlds. Our ultimate goal is to reunite with the Creator's consciousness, from the Divine light that shattered into millions of pieces, a light which we are all part of.

The Tree of Death is a mirrored reflection of the Tree of Life, moving in the opposite direction and further away from the spiritual origins of life, towards, what some would call the pits of hell. A perception of reality full of division, disharmony, immorality, disunity and materialism. A place where black magic and demons run amok, pulling anyone who goes there away from their Divine roots and into a downward spiral of negative emotions and emptiness. While the Tree of Life has many pathways with ten spiritual energy centres known as Sefirot, each assigned with angels guarding their spiritual dominion and place within the heavens, the Tree of Death has energy centres called Qliphoth. These Qliphoth come with an array of demons and dark entities eager to attach themselves to anyone's conscious perception, in order to feed off their Divine spark residing within, pulling them towards a miserable husk like existence culminating in spiritual death.

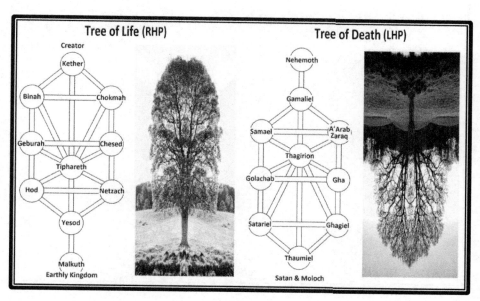

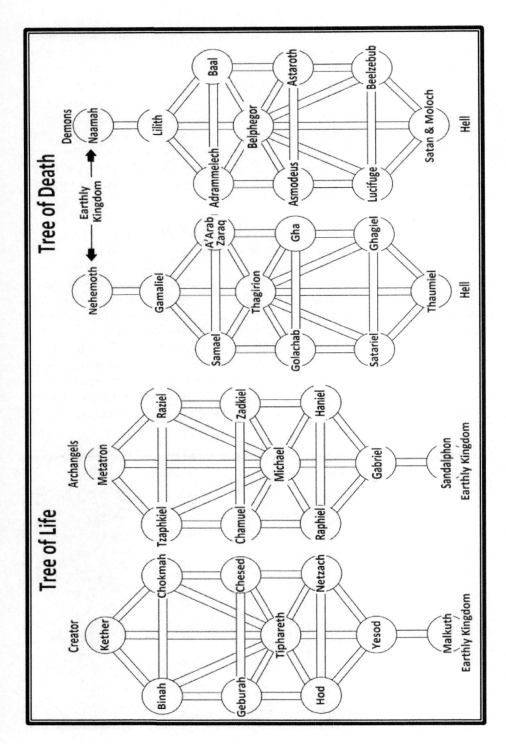

Each path between the ten Sefirot has different characteristics, depending on its position up the Tree of Life and the relevant Sefirot between those pathways. For example, from Malkuth, at the bottom of the tree, in the earthly realm, the path towards Yesod, ruled by the Moon, could be viewed as the first step into the world of the inner self and the spiritual subconscious. A righteous path which opens one's whole perception of life towards spirituality, moving one step closer to a conscious union with the Creator. Because Kabbalah is the esoteric foundation to many occult practices, it is no surprise to find that tarot cards fit neatly onto the ten Sefirot and the numerous pathways leading to the top of the tree towards the crown of the Supernal Triad. Furthermore, each of the 22 pathways, connecting the Sefirot, on the Tree of Life, are given one of the 22 letters of the Hebrew alphabet.

"In the beginning was the Word, and the Word was with God, and the Word was God. He was with God in the beginning. Through him all things were made; without him nothing was made that has been made. In him was life, and that life was the light of all mankind. The light shines in the darkness, and the darkness has not overcome it." - John 1 : 1-5 (NIV)

If we consider all the major religions, in relation to their adopted planets, and view them from their corresponding positions on the Tree of Life, the tree's profound overall esoteric correlations begin to make a little more sense. From the first pathway to the Sefirot Yesod we develop a conscious connection with our inner subconscious mind. This first path towards spirituality, tied to the Moon, can be seen in the everyday lives of monks (moonks), as they observe and adhere to the Moon's phases and cycles, while learning the ancient art of meditation. From Yesod, the pathway to the Sefirot Hod, ruled by Mercury, is one in which the inner subconscious learns to communicate with the spiritual realm. Budha, with one 'd', is sanskrit for the planet Mercury. Consequently, Buddhism is very much tied into the Sefirot of Hod, which is the Mercurian energy vortex of communication. Once an individual has mastered the art of meditation, one can move up the Tree of Life by learning to communicate with their inner spiritual side, connecting them to the Creator. Hod is the Sefirot of splendour, which means magnificence, grandeur, opulence, luxury, riches, fineness, beauty and elegance, a word who's description accurately describes most traditional ornate Buddhist Temples with their gold Buddha statues and elegant architecture. Hod is also the 8th Sefirot. Could this be the real source behind the Buddhist's eighth fold path?

The next Sefirot is Netzach, ruled by Venus, a planet synonymous with Islam. This Sefirot is all about victory, a word used to describe the ambitions of faithful Muslims over non-believers or infidels. Netzach is the 7th Sefirot, maybe the real reason why Muhammad celebrated his victory in Mecca by walking around the

Kaaba seven times. The Quran refers to the concept of victory in numerous texts.

"Allah was much pleased with the believers when they swore fealty to you under the tree. He knew what was in their hearts. So He bestowed inner peace upon them and rewarded them with a victory near at hand." - Quran, Surah Al-Fath 48 : 18-26

"And another (favour will He bestow,) which ye do love,- help from Allah and a speedy victory. So give the Glad Tidings to the Believers." - Quran, sūrat I-ṣaf 61 : 13. Yusuf Ali.

"When there comes the help of Allah and victory." - Quran, Sura Nasr 1.

Chesed is the Sefirot ruled by Jupiter, the planet associated with Christianity. Chesed's energy vortex appears on the pillar of mercy, and being the Sefirot of mercy, its influence can be seen throughout the Christian Bible and religious ideology.

"Let us then approach God's throne of grace with confidence, so that we may receive mercy and find grace to help us in our time of need." - Hebrews 4 : 6 (NIV)

"All the paths of the Lord are mercy and truth unto such as keep his covenant and his testimonies." - Psalms 25 : 10 (KJV)

"Be ye therefore merciful, as your Father also is merciful." - Luke 6 : 36 (KJV)

"The merciful man doeth good to his own soul, but he that is cruel troubleth his own flesh." - Proverbs 11 : 17 (KJV21)

Judaism holds the highest position of all the monotheistic religions on the Tree of Life, being aligned with the Sefirot Binah, an energy vortex ruled by Saturn. It is the closest religion to the Creator, within what is referred to as the Supernal Triad. Could this be the reason why the Jews are referred to as 'God's chosen people'?

Binah is the Sefirot of understanding, also associated with the colour black. Coincidentally, those with knowledge and understanding graduate from years of study with squared black mortar boards and black gowns. Judaism is a religion which promotes scholarship and knowledge, this offers scholarly Jews a deep metaphysical understanding of their conscious relationship with the Creator.

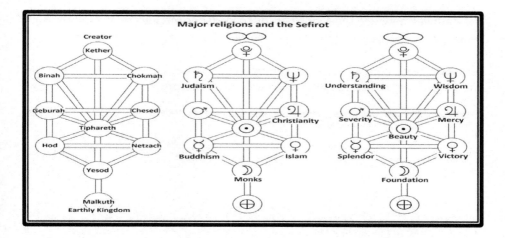

Major religions and the Sefirot

"Human beings are human by virtue of our being in covenantal relationships with other human beings, with the earth, and with God. And Torah is our evolving understanding of what that practically means." - "If Torah is our understanding of being in covenant, mitzvah is our acting out of being in covenant." - Rabbi Brian Field, October 2016. [2]

There are three pillars to the Tree of Life, which descend from the Creator at the crown. On the left side of the Tree of Life, (NB not the left hand path) ranging through Binah and Geburah to Hod, is the pillar of severity, incorporating the maleficent planets of Saturn and Mars. On the right side is the pillar of mercy, incorporating benefic planets like Jupiter and Venus. In the middle is the pillar of equilibrium, this is the easiest path to the Creator, which includes the father, the Sun and the Moon (holy spirit). When the Tree of Life is viewed from this perspective, it becomes a little clearer as to why various monotheist religions align themselves to particular traditions. These traditions reflect behavioural patterns, ceremonies and beliefs, all of which try to promote spiritual ascension up the Tree of Life, while at the same time restrict any subversive influence from demonic entities that frequent the Tree of Death's energy vortices, known as Qliphoth.

In the Old Testament, 1 Chronicles 29:11 outlines the lower seven Sefirot with the Lord exalted above them in the Supernal Triad.

"Thine, O Lord is the greatness *(Chesed)***, and the power** *(Geburah)***, and the glory** *(Tiphareth)***, and the victory** *(Netzach)***, and the majesty** *(Hod)***: for all that is in the heaven and in the earth** *(Yessod)* **is thine; thine is the kingdom** *(Malkuth)***, O Lord, and thou art exalted as head above all** *(Kether)***." -** 1 Chronicles 29 : 11 (KJV), emphasis added.

148

The pathway between the Moon Sefirot Yesod (subconscious mind) and the Sun Sefirot Tiphareth (focal mind) is represented, in tarot, as the temperance card.

Temperance definition : restraint or moderation, especially in not yielding to one's appetites or desires. Abstinence from alcoholic drinks.

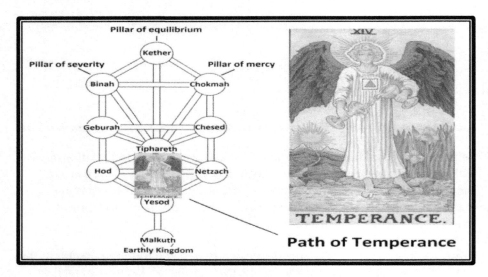

Path of Temperance

As can be seen in this basic explanation of Kabbalah, all the virtues in life concerning one's behaviour, temperament and outlook have the potential to lead a person up the righteous path on the Tree of Life towards union. While, conversely, all the vices in life will do the exact opposite and lead one further and further down the Tree of Death, away from the Creator's desire to bestow, which inevitability restricts a person's ability to receive Divine light, resulting in the detachment of the spirit and the slow death of the soul.

There are many opportunities in modern society which can lead someone down the Tree of Death. It is my opinion that over the past few decades society has been purposely steered down this dark and sinister path by its ruling classes, many of whom are wilfully ignorant as to what is unfolding. The reason for this is multifaceted and will be discussed in greater detail later. However, without realising it, each new generation is becoming more materialistic and egocentric, drifting further away from a healthy balanced spiritual attachment with their Creator. According to Jewish tradition, after Cain killed Abel, Adam separated from Eve for a period of 130 years. During this time he was seduced by Lilith and Naamah producing many demonic children who went on to plague the future of mankind.[3] These demonic entities could very well be connected to the Archonic entourage of the Demiurge. Both Naamah and Lilith can be found on the first path leading down the Tree of Death. Lilith is the mother of all demons, and both her and her sister Naamah (the queen of the night) seduce all who enter and walk their first steps down the Tree of Death and into the abyss.

"The Spirit of Defilement comes from the corrupt Serpent, which is Lilith." - Vayishlach: Passages 76, 79

"Lilith is a wicked bondwoman that is insolent, has no humility and no modesty, and she is the mother of a mixed multitude. Solomon refers to her when he said, "A virtuous woman is a diadem to her husband, but she that acts shamefully is as rottenness in his bones" (Mishlei 12:4). - Furthermore, Lilith has neither humility nor modesty before God. Her children are similar, being a mixed multitude. In the future God will remove her and her children from the world, for they are bastards, born of the nine attributes, as described by the sages. The nine attributes for which children are considered bastards by the Torah are:

- **A wife raped by her husband.**
- **A wife hated.**
- **A woman menstruating at the time of intercourse.**
- **A wife whose husband at the time of intercourse thought she was someone else or his other wife.**
- **A wife who is rebellious (at the time of intercourse).**
- **A husband drunk at the time of intercourse.**
- **Having intercourse with a wife divorced in her heart.**
- **A wife who is insolent.**
- **A wife who had relations immediately prior to her marriage."** - Pinchas passage 327

"Samael and his female Lilith were servants to God, but later made themselves into deities. God will remove them out of the world and wipe them away. Lilith is called filthy refuse, because she is excrement mixed with different types of filth and vermin into which dead dogs (the uncircumcised) are buried. She is a grave for idolatry. She is the reason the dead dogs (the uncircumcised) and vermin become a bad smell." - Ki Tetze: Passages 39, 113, 123

Sexual desires within the Tree of Death can never be satisfied, as lust is loveless, this form of sex promotes greater promiscuity together with a greater desire for more deviant perversions. Only those who can control the cravings of the mind can raise their energetic serpent, by conquering the dragon within and then to thereby transform themselves from intellectual animals to the greatest spiritual version of themselves.

"Desire is never satisfied by the enjoyment of the objects of desire. It grows from more to more, as does the fire to which fuel is added." – Dada J.P.Vaswani

There are many ways to seduce a person, setting in motion their descent down the Tree of Death. A journey which few recover from. As the path to the Moon Sefirot, on the Tree of Life represents our vulnerable emotional subconscious, it is also the key to the seduction of our emotions which can lead to our downfall. It is therefore vitally important that the conscious mind steers the vulnerable subconscious away from corruption and temptation.

"Enter through the narrow gate. For wide is the gate and broad is the road that leads to destruction, and many enter through it. But small is the gate and narrow the road that leads to life, and only a few find it." - Mat 7 : 13-14 (NIV)

"Our Father in heaven, hallowed be your name, your kingdom come, your will be done, on earth as it is in heaven. Give us today our daily bread. And forgive us our debts, as we also have forgiven our debtors. And lead us not into temptation, but deliver us from the evil one." - The Lords Prayer, Matthew 6 : 9-13 (NIV)

Pornography, freely available, on the internet, together with the establishments sexualisation of our children's minds, imposed upon them by the modern schooling curriculum, are both contributing to the undermining and deviation of societies morality and sexual behaviour. Stimulating a variety of addictions and perversions which easily opens the door down the left hand path. As the Anus is ruled by the base chakra, which in turn is ruled by Saturn, it is therefore no coincidence to see the promotion of anal sex and sodomy throughout all levels of this globalisation project.

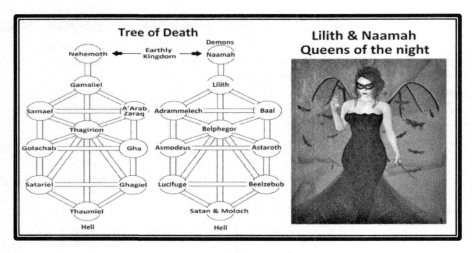

Corrupting society down the left hand path

Sandalphon, the Archangel which guards the first path from the earthly realm to the Moon Sefirot, is one of a handful of Archangels who's name does not end in EL, instead it ends in 'phon'. Sandalphon is the archangel of music, ruling over all music in heaven. He also helps people on Earth to communicate with the Creator through music.[4] Consequently, spiritual music generally resonates at higher frequencies, with the aim of uplifting the internal spirit towards greater union with the Creator. However, when music is bastardised, towards bass frequencies, which only energise the soul and our base animal instincts, those frequencies have the capacity to drive the subconscious down towards the Tree of Death.

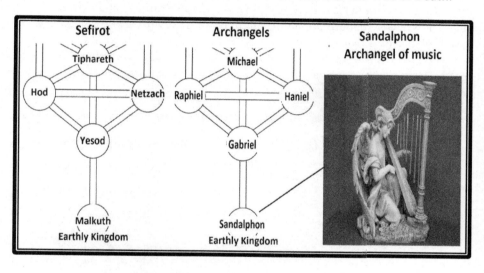

Music has been used for thousands of years to inspire and motivate people in various ways. National anthems and patriotic music have the ability to resonate deep within the subconscious, prompting significant emotional sensations. Today, it is becoming clear to most people that the majority of modern music has changed, not only in lyrical content, but also in sophistication. Much of it has become repetitively simple, lacking inspiration and the ability to uplift an individual spiritually. Modern music tends to promote themes of materialism, sex and selfishness, as though it is being influenced by the demonic duet Lilith and Naamah. The first Qliphoth down the Tree of Death is Nehemoth, it is responsible for frightening sounds in strange places, where beautiful music becomes perverted.

The next Qliphoth down the left hand path is Gamaliel, opposing the Sefirot Yesod (foundation). This Qliphoth is responsible for the corruption of all forms of visual art.

"The Gamaliel are the Misshapen and polluted images that produce vile results." - Gamaliel, Qliphoth, Wikipedia.[5]

Modern art, films, and various forms of visual expression have and are becoming more satanic, expressing a more materialistic perspective as opposed to the spiritual. Visual stimulation, in the form of art easily finds its way into the garden of the subconscious, influencing each generation's habitual nature through the corruption of their emotional coordinates. Still under the influence of Lilith, we see a great deal more sexualisation and perverted distortions occurring in the modern film industry and art world in general.

While Hod (splendour) is the creator of form, its counterpart Samael is the desolation of God. Where the nature of morality is perverted into a version of moral relativism; a place where common or traditional social morality is discarded in favour of one's own unique and distorted interpretation of acceptable morality. Samael and Lilith created a host of demon children, one being Asmodai 'the sword of Samael'.

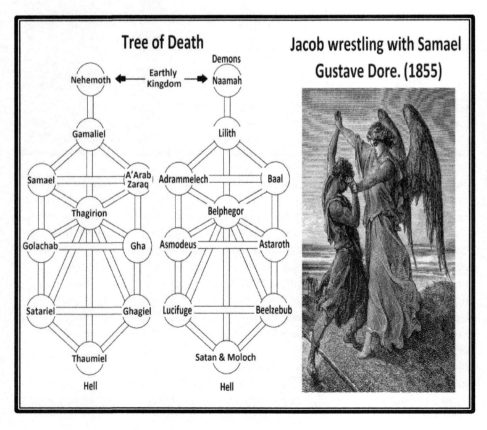

153

The Sefirot Netzach (Victory) is ruled by Venus, the planet associated with Islam. Here, in return for putting your faith in God, where the Creator bestows ample energy and strength in all your daily needs. The Qliphoth opposing Netzach is A'Arat Zaraq or Harab Serapel, with its demon Baal. Baal is the maker of sharp weapons, promoting violence in society. Furthermore, it helps to desensitise most people towards appalling acts of violence. Baal is also referred to as 'Lord of darkness', and linked to Tubal-cain mentioned in the Bible.

"Zillah also had a son, Tubal-Cain, who forged all kinds of tools out of bronze and iron. Tubal-Cain's sister was Naamah." - Genesis 4:22 (NIV)

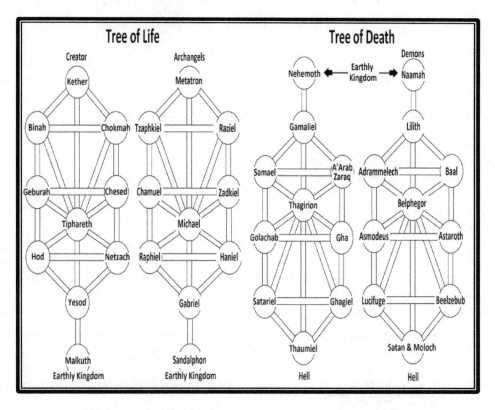

Ruling the 6th Sefirot, we find Archangel Michael, presiding over Tiphareth the energy centre of beauty. The opposite Qliphoth, Thagirion, is ugliness, the inverse of beauty. The demon ruling Thagirion is Belphegor, Lord of the dead, and the chief demon of laziness. This Qliphoth promotes all things ugly, distorting societies traditional and acceptable norms concerning beauty. It is responsible for the change in social attitudes in areas such as body image acceptance, transgenderism, tattoos, vulgar body piercings and ugly behaviour in general.

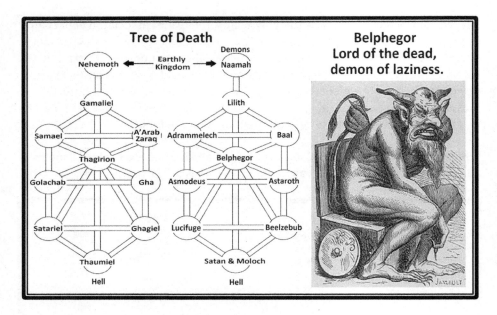

Tree of Death

Demons

Nehemoth ← Earthly Kingdom → Naamah

Gamaliel — Lilith

Samael — A'Arab Zaraq — Adrammelech — Baal

Thagirion — Belphegor

Golachab — Gha — Asmodeus — Astaroth

Satariel — Ghagiel — Lucifuge — Beelzebub

Thaumiel — Satan & Moloch

Hell — Hell

Belphegor
Lord of the dead,
demon of laziness.

Geburah (Severity), is associated with the planet Mars, a planet of proactive energy and movement in a specific direction and promotes power to rule in righteousness. The opposing Qliphoth, Golachab is associated with the burning of bodies. Its demons and entities enforce their will upon others through brutal strength not righteousness. The assigned demon Asmodeus is attributed to 'one who is adorned with fire'. In practical terms, this Qliphoth will promote harsh laws on those who take the righteous path, corrupting those in power to abuse society in a ruthless, aggressive and inhuman manner. Asmodeus is the prince of the demons, and one of the seven princes of hell. Each of these seven princes are said to represent the seven deadly sins and/or vices associated with the traditional seven planets.

Asmodeus prince of the demons

Seven deadly sins / vices

Lust	Venus
Gluttony	Jupiter
Greed	Saturn
Sloth	Moon
Wrath	Mars
Envy	Mercury
Pride	Sun

Chesed (mercy), is the Sefirot associated with Christianity. It promotes kindness and compassion through God's mercy. Ruled by Jupiter, it is the source of abundance, bounty and optimism. Its opposing Qliphoth, Gha or Gamchicoth, are known collectively as the devourers. They seek to waste the substance and thought of creation, while seducing men by means of laziness and self doubt. Asteroth, the demon assigned to this Qliphoth is the Prince of Accusers and Inquisitors. From a social perspective, this Qliphoth will eradicate inspiration, imagination and critical thinking, promoting uniformity and regimentation within society, together with the inability to think outside the box.

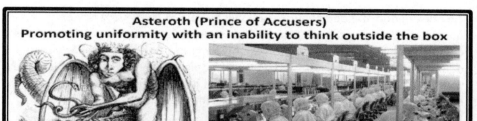

Asteroth (Prince of Accusers)
Promoting uniformity with an inability to think outside the box

The Sefirot Binah (understanding), is ruled by Saturn, associated with the colour black and the religion of Judaism. Its Archangel is Tzaphkiel. Binah is attributed to the Divine feminine or the great mother of the cosmos, referred to as the eternal womb, which gives birth and shape to the infinite spirit of the Creator. Binah is one of the three Sefirot within the Supernal Triad, together with Chokmah and Kether. Binah's counterpart or Qliphoth, on the Tree of Death, is Satariel, which is the domain of the demon Lucifuge (one who flees the light). In practical terms, this would manifest as an attempt to conceal the Creator by promoting Atheism.

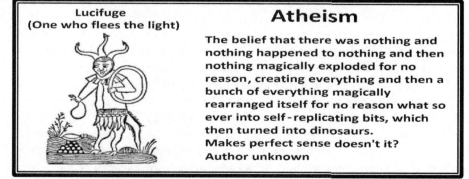

Lucifuge
(One who flees the light)

Atheism

The belief that there was nothing and nothing happened to nothing and then nothing magically exploded for no reason, creating everything and then a bunch of everything magically rearranged itself for no reason what so ever into self-replicating bits, which then turned into dinosaurs.
Makes perfect sense doesn't it?
Author unknown

The second Sefirot Chokma is ruled by Neptune, one of the outer planets associated with spiritual matters, dreams and illusions. Chokma is the Sefirot of wisdom, and the Divine masculine, located at the top of the pillar of mercy. Its Archangel is Raziel, the keeper of secrets and the angel of mysteries. Chokma's counterpart, on the Tree of Death, is the Qliphoth Ghagiel (the confusion of the power of God), a place empty of the Creator. Assigned to this Qliphoth is Beelzebub, a demon with the ability to fly. Consequently, he was know as 'Lord of the flyers' or 'Lord of the flies'. In the New Testament, Jesus mentions the destructive power of division within the godless realms on the Tree of Death.

"Every kingdom divided against itself will be ruined, and every city or household divided against itself will not stand. If Satan drives out Satan, he is divided against himself. How then can his kingdom stand? And if I drive out demons by Beelzebub, by whom do your people drive them out? So then, they will be your judges. But if I drive out demons by the Spirit of God, then the kingdom of God has come upon you." - Matthew 12 : 25-28 (NIV)

Beelzebub (Lord of the flies)

"But some of them said, He casteth out devils through Beelzebub the chief of the devils." - Luke 11:15 (KJV)

"If Satan also be divided against himself, how shall his kingdom stand? Because ye say that I cast out devils through Beelzebub. And if I by Beelzebub cast out devils, by whom do your sons cast them out? therefore shall they be your judges." - Luke 11:18-19 (KJV)

The crown or Divine Sefirot Kether, is the seat of the Creator, where all infinite potential of Divine consciousness begins. Archangel Metatron, also known as Mitatrush in Islam, is the highest angel, serving the Creator as a celestial scribe. While the crown Sefirot is concerned with unity, within an all encompassing oneness within universal consciousness with the Creator, its counterpart, down the Tree of Death, is all about division, separation, duality and godlessness. Because of its divisive nature, the Qliphoth, Thaumiel (division of that which is perfect in unity), is ruled by two of the highest demons within the underworld, Satan and Moloch. In Hebrew Satan is a generic noun which means the accuser or adversary. Moloch, on the other hand is an ancient Canaanite God associated with child sacrifice. Together both Satan and Moloch are the apex of the demonic world, a materialistic world of divide and rule, where the Divine spark within humanity is extinguished, in favour of an inferior, artificially created divinity.

Over the past 2000 years all the main monotheistic religions have tried to steer their followers on a path of righteousness. Occasionally falling foul to the temptations and distorted divisions promoted by the left hand path. Although Judaism, associated with the Sefirot Binah was, on the whole, concerned with righteousness and union with the Creator, something changed during the 17th century, bringing forth a new interpretation of Kabbalistic teaching; a perspective which saw both good and evil as equal expressions of God. Through the Binah Sefirot, on the Tree of Life, and the Sathariel Qliphoth on the Tree of Death, the new Kabbalists believed that a new Messiah could be encouraged to come forth into this earthly realm.

Origins of Kabbalah

The Jewish Kabbalah purports to be a uniquely Jewish creation given to God's chosen people by Moses, Abraham and even Adam. Resurrected from 2nd century Jewish lore and compiled by rabbinic elders, bestowed by God as a means to communicate and unite with Divine consciousness on a spiritual level. However, the truth of its origin appears to be slightly different. A more plausible explanation of its introduction comes during the Jewish spiritual renaissance of the 13th century, at a time when ancient manuscripts and writings were being translated by Muslim scholars during the Golden Age of Islam. An Age which began in the 8th century and lasted up until the collapse of the Abbasid Caliphate due to Mongol invaders, culminating in the Siege of Baghdad in 1258. During this time the Muslims created the great library in Baghdad, bringing together some of the greatest written works throughout their empire and the known world. Great works from ancient Greece, Persia and India were translated into Arabic, creating a vast athenaeum of ancient knowledge, works from some of the greatest minds in world history. At this time both Jewish and Sufi (Islamic mystics) thinkers laid the foundations for the emergence of Kabbalah.[6]

"Though presented by the original authors as a series of venerable spiritual teachings ascribed to ancient Jewish masters of the early centuries of the Christian era, it was not; it bloomed into existence at the very time that it was claimed to be "uncovered." And it was, of course, said to be wholly Jewish-employing the language and (alleged) tale, myth, law and symbolism of second century Hebrew and Aramaiciv as an entrance into the mysteries of spiritual union with God." - Tom Block, A question of Sufi influence on the early Kabbalah.[6]

At this time Sufism was widespread throughout the Islamic Empire, especially around the Mediterranean basin. Islamic mystics had already paved the way, with their knowledge of astro-magic and ancient esoteric wisdom from which Kabbalah would eventually follow.

"It was no coincidence that the earliest Kabbalistic writings and the work of (Sufi philosopher) Ibn Arabi appeared around the same time (late 12th-early 13th-centuries). Jewish refugees from Muslim Spain were breathing new life into the doctrines and imagery developed by the Sufis in Baghdad and later in Andalusia, creating the new system of mysticism known as the Kabbalah." - Michael McGaha, *Medieval Encounters III.*[7]

Jewish Kabbalism evolved from a collection of ideas, myths and writings, which grew during this time period. Writings such as :

- Sefer Yetzirah - 'Book of Creation'. The earliest book on Jewish esotericism, ascribed to the patriarch Abraham.
- Sefer Bahir - 'Book of Bright'. An anonymous early Jewish esoteric mystical work, which led to Kabbalah.
- Sefer ha-Lyyun - 'Book of Principles'. A 15th century work, outlining the principles of Judaism.
- The Zohar - 'Splendor or Radiance'. A comprehensive work laying the foundation of Jewish Kabbalistic mysticism.

"The Sefer Yetzirah emerged during a wonderfully amicable time between the two Biblical cousins, when Jews were included even in the highest intellectual circles of the Islamic caliph's court in Baghdad." - **"An Islamic text of virtually the same name, *Secret of Creation*-a book said to have been written during the time of the Caliph al-Mamun (813-833) - predated the Sefer Yetzirah by a century or so."** - Tom Block, A question of Sufi influence on the early Kabbalah.[6]

"The technique of magical and mystical calligraphy current among Muslims around Damascus and Baghdad beginning in the ninth century found its way into Jewish mystical traditions in the 12th and 13th centuries. This technique of mystical calligraphy in Islam was based on Sufi teachings on divine names." - Ariel[8]

According to Mark Verman, in his book *The Books of Contemplation (Medieval Jewish Mystical Sources)* he suggests that the Zohar was written by the Spanish Rabbi and Kabbalist known as Moses de Leon (1240 - 1305). His conclusion is based on Loen's wife's own confession alluding to this.[9] Many of the concepts found in Leon's Zohar mirror the works of the Spanish Sufi Muhammad ibn Masarra (883 - 931), who's work must have had some kind of influence over Moses de Leon.

It is worth mentioning, at this stage, a prominent central figure in the development of Jewish Kabbalism, a man by the name of Moses ben Jacob Cordovero (1522 - 1577). He was the leader of a mystical renaissance of the 16th century, along with a mystical school in Sefed, Ottoman Syria. He was also responsible for bringing different schools of thought, on the subject of Kabbalah, together, to produce the first fully integrated interpretation of Kabbalism. Following on from Cordovero's work was non other than Isaac Luria, the father of Lurianic Kabbalism. The interesting thing here is Moses' surname 'Cordovero', a name taken from the Southern Spanish city of Cordoba; a city which was once at the forefront of progress and sophistication, during the Golden Age of Islam, when Muslims were united and powerful. The name Cordavero indicates his family origins to the Spanish city, which most likely ended with their expulsion in 1492 as a result of the Spanish Inquisition.

There are different ways to spell the word Kabbalah, depending upon which ideology is interpreting the system. Jewish Kabbalism is spelt with a 'K', Christian Cabala is spelt with a 'C', and western Hermetic Qabalism is spelt with a 'Q'. It is not an exclusively Jewish discipline.

How did this profound esoteric and occult discipline, of trying to comprehend human spiritual connection to the Creator become perverted into a divisive, destructive form of black magic, which, I suspect, is a major contributing factor, leading society towards the left hand path and down the Tree of Death?

Lurianic Kabbalism was the underlying influence which spawned Sabbatai Zevi's interpretation of this ancient knowledge. To understand Zevi's perspective, further examination is necessary concerning the Sefirot Binah, a Sefirot ruled by Saturn, the planet adopted by Judaism.

Saturn Binah and the Messiah

Binah is the third Sefirot, within the Supernal Triad of Father, Son and Holy Spirit. It is considered to be the Divine feminine, a power which presides over the seven lower Sefirot, and the source from which they emanate.

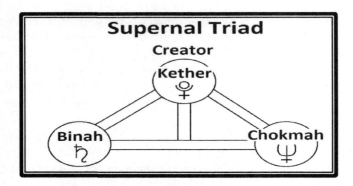

"Binah is the great revealing one who bestows the structure of the absolute onto the created." - Binah (Ascension glossary)[10]

"The King Messiah is the secret of Binah, and when the time for the Redemption of Israel will arrive, the Holy One, blessed be He, who is K [eter]-'E[lyon] will cause him to smell all those fine smells and perfumes ... that attribute called Messiah as it is written 'and the spirit of Elohim is hovering over the face of the water this is the spirit of the Messiah ... Then, the Binah which is Messiah, judges the poor in a right manner, namely Knesset Yisrael, because she arouses stern judgement and justice onto the nations of the world." - Saturn's Jews, page 59.[11]

"Thus, we find in the emphasis on the redemptive nature of the third sefirah, designated as the Redeemer and higher Messiah, a clear tendency to depict the return of the emanative process to the source, a restoration of the primordial, a circular concept of what I propose to call a 'cosmic macrochronos', and not a historical rectilinear vision of history which ends, or culminates in, the messianic era." - Saturn's Jews, page 60.[11]

According to Judaic Kabbalism, Saturn, Binah and redemption are related to one another. The name Sabbatai is Hebrew for the planet Saturn.

"His name literally meant the planet Saturn, and in Jewish tradition "The reign of Sabbatai" (The highest planet) was often linked to the advent of the Messiah." - Sabbatai Zevi (Wikipedia)

"And since it is higher than all the seven planets it is appointed upon religions and buildings ... And because [the planet of Sabbatai] is appointed over the perpetuation, when it will arrive to the ascent, it will not decline forever, as it is said that 'the spirit of God dwells upon him, the spirit of Hokhmah and of Binah'. See and understand that this is the secret of 'Mashiyah YHWH ... This is the reason why every ascent of Israel is but by the means of commandments, when they draw upon themselves the power of the Binah ... See and understand that the planet Sabbatai has the crown of Binah." - Joseph ben Shalom Ashkenazi (14th century Spanish Kabbalist)[11]

It is thought that Sabbatai Zevi was initially named Sabbatai because he was born on the Sabbath, Saturn's day. This was a custom at the time, which possibly contributed and influenced his own beliefs, seeing himself as the new Messiah, which ultimately led to his Kabbalist movement of Sabbateans, a movement which evolved from the foundations laid by the Lurianic Kabbalists.

It is plausible to assume that because Jewish Kabbalists saw the third Sefirot as the seat of Messianic power, which would initiate the manifestation process, that Jesus, the ambassador of Christianity, aligned to the fourth Sefirot Chesed, could not be their Messiah and therefore rejected him. Coincidentally, it is worth pointing out that, as Kabbalism is the foundation of many occult and esoteric practices, that the glyph for Jupiter, the crescent over the cross, is also a symbol used to represent the number 4.

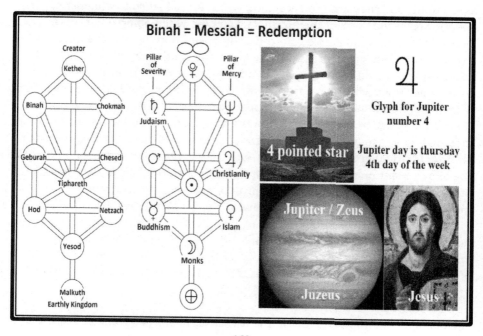

While Jewish Kabbalists regarded Saturn and Binah as the Divine feminine, the Messiah and the seat of Divine manifestation, many Greek and Arab astrologers considered Saturn to be a maleficent and malignant planet, viewing those who worshipped it to be contaminated by its wicked nature.[12]

"Since Saturn is the cause of sorcery and of pagan worship ... our master Moses, of blessed memory, had to stand in the breach and guard Israel in the matter of the Torah and commandments which issue from the sefirah of Tiferet and from all kinds of pagan worship. All kinds of sorcery issue from Saturn." - Rabbi Yahanan Alemanno, Hesheq Shlomo.[11]

Sabbat of Witches

"I know thy works, and tribulation, and poverty, (but thou art rich) and I know the blasphemy of them which say they are Jews, and are not, but are the synagogue of Satan." - Revelations 2:9 (KJV)

"It is well known in the science of the planets, that when someone makes a peculiar image from a peculiar matter which is connected with a peculiar planet, as they [the ancestors] said: 'There is no [leaf of] grass on earth etc.,' and he will place it under the power of the above-mentioned planet, when the latter is at its ascendant, and in the house of its glory, then will the power of the star pour upon that image and it [the image] will speak and perform certain operations, and they are the Teraphim, which From Saturn to Melancholy are mentioned in the Book of the Prophets. Likewise when a person prepares himself for that, for example to receive the power and the spiritual force of the planet Saturn, he would dress [in] black and he would wrap himself in black [clothes] and would cover the place he stood upon with black clothes and would eat things which increase the dark bile, which are under the dominion of Saturn and he should smell things that are attributed to it and will compose of them a perfume to burn incense from the above-mentioned things so that the incense would rise to heaven to the above-mentioned planet, and the light of another planet would not intercede. Then the power and the spiritual force of the above-mentioned planet will pour upon the person. And this is the essence of the prophecy of the Ba'al and the prophets of Ashtoret and similar [phenomena]." - Solomon Maimon, Jewish philosopher, late 18th century.[13]

According to Moshe Idel, in his book *Saturn's Jews,* he points out that the majority of references, made by Jews, regarding the planet Saturn are almost all of a negative nature. This only changes after the 12th century, when Saturn is referred to in a more positive light.

"I would like to emphasize that in the few cases of astrological discussions

163

where Sabbatai is mentioned by Jewish authors before the impact of Arabic astrology is discernible, all the descriptions of Saturn are negative. Positive qualities may be added to the negative ones only after the twelfth century, and it seems to me that only this positive addition may explain the subsequent developments in Judaism insofar as messianism is concerned." - Moshe Idel, Saturn's Jews.[11]

With this new Jewish renaissance in Kabbalistic matters, especially concerning redemption and the arrival of the long awaited Messiah, Kabbalistic practices may have been seen in the same light as astro-magic and black magic, giving rise to a link between some Jews, Saturn, Sabbatai and the Sabbat of witches. Some ignorant Christians at that time, having no knowledge of Kabbalah, could have viewed anything they did not understand as a form of Satanic ritual, which ultimately fell under the Catholic Church's laws concerning heresy. For the Catholic Church to come down so heavily on sorcery, black magic, astro-magic and particular interpretations of Kabbalism would seem to suggest that in certain hands and under certain circumstances, these practices must have had some element of power, which had the potential to undermine the church's own ambitions and authority.

Witchcraft, especially Sabbath witches, would align their conscious attachment with the Tree of Death's demonic forces, by conducting their rituals on Saturn's day, the Sabbath. Witching rituals usually take place from nightfall on Friday to nightfall on Saturday. Witches and Satanists from all over the world still, to this day, join together, at numerous locations, with the intention of summoning forth dark energies and entities associated with the left hand path and the Tree of Death.

It is generally understood that the redemption and the Messiah would ascend from the third Sefirot Binah. It is also the belief of some Kabbalists, that both the left and right hand path originate from God. Therefore, a Messiah, whether he comes from the 3rd Sefirot on the Tree of Life or the 3rd Qliphoth on the Tree of Death, is not important, because good and evil are just relative concepts. All that matters, to some Kabbalists is that all the circumstances are in place for the new Messiah to appear. I will once again refer to the following quote from the Talmud, stating that a Messiah will come during a time when the people are either all good or all bad. In my opinion, elements of the new ruling classes are promoting the latter, because promoting moral degradation runs in line with their divide and rule policy, a policy which has been underpinning the globalisation project since its conception.

"R. Johanan said: When you see a generation ever dwindling, hope for him [the Messiah], as it is written, And the afflicted people thou wilt save. R. Johanan

164

said: When thou seest a generation overwhelmed by many troubles as by a river, await him, as it is written, when the enemy shall come in like a flood, the Spirit of the Lord shall lift up a standard against him; which is followed by, And the Redeemer shall come to Zion. R. Johanan also said: The son of David will come only in a generation that is either altogether righteous or altogether wicked. 'in a generation that is altogether righteous,' — as it is written, Thy people also shall be all righteous: they shall inherit the land for ever. 'Or altogether wicked,' — as it is written, And he saw that there was no man, and wondered that there was no intercessor; and it is [elsewhere] written, For mine own sake, even for mine own sake, will I do it." - Talmud, Sanhedrin 98a[14]

It is worth looking at the astrological zodiac chart for the start of 1666, the year Sabbatai Zevi publicly claimed to be the new Messiah, sent by God to lead all the Jews into their new paradise.

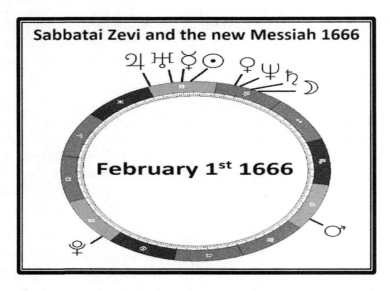

The interesting thing about the zodiac chart of February 1666 are the number of planets in Aquarius and Capricorn. Almost all the planets except Mars and Pluto are in Aquarius and Capricorn and Pluto was not part of traditional astrology at that time anyway. In traditional astrology both Aquarius and Capricorn are ruled by Saturn. As astrology was a major part of the learned classes knowledge base at that time, this chart formation must have appeared even more compelling, supporting Sabbatai's belief in his Messianic claim.

The Holy Land

What is it about the Holy Land which makes it so holy? Maybe there is a link

165

between the ancient esoteric wisdom contained in Kabbalah and land considered holy to Jews, Muslims and Christians alike? There are a few clues within both Kabbalah and some old written descriptions concerning this matter. It is possible that during the early development of Kabbalah, a physical geographical area of land was adopted to represent Kabbalistic metaphysical components, incorporating Jerusalem as the Supernal Triad or God Head. Leading from Kether, the crown Sefirot, is one of the longest pathways between Sefirots, known as Gimel, a Hebrew word which means camel. This path from the Divine spirit of Kether to the soul/Sun of the 6th Sefirot Tiphareth, terminates in the middle/medi on the Tree of Life. Could this be the true origins behind the name of the city Medina? Before the 20th century, the only practical way to travel from Jerusalem to Medina was by camel, across what was referred to as an abyss, an inhospitable and barren desert region which made for a long, arduous and sometimes dangerous journey between the two cities. This part of the Kabbalah tree is also referred to as the abyss.

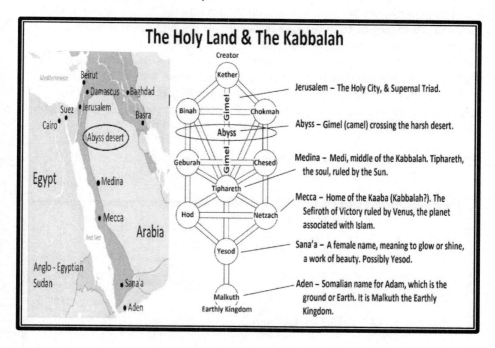

The Holy Land & The Kabbalah

Jerusalem – The Holy City, & Supernal Triad.

Abyss – Gimel (camel) crossing the harsh desert.

Medina – Medi, middle of the Kabbalah. Tiphareth, the soul, ruled by the Sun.

Mecca – Home of the Kaaba (Kabbalah?). The Sefiroth of Victory ruled by Venus, the planet associated with Islam.

Sana'a – A female name, meaning to glow or shine, a work of beauty. Possibly Yesod.

Aden – Somalian name for Adam, which is the ground or Earth. It is Malkuth the Earthly Kingdom.

South of Medina is Mecca, an ancient trading city, and the home of the Kaaba (Kabbalah?). When Muhammad took over the city, with his Muslim army, he threw out 360 idols in favour of a meteorite which possibly fell to Earth from Venus, as it changed orbit, many years ago. Before this, Muhammad circled the Kaaba seven times, Why seven? Was he paying homage to the seven lower Sefirot before dedicating the Kaaba solely to the worship of Venus and the 7th Sefirot Netzack, the Sefirot of victory? Continuing south there is a city called

Sana'a, a female name meaning to shine or glow. Could this represent Yesod, the Sefirot ruled by the Moon? At the lowest point, in the south west corner of Arabia we find the city of Aden, a Somalian word for Adam, who represents the earthly kingdom of Malkuth. The Sumero-Akkadian name for Jerusalem 'Uru-Salim' means 'foundation of the God Shalim'. All in all, this is more than just a remarkable coincidence.

At the end of the 13th century, the medieval Kabbalist Abraham ben Samuel Abulafia, another character who believed he was, not only a prophet, but also the Messiah, wrote about the land of Israel together with references to Saturn; texts which, I presume, were written after the last of the Christian crusades, around the time of the Siege of Acre in 1291.

"The Land of Israel is higher than all the lands ... the known land, whose sign is one thousand two hundred and ninety, and this is the Land of Israel , which was the land of Cana'an ... And it is known that among the stars, the power of Sabbatai corresponds to it because it [Saturn] is the highest among its companions, and behold, the supernal entity appointed upon another supernal entity, and the nation of Israel is superior to all the nations, 'for there is one on high who watches over him that is high, and that there are yet higher ones'. And the high is the dust of the Land of Israel, and higher than it, which is appointed on it, is Sabbatai, and Israel are higher than them." - Abraham ben Samual Abulafia.[17]

It is worth pointing out here that the name ISRAEL is made up of a triad of its own. ISIS - RA - EL, yet another reference to the Supernal Triad.

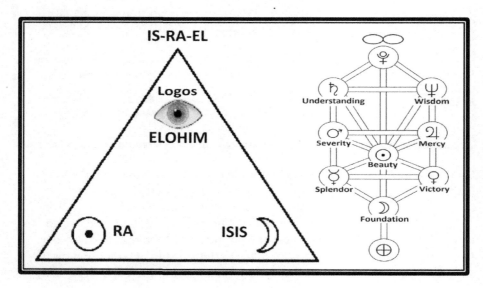

The pathway between the crown Sefirot, Kether, and Binah, the messianic Sefirot, is know as Beth. It is described as the first action in the creation process, the beginning of duality, where the Creator initiates the created. Coincidentally, the place of birth for Jesus, the Messiah of the Piscean Age was Bethlehem, only 9km south south west of Jerusalem.

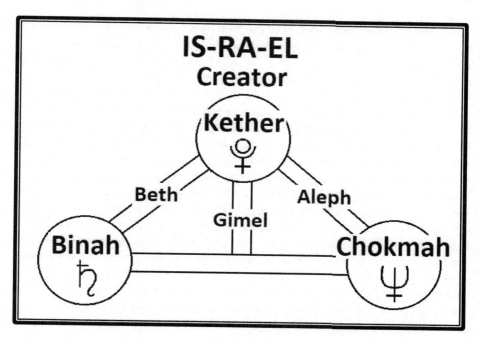

Is it the case that our kabbalistic ancestors, throughout the Middle East, saw Israel, and the Hejaz (west coast of Saudi Arabia), as the physical earthly expression of the Tree of Life, with the Red Sea separating it from Egypt. And is it the case that the Hebrews regarded Egypt as the physical manifestation of the Tree of Death? The fact that the name Suez is Zues/Jupiter spelt backwards, could give some credence to this proposal. When revisiting the story of Exodus, where Moses parted the Red Sea, saving the Israelites from the Egyptians, it could, in this context, be considered as a metaphorical explanation for a person's journey back up the Tree of Life after seemingly becoming trapped down among the Archons and demigods associated with the Tree of Death. In the Red Sea crossing, a passage in Exodus 14 mentions a character called Baal Zephon, furthermore the Exodus story mentions 42 stations, or locations, visited by the Israelites, as they made their way towards Israel and the Holy Land. There are 22 pathways on each tree, and if the earthly pathway is not included and counted twice, then we have all the pathways from hell, at the bottom of the Tree of Death, to the Creator, at the top of the Tree of Life. Bearing in mind, that Mars is the planet of proactive energy, and physical movement, in a specific direction.

Moses could very well be the personification of the planet Mars! (Mars - Marses - Moses).

"No tree, it is said, can grow to heaven unless its roots reach down to hell." - C G Jung

"Then the Lord said to Moses, "Tell the Israelites to turn back and encamp near Pi Hahiroth, between Migdol and the sea. They are to encamp by the sea, directly opposite Baal Zephon. Pharaoh will think, 'The Israelites are wandering around the land in confusion, hemmed in by the desert.' And I will harden Pharaoh's heart, and he will pursue them. But I will gain glory for myself through Pharaoh and all his army, and the Egyptians will know that I am the Lord." So the Israelites did this. When the king of Egypt was told that the people had fled, Pharaoh and his officials changed their minds about them and said, "What have we done? We have let the Israelites go and have lost their services!" So he had his chariot made ready and took his army with him. He took six hundred of the best chariots, along with all the other chariots of Egypt, with officers over all of them. The Lord hardened the heart of Pharaoh king of Egypt, so that he pursued the Israelites, who were marching out boldly. The Egyptians—all Pharaoh's horses and chariots, horsemen and troops—pursued the Israelites and overtook them as they camped by the sea near Pi Hahiroth, opposite Baal Zephon. As Pharaoh approached, the Israelites looked up, and there were the Egyptians, marching after them. They were terrified and cried out to the Lord. They said to Moses, "Was it because there were no graves in Egypt that you brought us to the desert to die? What have you done to us by bringing us out of Egypt? Didn't we say to you in Egypt, 'Leave us alone; let us serve the Egyptians'? It would have been better for us to serve the Egyptians than to die in the desert!" Moses answered the people, "Do not be afraid. Stand firm and you will see the deliverance the Lord will bring you today. The Egyptians you see today you will never see again. The Lord will fight for you; you need only to be still." Then the Lord said to Moses, "Why are you crying out to me? Tell the Israelites to move on. Raise your staff and stretch out your hand over the sea to divide the water so that the Israelites can go through the sea on dry ground. I will harden the hearts of the Egyptians so that they will go in after them. And I will gain glory through Pharaoh and all his army, through his chariots and his horsemen. The Egyptians will know that I am the Lord when I gain glory through Pharaoh, his chariots and his horsemen." Then the angel of God, who had been traveling in front of Israel's army, withdrew and went behind them. The pillar of cloud also moved from in front and stood behind them, coming between the armies of Egypt and Israel. Throughout the night the cloud brought darkness to the one side and light to the other side; so neither went near the other all night long. Then Moses stretched out his hand over the sea, and all that night the Lord drove the sea

back with a strong east wind and turned it into dry land. The waters were divided, and the Israelites went through the sea on dry ground, with a wall of water on their right and on their left. The Egyptians pursued them, and all Pharaoh's horses and chariots and horsemen followed them into the sea. During the last watch of the night the Lord looked down from the pillar of fire and cloud at the Egyptian army and threw it into confusion. He jammed the wheels of their chariots so that they had difficulty driving. And the Egyptians said, "Let's get away from the Israelites! The Lord is fighting for them against Egypt." Then the Lord said to Moses, "Stretch out your hand over the sea so that the waters may flow back over the Egyptians and their chariots and horsemen." Moses stretched out his hand over the sea, and at daybreak the sea went back to its place. The Egyptians were fleeing toward[c] it, and the Lord swept them into the sea. The water flowed back and covered the chariots and horsemen—the entire army of Pharaoh that had followed the Israelites into the sea. Not one of them survived. But the Israelites went through the sea on dry ground, with a wall of water on their right and on their left. That day the Lord saved Israel from the hands of the Egyptians, and Israel saw the Egyptians lying dead on the shore. And when the Israelites saw the mighty hand of the Lord displayed against the Egyptians, the people feared the Lordand put their trust in him and in Moses his servant." - Exodus 14, The Res Sea crossing. (NIV)

The name Red Sea also has a metaphysical significance, which could represent a metaphorical crossing from one tree to another, a symbolic barrier. Red is the colour synonymous with seduction, the underworld and objects moving away from one another, as in the Doppler Shift. In this case it is the created creature moving further away from the Creator.

Is it the case that thousands of years ago the Demiurge and its demonic creations ruled parts of the ancient world? A world of megaliths, giants and various god like entities, requiring human obedience, respect and sacrifice. A pantheon of idols and gods who, through either a cosmic cataclysm or Divine intervention, were washed away in a great global catastrophe. Some artefacts and megalithic remnants, of this once powerful civilisation, still remain, paying homage to the Demiurge, the gods who once walked amongst men, masters of an extremely advanced materialistic civilisation.

Once monotheism, in all its forms, evolved, utilising the knowledge of Kabbalah, humanity found a way to escape the bondage and desolation found within the Tree of Death. By understanding their relationship to the Creator, through the use of Kabbalah, they were able to free themselves by crossing the Red Sea and ascending up the Tree of Life, towards a more righteous and optimistic path. If there is any credence in this idea, it means that the ancient knowledge of

Kabbalism has been around for thousands of years, giving Muhammad his unique perspective on how to unify his people and promote them up the righteous tree.

"And it came to pass, that at midnight the Lord smote all the firstborn in the land of Egypt, from the firstborn of Pharaoh who sat on his throne, unto the firstborn of the captive who was in the dungeon, and all the firstborn of cattle. And Pharaoh rose up in the night, he and all his servants and all the Egyptians; and there was a great cry in Egypt, for there was not a house where there was not one dead. And he called for Moses and Aaron by night and said, "Rise up, and get you forth from among my people, both ye and the children of Israel! And go, serve the Lord, as ye have said. Also take your flocks and your herds, as ye have said; and be gone, and bless me also." And the Egyptians were urgent upon the people, that they might send them out of the land in haste; for they said, "We are all dead men."" - Exodus 13 : 29 -33 (KJV21)

If the Holy Land and the Hejaz represent the Tree of Life and the path to spiritual enlightenment, then we can assume Egypt, the land west of the Red Sea, to be an area associated with the Tree of Death, its Qliphoths, and all those pathways which lead to the Demiurge. Egypt in Arabic is 'Misr', meaning country with government, laws and order. The Quran also refers to Egypt as 'Misr', the country with government. Mizraim is an old name for Egypt, and being the son of Ham and grandson of Noah, Mizraim's offspring led to the Hemite branch of Noah's descendants. The name Egypt also comes from the Greek Aegyptus, which is the Greek way of pronouncing 'Hwt-Ka-Ptah', a name which means 'Temple of the soul of Ptah'. According to some scholars Ptah was the ancient Egyptian demiurge of Memphis, the god of both craftsmen and architects. In the Triad of Memphis, the old capitol of Lower Egypt, Ptah was the husband of Sekhmet and the father of Nefertum.[15] This triad is similar to the Supernal Triad, at the top of the Tree of Life, but this path leads to the rulers of the Tree of Death, down into the arms of the Demiurge via Satan and Moloch. The ancient Egyptians used the name Kemet/Kemit as the name of their country, this translates as 'black country', with the people referring to themselves as 'remetch en Kemet', meaning 'people of the black country'. Although orthodox historians regard the term black as a reference to the colour of the soil on either side of the Nile; could it be that the true meaning behind black country is really a reference to the dark satanic side of esoteric mysticism and the Tree of Death? Although Egyptian society lasted thousands of years, it eventually degenerated through the abuse of black magic with the Pharaohs becoming tyrannical over their subjects.

Around 700BC, when the city of Memphis became the administrative capital of a united Egypt, a text known as the *Memphis Creation Myth* was written.[16] In this myth it states that Ptah, who was regarded as the god of the Earth, created nine other deities, referred to as Ennead (a group of nine deities in ancient Egyptian mythology). This is quite astonishing, when considering there are ten Qliphoth within the Tree of Death. Consequently, it is possible that Ptah and his Ennead are the Egyptian equivalent of the ten Qliphoth associated with the Tree of Death.

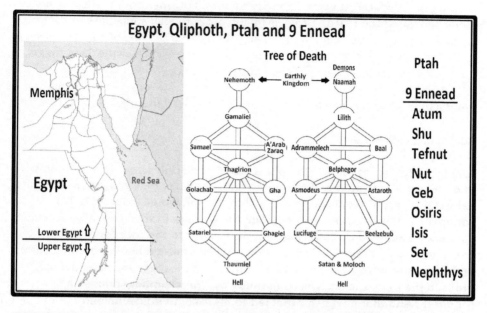

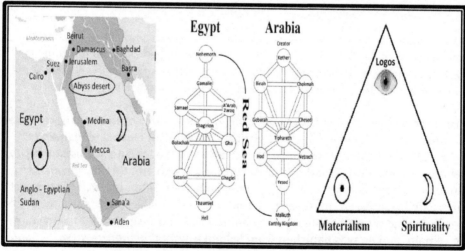

Once the Israelites had crossed the Red Sea, they were made to wander the wastelands of the desert for 40 years, until those who had done evil things had died.

"The Lord's anger burned against Israel and he made them wander in the wilderness forty years, until the whole generation of those who had done evil in his sight was gone." - Numbers 32 : 13 (NIV)

In traditional Judaism, it was customary to only allow men over the age of 40 to study Kabbalah. The reason being, is that in order to fully appreciate its esoteric wisdom, only the mature mind of the 40 year old was capable of comprehending it. Sabbatai Zevi declared himself Messiah at the age of 40. For the Sabbateans, 40 was a very significant age, the age of true maturity.

"And a man of 40 is ready for Binah - understanding." (Avot 5:24).

Continuing with Sabbatai Zevi

"Sabbatai Zevi went too far; he took a group of disciples into the mountains and attempted to command the sun to halt. For a day they prayed, with Sabbatai Zevi confidently announcing that the sun would respond to his commands. This blasphemy earned him the censure of the local religious court; Sabbatai responded by declaring himself superior to the court and excommunicating them. This impudent response earned him excommunication and banishment from Smyrna. Other contemporaries recount that Sabbatai aroused the ire of the Smyrna community by "'proclaim[ing] himself a prophet,'" and that it was this that led to his excommunication and banishment." - Paul Benjamine, on Sabbatai Zevi[17]

After his banishment form Smyrna, he made his way to Salonika in Greece, another hub of Kabbalistic learning. In the beginning he assimilated, fitting in well with the other Rabbis and the community as a whole, However, after some time his mental illness erupted unveiling his maniac and eccentric nature.

"His mania soon returned, and with it his transgressions of the law; once more he pronounced the divine name. Further, he staged an elaborate wedding ceremony and banquet, to which he invited all of the leading rabbis of the city, wherein he married a Torah scroll. According to Scholem, this ceremony appears to have had a profound personal impact on Sabbatai Zevi; for the rest of his life he spoke of the Torah as a bride and himself as its bridegroom. Once again, Sabbatai's odd behavior was deemed as too transgressive to allow him to remain, and he was banished from Salonika sometime before 1658." - Paul Benjamine, on Sabbatai Zevi[17]

From Salonika he spent some time in Greece before making his way to Constantinople. As before, he was accepted as a normal member of the Jewish community, until he purchased a large fish, dressed it up like a baby and placed it in a cradle. To Sabbatai Zevi, this act symbolised the new Messiah in the Age of Pisces. The Rabbis of Constantinople were not impressed, they ordered him to be flogged along with a modest period of excommunication.

During his time on the move, it is suspected that he had visions, which told him to violate normal Jewish law, concluding that such violations were necessary and sacred. His reason for doing this was to collect any Divine spark, encased in sin, which had found its way into the husk like shells of the Qliphoth, down the Tree of Death. And it was the duty of the Jews to redeem the sparks from their material prisons and bring them back towards holiness. In Zevi's view the only way to redeem the world was to sin, in an attempt at acquiring all those imprisoned Divine sparks. He believed his task, as Messiah, was to transcend all earthly boundaries by operating in an entirely new way.[17] His followers saw his conversion to Islam as a necessary way of freeing the Divine spark trapped within the religion.

Upon Sabbatai Zevi's death his brother in law, Yakub Celebi, took over the role of leading the Donmeh. Not only was he a close friend to Sabbatai Zevi, but he was specifically selected by Zevi to become his successor. The wife of Sabbatai Zevi, and sister to Yakub Celeb, testified that her brother underwent a three day transformation, where the spirit of Sabbatai Zevi had entered into him, in a process of spiritual rebirth, essentially becoming the new Messiah. Gradually cracks began to appear in his authority and capability to lead the Donmeh as a unified group. Because he offered a pragmatic style of leadership, promoting assimilation within the Islamic Ottoman culture, he was regarded, by some followers, as too much in favour of Islamic principles, putting the teachings of Sabbatai Zevi in second place. With the initiative of Mustafa Celebi, another leading light, the Donmeh split, with a new group adopting a boy named Osman Baba as their replacement Messiah. This new group known as the Karakas, believed that the spirit of Sabbatai Zevi had reincarnated within the boy, thus giving him Divine powers. While the Yakubi were assimilating successfully within Islamic culture, spreading out from Salonika and dressing accordingly, the Karakas kept their own identity, staying true to the legacy of Sabbatai Zevi. They had more in common with the Sufi orders of Islam, forming close ties, as they existed in a more underground fashion. When Osman Baba was forty years old he was officially declared as the new Messiah. Tension began to mount within the ranks of the Karakas, as some of its top leaders did not regard Osman Baba as Sabbatai Zevi's replacement, and when Baba died a few years after his 40th birthday, another split occurred promoted by Ibrahim Agha. Believing Baba to be the Messiah, the Karakas didn't think his body would decay like an ordinary man. Consequently, Ibrahim Agha and his followers wanted Baba's body unearthed to see if it had rotted, if so they would be vindicated in their belief that he could not be the Messiah. After much in-fighting and disagreement, the body was finally exhumed, only to discover that it had rotted, just like every other corpse in the cemetery. In the mind of Ibrahim Agha, and his followers, it was a clear indication that Osman Baba was no Messiah. Consequently, they split with the Karakas, forming yet another group of Donmeh known as the Kapanci.[17]

Both the Karakas and the Kapanci believed and promoted the doctrine of 'Torah of Emanation'. Part of the teachings of Sabbatai Zevi, in which all prohibitions of the Torah were reversed into commandments to commit acts of sin, all in an attempt to repatriate fragments of Divine sparks concealed within the Qliphoth, down within the Tree of Death. It is likely that this doctrine lay behind the promotion of perverted sexual acts, wife swapping orgies and incest. It is also suspected as being one of the factors, together with Sabbatai Zevi's bipolar personality which led to his bizarre, sometimes outrageous, behaviour. The Donmeh believed that only through the act of sinning could the world be truly elevated, finally fulfilling God's ultimate plan.

Jacob Frank, another leading figure in the Sabbatean Kabbalistic movement, converted to Islam in order to become a member of the Karakas movement. Frank was another charismatic leader who considered himself to be the spiritual reincarnation of Sabbatai Zevi, and consequently another Messiah. When he and many of his followers found themselves excommunicated from mainstream traditional Judaism, they moved to Europe to claim leadership of the Polish contingent of the Sabbateans. Once in Poland, the Frankists converted to Catholicism, becoming a form of Christian Donmeh. Frank also promoted his daughter Eve as their sects version of Mary, the Holy Mother. On Frank's death Eve took over the sect, however, producing no children of her own left the sect with no successor and so it began to fizzle out, eventually dissolving by the late 19th century.

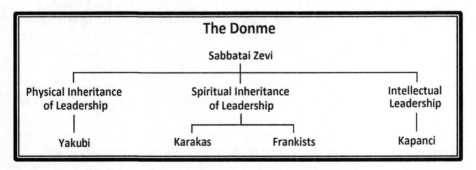

The Kapanci, differed slightly from the other groups, in the way in which they chose their leadership. Instead of looking for a physical or spiritual replacement for Sabbatai Zevi, they chose to focus their movements leadership and structure based entirely on the teachings and wisdom left by Sabbatai Zevi. This gave an element of stability to the group preventing future charismatic leaders from undermining the core teachings of their Messiah. This approach produced a sect which was relatively successful within the host country, allowing broad and extensive trade to prosper as they dealt with all sides. As the Kapanci climbed the economic ladder along with their merchants and professionals, they became part of the upper and middle classes. The Yakubi were also successful due to their ability to assimilate with the broader Ottoman society. Because the Karakas relied on the personality of their leader, the reincarnation of Sabbatai Zevi, and the Messiah, they were open to deviations brought about by their leaders unique personality and interpretation of Sabbatai Zevi's teachings. This is partly why the Frankist movement was regarded as an extreme and perverted cult of Sabbatean Judaism, a movement rejected by Rabbis within the Council of Four Lands and the majority of Jews faithful to the Torah and traditional Judaic laws. This culminated in claims of Incest, blasphemy, heresy and an overall attempt to invert and pervert Judaism. In 1759, this ultimately led to 2,000 Frankists, within the city of Lvov, being excommunicated by the moderate mainstream Jewish community of the time. This policy of excommunication put a great deal of pressure on those within the Frankist movement. The ban included the following statement:

"We shall not rent a house to or from them; we shall not buy from them or sell to them; we shall not teach their children, nor bury them nor circumcise them".
- Council of Four Lands, ban on the Frankists. Sacred Orgies: the Extremist Sabbatean Sect of Jacob Frank[18]

This added pressure contributed to Jacob Frank's decision to convert over to Catholicism, persuading thousands of his follows who later followed suit. Publicly they would appear to be Catholics, but privately, many of them despised the church, and continued to practice and promote their extreme version of Sabbatean mysticism. As part of the conversion process, they were asked to declare the Talmud as nonsensical and a pack of lies, while still maintaining their recognition for the Zoha. They also had to admit that their fellow Jews did indeed use the blood of Christian children to make Matzot (unleavened bread for the Passover). Jacob Frank once addressed his followers with these words:

"I came not to elevate your spirits, but to humiliate you to the bottom of the abyss, where you can get no lower, and where no man can rise from by his own forces, but only God can pull him with his mighty hand from the depth." - Jacob Frank[18]

Furthermore, the Sabbateans, in their pursuit of sinning, would bless one another with this perverted verse :

"Blessed art thou, Lord, who cancels and allows the prohibitions." - Sabbataen blessing[18]

Although mainstream rabbinical authorities were essentially at war with the Frankist movement, throughout the 18th century, Sabbatean and Frankists groups continued to spring up, growing all over Eastern Europe and the Middle East. In 1760 Jacob Frank was arrested and charged with feigned conversion of Catholicism, together with the spreading of pernicious heresy. After being found guilty by the Church, he was sentenced to 13 years in prison, which, over the years, increased his mystical qualities and popularity, ultimately elevating him to the status of martyr. Following his release, in 1772, he moved to Moravia, in Czech Republic, where he lived until 1786. From Moravia he moved to Offenbach, a town on the outskirts of Frankfurt. Here he was given the title of Baron of Offenbach, now a wealthy nobleman, he lived a comfortable retirement on frequent donations given to him by his many followers. Here he stayed until his death, in 1791, upon which, his daughter took over the running of the Frankist movement.

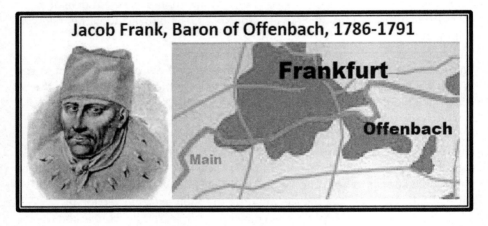

Jacob Frank, Baron of Offenbach, 1786-1791

The important and interesting thing to note here, which will be explored in the following chapters, is that Frankfurt was also the home of the Rothschild banking dynasty (well known Jews) and Adam Weishaupt, the founder of the Bavaria Illuminati, who, coincidentally, also happened to be a descendant of Jewish converts to Christianity.[19]

"For the Sparks of the holy which are scattered among all peoples must be brought home if everything is to return to its proper place and the redemption thereby be complete." - Gershom Scholem, *The Messianic Idea in Judaism: And Other Essays on Jewish Spirituality.* Page 61.

Notes for chapter 6

(1) Rav Michael Laitman, The difference between Kabbalah and religion. Kabacademy.eu. https://kabacademy.eu/uk/wp-content/uploads/sites/5/2018/08/Lesson-8-Part-1-Transcript.pdf

(2) Rabbi Brian Field, The Four Fundamentals of Jewish Spirituality, Judaism Your Way. https://www.judaismyourway.org/four-fundamentals-jewish-spirituality/

(3) Naamah demon, wikipedia, https://en.wikipedia.org/wiki/Naamah_(demon)

(4) Sandalphon, Meet Archangel Sansalphon, Archangel of music. Learn Religion, 2017. https://www.learnreligions.com/meet-archangel-sandalphon-124089

(5) Qliphoth, Wikipedia. https://en.wikipedia.org/wiki/Qliphoth

(6) Tom Block, A question of Sufi influence on the early Kabbalah. The Journal of Traditional Studies, Oakton, VA, Winter, 2007-2008, http://www.tomblock.com/shalom_sofia

(7) Michael McGaha, *Medieval Encounters III,* (1997), pg. 57.

(8) Ariel, in Approaches to Judaism in Medieval Times II, (Scholars Press, 1985), pg. 158-159.

(9) Mark Verman, The books of contemplation, medieval Jewish mystical sources, Sunny Press, 1992. https://books.google.co.th/books/about/The_Books_of_Contemplation.html?id=R_3rEJCX7CwC&redir_esc=y

(10) Binah, Ascension glossary. https://ascensionglossary.com/index.php?title=Binah&mobileaction=toggle_view_desktop

(11) Moshe Idel, Saturn's Jews. Page 59. file:///D:/Downloads/Saturn_s_Jews_On_the_Witches_Sabbat_and.pdf

(12) Shlomo Sela, Saturn and the Jews, 2017, Katz Center, University of Pennsylvania, https://katz.sas.upenn.edu/blog/saturn-and-jews

(13) Solomon Maimon quote, presented in Jacob Neusner's 1992 book, Religion, science and magic, in concert and in conflict. https://www.amazon.com/Religion-Science-Magic-Concert-Conflict/dp/0195079116

(14) Sanhedrin 98a, Talmud. http://www.come-and-hear.com/sanhedrin/sanhedrin_98.html

(15) Ptah, Wikipedia, https://en.wikipedia.org/wiki/Ptah

(16) Ptah, Mythology.net. 2016, https://mythology.net/egyptian/egyptian-gods/ptah/

(17) Paul Benjamine, And the Spirit of Sabbatai Zevi, Moved Upon the Waters Modes of Authority and the Development of the Donmeh Sects, 2012, Pdf, Scholarship.tricolib.
https://scholarship.tricolib.brynmawr.edu/bitstream/handle/10066/8207/2012BenjaminP_thesis.pdf?sequence=1&isAllowed=y

(18) Ushi Derman, Sacred Orgies: the Extremist Sabbatean Sect of Jacob Frank. Museum of the Jewish People at Beit Hatfutsot. https://www.bh.org.il/blog-items/sacred-orgies-extremist-sabbatean-sect-jacob-frank/

(19) Isabel Hernandez, Meet the man who started the Illuminati. History Magazine, National Geographic.
https://www.nationalgeographic.com/archaeology-and-history/magazine/2016/07-08/profile-adam-weishaupt-illuminati-secret-society/#close

Chapter 7. Jacob Frank, the Illuminati, the Rothschilds & secret societies

Gershom Scholem, one of the world leading authorities on Jewish Kabbalah wrote about Jacob Frank :

"Jacob Frank (1726-91) will always be remembered as one of the most frightening phenomena in the whole of Jewish history: a religious leader who, whether for purely self-interested motives or otherwise, was in all his actions a truly corrupt and degenerate individual." - Gershom Scholem (1897 - 1982, German born Israeli philosopher and historian, professor of Jewish mysticism)

After Franks release from prison in 1772, he initially settled in Gino (Bruenn) Morovia, in the now Czech Republic. Here he lived with his relatives Solomon and Sheindel Dobrushka. Solomon was a wealthy business man, owning both the potash and tobacco monopolies in Moravia. Throughout this period Frank would give his wife and daughter over to his Sabbatean sect, to be used for immoral sexual acts in orgies and satanic rituals. Solomon and Sheindel had 12 children, all of which were Frankists. Of the eight who openly converted to Christianity, six eventually gained titles of nobility. Once out of prison Frank was free to circulate among the rich and influential elements of European Jewish society, no doubt, in an attempt to spread his Sabbatean philosophy and to recruit new sponsors.

"Where Frank obtained the money for the upkeep of his court was a constant source of wonder and speculation and the matter was never resolved; doubtless some system of taxation was organized among the members of the sect. Stories circulated about the arrival of barrels of gold sent, some say, by his followers, but according to others, by his foreign political employers." - Encyclopedia.com (Frank, Jacob and the Frankists).[1]

"The Frankist elite consisted of a circle of very gifted intellectuals, theologians and men of letters, as well as a group of men of great financial means who were for the most part great merchant bankers and exerted tremendous influence in their day in the highest financial circles of Europe." – Robert Akers, *Sibling Rivalry on a Grand Scale: The Devil's in the Details.* 2011.[1b]

During this period, he visited many cities especially Vienna, taking his daughter with him. Around this time, while he networked himself among the rich and wealthy, Frank come into contact with Adam Weishaupt, a German philosopher, professor and founder of the Bavarian Illuminati (1776). Weishaupt was born in 1748, in Ingolstadt, Bavaria, to the descendants of Jewish converts to Christianity.[2]

"Freemasonry was steadily expanding throughout Europe in this period, offering attractive alternatives to freethinkers. Weishaupt initially thought of joining a lodge. Disillusioned with many of the Freemasons' ideas, however, he became absorbed in books dealing with such esoteric themes as the Mysteries of the Seven Sages of Memphis and the Kabbalah, and decided to found a new secret society of his own." - Meet the man who started the Illuminati.[2]

On his travels, Jacob Frank would outline his perverted ideologies in sermons, meetings and presentations, providing an overview, to future converts, as to what to expect from the cult which he was promoting. Not only was he inverting all those righteous and positive messages found in the traditional Judaic interpretation of the Torah, but he wanted to destroy all existing systems of both religious and social structures, with a view to creating a new order from the chaos which he and his followers hoped to foment.

"Wherever Adam trod a city was built, but wherever I set foot all will be destroyed, for I come into this world, only to destroy and to annihilate, but what I build will last forever." - Jacob Frank.

Frank was under the impression that in order for humanity to ascend to greater levels of conscious awareness, they must first descend down to the very bottom rung of existence. Only from the bottom of the mountain can humanity climb to the very top, where infinite consciousness can be grasped and understood. The Frankists aspired to a future time when every righteous religious belief system had been eradicated, initiating a global revolution which could sweep away the past and begin the process of rebuilding society from the very bottom.

"I did not come into this world to lift you up but rather to cast you down to the bottom of the abyss, further than this it is impossible to descend, nor can one ascend again by virtue of one's own strength, for only the Lord can raise one up from the depths by the power of his hand." - Jacob Frank

"Since we cannot all be saints, let us all be sinners" - Jacob Frank

All this pessimistic rhetoric which Frank promoted, influenced many impressionable minds throughout Europe prior to the French Revolution, a revolution which would ultimately dismantle the old custodians of traditional standards of morality.

In 1786 Frank moved from Morovia to Offenbach on the outskirts of Frankfurt, the same city where the Rothschild banking cartel began and the home of Adam Weishaupt. For these three to be in the same city at the same time, in my view, is not a matter of innocent coincidence. It opened up an opportunity which allowed the coordination of big projects to manifest easily with big money. In Offenbach, Frank lived a regal lifestyle underpinned by some of the biggest banking houses in the city. He was even given the title of 'Baron of Offenbach'.

After Jacob Frank's death in 1791, his nihilistic Frankist nephews Moses and Emanuel Dobruschka went to Paris to join the Jacobins, a group of political revolutionaries promoting anti royal sentiments together with the dismantlement of the old political order. Both Moses and Emanuel changed their surnames to Frey, and became heavily involved in the French Revolution. By 1794, with the end of the 'reign of terror', both brothers were executed for treason, using a new execution device called the guillotine.

"As long as the last divine sparks of holiness and good which fell at the time of Adam's primordial sin into the impure realm of the Qliphoth have not been gathered back again to their source so the explanation ran the process of redemption is incomplete. It is therefore left to the Redeemer, the holiest of men, to accomplish what not even the most righteous souls in the past have been able to do: to descend through the gates of impurity into the realm of the Qliphoth and to rescue the divine sparks still imprisoned there. As soon as this task is performed the Kingdom of Evil will collapse of itself, for its existence is made possible only by the divine sparks in its midst. The Messiah is constrained to commit "strange acts" of which his apostasy is the most startling; all of these, however, are necessary for the fulfilment of his mission." - Sabbatean and Frankist philosophy towards redemption, *Redemption Through Sin* By Gershom Scholem[3]

The Sabbatean Frankists believed that a new world order had begun with the arrival of their Messiah Sabbatai Zevi, who's Messianic soul reincarnated into Jacob Frank. To the Frankists this meant everything to do with the old world, its systems of religion and political order, had to be dismantled, a process which they thought must be achieved through any means necessary. Furthermore, because their Messiah had set a precedence of concealing his true intentions, through apostasy, hiding behind another religion, his followers were also expected to conceal their true leanings towards nihilistic Frankism. In their own words the Torah of Beriah (world of creation) was to be violated while the Torah of Atzilut (World of souls) was to be observed in secret, a philosophical ideology which would underpin many future secret societies.

For the Frankists to believe that the more they sinned the more they hastened the coming of redemption is contrary to all those who were trying to climb the Tree of Life, walking a difficult path of righteousness and high standards of morality. This includes traditional Judaism as well as Muslims, Christians and Buddhists alike.

According to Gershom Scholem, Sabbatean nihilists regarded violating the Torah of Beriah, on the most consecrated ground of all, Israel, the Supernal Triad, to be the pinnacle of sinning, which would bring about special significance with profound revelations. For those on the side of righteousness, they regarded anyone who attempted to descend down the Tree of Death, for whatever reason, even if they were trying to destroy the Qliphoth with their holiness, were deluded. It is believed that once a person falls into the arms of Satan and his entourage, they would find it virtually impossible to return, a position where even the Lord will not pardon them.

"Watch and pray so that you will not fall into temptation. The spirit is willing, but the flesh is weak." - Matthew 26 : 41 (NIV)

"Those who want to get rich fall into temptation and a trap and into many foolish and harmful desires that plunge people into ruin and destruction." - 1 Timothy 6 : 9 (NIV)

"Flee from sexual immorality. All other sins a person commits are outside the body, but whoever sins sexually, sins against their own body." - 1 Corinthians 6 : 18 (NIV)

"The acts of the flesh are obvious: sexual immorality, impurity and debauchery; idolatry and witchcraft; hatred, discord, jealousy, fits of rage, selfish ambition, dissensions, factions and envy; drunkenness, orgies, and the like. I warn you, as I did before, that those who live like this will not inherit the kingdom of God." - Galatians 5 : 19-21(NIV)

The Illuminati

In the second half of the 18th century Jesuits (Society for Jesus, a Roman Catholic order of priests) were being expelled from a number of Catholic countries around the world due to an internal conflict within the church. As a result, in 1773, Pope Clement XIV (1705 - 1774) issued a papal brief known as 'Dominus ac Redemptor', which essentially suppressed the Jesuit order's influence throughout Christendom.[4] This papal order opened up influential positions throughout society which were once filled by Jesuits. One of these positions was Professor of Cannon Law at Ingolstadt University, a city 300 km SE of Frankfurt. Adam Weishaupt, who had graduated in law at the university in 1768, had studied ancient Greek and Eleusian Mysteries, together with the mystical doctrines of the Greek philosopher Pythagoras. He eventually became a professor of Law within the ranks of the university's staff. In 1773, Weishaupt took over the position of Professor of Cannon Law, becoming the only non-clerical professor at the institution which, on the whole, was run by Jesuits.[5] At this time, a period viewed as an era of enlightenment, saw many people trying to break free from the controls and rigidity imposed on them by the old order, which mainly consisted of Catholicism and the rule of the monarch. This period of relative enlightenment promoted thoughts of atheism together with a nihilistic view towards the establishment.

Freemasonry was already well established by this time, and seen by some as an old boys network, which ultimately made up part of the establishment's fringe tentacles. Weishaupt was interested in Freemasonry, but saw many of its members lacking in occult knowledge and understanding of its ancient pagan religious roots. He therefore decided, in 1776, to form his own exclusive and elite secret society, based around the Freemason model, this became known as the Bavarian Illuminati, adopting the Owl of Minerva as its symbol. At the beginning there were only a handful of members, who were at a similar end of the radical and free thinking spectrum as Adam Weishaupt. However, after ten years this had risen to well over 2,000. New members were referred to as Minervals, after the Pagan Goddess of wisdom, reflecting the orders symbol of a wise old owl.

In 1777, Weishaupt joined the Masonic Lodge of the Strict Observance Rite, Lodge Theodore of Good Council (Theodor zum guten Rath), in Munich, an order which practised a form of neo-Templar-Masonry. His radical philosophy was similar to that of the Frankists, in the sense they both desired to do away with the old systems of governance, in favour of creating an order out of its demise. Weishaupt wrote :

"At a time, however, when there was no end of making game of and abusing secret societies, I planned to make use of this human foible for a real and worthy goal, for the benefit of people. I wished to do what the heads of the ecclesiastical and secular authorities ought to have done by virtue of their offices." - Adam Weishaupt[6]

Within the order of the Illuminati Adam Weishaupt adopted the name of 'Brother Spartacus'. A name which came from a 1st century BC Thracian gladiator who escaped bondage to lead a slave uprising against the then Roman Republic. This is interesting in itself, maybe Weishaupt considered himself as a new Spartacus, a modern gladiator in a battle with Rome's successors, the Catholic Church and the Holy Roman Empire. The initial objectives of the organisation appear to have wanted to promote equality and freedom throughout society, and in order to achieve this aim the authority of religious doctrines needed to be replaced by rationalism. As the order of the Bavarian Illuminati grew, its inner circles, a sophisticated network of spies and counter spies, became detached from the outer circles of less important members. Like most secret society structures, this would keep the important overriding objectives concealed. It is suspected that Weishaupt's underlining motive for joining the Freemason lodge in Munich was to attract new recruits for his own organisation. The contradiction faced by most movements seeking enlightenment through the process of free thought and rationalism, was in itself restricted by the order's internal rules and regulations, which ultimately came from those within its inner core and ruling council. For the first eight years of the Illuminati's existence it grew rapidly, spreading out from Bavaria into neighbouring cities and countries. As it spread into France, Italy and the Austria-Hungarian Empire, its members mainly came from the upper and middle classes, attracting aristocrats and even royals. Another contradiction arises when one considers Adam Weishaupt's vision of a future without monarchy, private property, social inequality, national identity and religious attachment. Although he aspired to all the concepts mentioned, he filled the ranks of his organisation with the very kinds of people which he desired to undermine. While Christians of good standing and character were actively encouraged to join, Jews and Pagans were not.[5] In 1779 Adam Weishaupt was persuaded to set up his own branch of Freemasonry, which was named 'Theodore of Good Council'. This new lodge was filled with members of the Illuminati, and used as a springboard to influence and infiltrate other masonic lodges with Weishaupt's radical beliefs. As Weishaupt's lodge networked itself among other masonic lodges, it grew in stature becoming accepted as an independent mother lodge affiliated to both the Union Lodge in Frankfurt and the Premier Grand Lodge of England. With this new status it was able to spawn masonic lodges of its own. The Illuminati continued to recruit by spreading their message of liberalism. However, this began to threaten the power base of both the clergy and the monarchy, which resulted in a reversal of various laws and policies, returning to a more traditional and hard line conservative approach. This U-turn, created resentment among the educated classes who were trying to promote their idea of liberalism, in what they regarded to be a new optimistic Age of Enlightenment. This frustration and resentment ultimately prompted more recruits into the arms of the Illuminati.

In 1783 Frederick the Great (ruler of Prussia from 1740 - 1786) was made aware of various documents belonging to the Illuminati, containing material of a revolutionary nature, which alarmed him. As a result, all of Berlin's masonic lodges were warned against the order, accusing the Illuminati of rejecting orthodox Christian theology, along with the desire to undermine existing religions, while at the same time attempting to turn Freemasonry into a political system. Consequently, 'The Three Globes', the oldest masonic lodge in Germany, sent out a call to reject the Illuminati and to no longer recognise them as fellow Freemasons. This began the decline of the Illuminati, as internal conflicts flared up resulting in resignations and a fall in membership. Their anti-religious and anti-monarchical stance now placed them in the firing line, as their secret society was slowly becoming public knowledge. It is claimed that in early 1785 an Illuminati courier, by the name of Lanze, was struck by lightening on his way to Ratisbon, carrying sensitive documents outlining plans for a revolution in France. Officials who found the documents passed them over to the government of Bavaria, who initiated an investigation into the affairs of the Order. Public resentment and suspicion increased casting doubt over positions of power occupied by members of the Illuminati within civic and state organisations. This put pressure on Charles Theodore (Prince Elector and Duke of Bavaria 1777 - 1799) to find a solution. Consequently, in March 1785, Theodore's government banned all secret societies including the Illuminati.[5] Adam Weishaupt lost his position at Ingolstadt University, and as a result, relocated to Regensburg, a town close to Ingolstadt, half way between Frankfurt and Vienna.

It is worth pointing out that this is the period when Jacob Frank moved to Offenback, a town on the outskirts of Frankfurt. Over the next few years raids took place on the homes and offices of Illuminati members by officials working for the Bavarian government. In 1787, only a few years before the French Revolution, when government agents had collected enough information on the matter, they published their findings in a 426 page book entitled *Einige Originalschiften des Illuminaton Ordens* (English translation : Some original letters of the Illuminaton Order).[7] According to New Dawn Magazine the publication resulted in the following conclusion :

"They revealed the full extent of the Illuminati's alleged plans to destroy Christianity, topple the monarchy, overthrow the civil governments of Europe and eventually extend their influence worldwide. Even though it was claimed these documents were blatant forgeries, as a result of their publication the Order was legally prohibited and membership of it could result in the death penalty." - New Dawn Magazine[8]

Frederick the Great Charles Theodore

Although the Illuminati were outlawed in Bavaria, some scholars believe that the movement's ideology, along with many members, went underground. Morphing into pockets of influence within other organisations and movements, holding on to what ever positions they had gained within the ranks of freemasonry. As a result of the ban, much of the Illuminati's writings were destroyed, giving rise to even more mystery and speculation surrounding the movement. The overriding intentions of the Illuminati could be viewed, in some ways, as altruistic, with a desire to advance civilisation towards socialistic rationalism underpinned by science and atheism. To achieve these objectives, most of the old societal norms of the day, based on religion and class, needed to be dismantled, thus posing a threat to the existing establishment.

To be part of a sophisticated group during that time, whether it be a secret society, a religious fraternity or masonic order, represented a person's standing within their community. It was a status symbol, reflecting how the individual wanted to be viewed by others, similar to today's status regarding car ownership or other symbols of success. To the men of the 18th century it gave them a sense of superiority, dressing up their egos, intellect and moral character, within an artificial world of mystery, magic and pseudo power. Many of these groups and organisations promised some form of enlightenment through knowledge which only a select few were allowed access to. Knowledge which had been kept, throughout the ages, by mystery schools, shamans and secret orders. A knowledge so valuable it could give, to those who understood it, paranormal powers beyond their wildest dreams. However, like most secret groups and orders, only those trusted ones, at the inner core, were given the keys to unlock these mysteries. In my view, it is plausible to assume that at the central core of these mechanisms of mysteries lay kabbalah, exposing the truth behind both the Tree of Life and the opposing Tree of Death.

At this time both the Illuminati and the Frankist Sabbateans were seeking dramatic changes within society. Although they came from different perspectives, they each had common goals towards the establishment, desiring an end to religious influence together with an end to the aristocracy and monarchical rule. They both saw revolution as the first step towards this objective, creating an opportunity for a new type of order out of the chaos which a revolution would bring. It is possible that elements of the Illuminati joined with elements of the Frankist movement in order to promote their common goals. Being so close to Frankfurt, the home of the Roshchild banking dynasty, made financing these objectives a great deal easier.

"I have heard much of the nefarious, and dangerous plan, and doctrines of the Illuminati, but never saw the Book until you were pleased to send it to me." - George Washington to William Russell, September 28, 1798, Library of Congress.

"It was not my intention to doubt that, the Doctrines of the Illuminati, and principles of Jacobinism had not spread in the United States. On the contrary, no one is more truly satisfied of this fact than I am." - George Washington, in Letter to the Reverend G. W. Snyder (24 October 1798)

"There is sufficient evidence that a number of societies, of the Illuminati, have been established in this land of Gospel light and civil liberty, which were first organized from the grand society, in France. They are doubtless secretly striving to undermine all our ancient institutions, civil and sacred. These societies are closely leagued with those of the same Order, in Europe; they have all the same object in view. The enemies of all order are seeking our ruin. Should infidelity generally prevail, our independence would fall of course. Our republican government would be annihilated." - Joseph Willard (1738-1804) U.S. Congregational clergyman, President of Harvard University

"I have been convinced that we, as an Order, have come under the power of some very evil occult Order, profoundly versed in science, both occult and otherwise, though not infallible, their methods being black magic, that is to say, electromagnetic power, hypnotism, and powerful suggestion. We are convinced that the Order is being controlled by some Sun Order, after the nature of the Illuminati, if not by that Order itself. We see our edifice crumbling

and covering the ground with ruins, we see the destruction that our hands no longer arrest...a great sect arose, which taking for its motto the good and the happiness of man, worked in the darkness of the conspiracy to make the happiness of humanity a prey for itself. This sect is known to everyone, its brothers are known no less than its name. It is they who have undermined the foundations of the Order to the point of complete overthrow; it is by them that all humanity has been poisoned and led astray for several generations...They began by casting odium on religion...Their masters had nothing less in view than the thrones of the earth, and the governments of the nations was to be directed by their nocturnal clubs...the misuse of our order...has produced all the political and moral troubles with which the world is filled today...we must from this moment dissolve the whole Order" - Duke of Brunswick, Grand Master of German Freemasonry, 1794

From Adam Weisehaupt's perspective, the crack down on his movement, in Bavaria, was not necessarily the end. It could be argued that the Illuminati had infiltrated other organisations to such an extent that there was no going back.

"Do you realize sufficiently what it means to rule—to rule in a secret society? Not only over the lesser or more important of the populace, but over the best of men, over men of all ranks, nations, and religions, to rule without external force, to unite them indissolubly, to breathe one spirit and soul into them, men distributed over all parts of the world?" - Adam Weisehaupt[9]

"The governments of the present day have to deal not merely with other governments, with emperors, kings and ministers, but also with the secret societies which have everywhere their unscrupulous agents, and can at the last moment upset all the governments' plans." – British Prime Minister Benjamin Disraeli

"From the days of Spartacus-Weishaupt to those of Karl Marx, to those of Trotsky, Bela Kun, Rosa Luxembourg, and Emma Goldman, this world wide conspiracy for the overthrow of civilization and for the reconstitution of society on the basis of arrested development, of envious malevolence and impossible equality, has been steadily growing. It played a definitely recognizable role in the tragedy of the French Revolution. It has been the mainspring of every subversive movement during the nineteenth century, and now at last this band of extraordinary personalities from the underworld of the great cities of Europe and America have gripped the Russian people by the hair of their heads, and have become practically the undisputed masters of that enormous empire." – Winston Churchill. Writing on 'Zionism versus Bolshevism' in the Illustrated Sunday Herald, February 1920.

"Surely these facts show that the Anarchists of France knew of the German Illuminati, and confided in their support. They also knew to what particular Lodges they could address themselves with safety and confidence.—But what need is there of more argument, when we know the zeal of the Illuminati, and the unhoped for opportunity that the Revolution had given them of acting with immediate effect in carrying on their great and daring work? Can we doubt that they would eagerly put their hand to the Plough? And, to complete the proof, do we not know from the lists found in the secret correspondence of the Order, that they already had Lodges in France, and that in 1790 and 1791 many Illuminated Lodges in Germany, viz. Mentz, Worms, Spire, Frankfurt, actually interfered, and produced great effects. In Switzerland too they were no less active. They had Lodges at Geneva and at Bern. At Bern two Jacobins were sentenced to several years imprisonment, and among their papers were found their patents of Illumination. I also see the fate of Geneva ascribed to the operations of Illuminati residing there, by several writers—particularly by Girtanner, and by the Gottingen editor of the Revolution Almanac." - (*Proofs of a conspiracy against all the religions and governments of Europe, carried on in the secret meetings of Freemasons, Illuminati, and reading societies.*) By John Robison, A. M. Professor of natural philosophy, and secretary to the Royal Society of Edinburgh. 1798[10]

House of Rothschild

Mayer Amschel Rothschild	Amschel Mayer Rothschild Frankfurt	Solomon Mayer Rothschild Vienna	Nathan Mayer Rothschild London	Carl Mayer Rothschild Naples	James Mayer Rothschild Paris

The Rothschild family dynasty came to dominate European banking from the late 18th century onwards and by the middle of the 1800s they had become the richest family in the world. They began in 1743, when Amshal Moses Bauer opened a money changing house in the Jewish ghettos of Frankfurt. To promote his money lending business, Amschel, hung a red shield from the front of his premises, from then on the local community referred to his business as the "**Red Shield Firm**". In 1755, after producing eight children, Amschel died, a premature death, from smallpox, leaving the family business to his fourth son Mayer Amschel Bauer. Eventually, Mayer Amschel Bauer change the family name to

Rothschild, reflecting the red shield which symbolised the business. Mayer soon discovered that lending money to royalty and governments was far more lucrative than lending to the general public, plus it had the added security because the loans were secured against future taxation. Mayer had ten children, five of which were boys. When the boys were old enough he sent them out to create private banks in five of the most prominent European countries, with the aim of dominating the world's banking system. Working together as a network of family banks, they would finance both sides of European political and military conflicts, collecting vast profits from all the chaos which they helped to support. Nathan in London took advantage of Napoleon's defeat at Waterloo by taking control of England's stock and bond markets. It is also suspected that this is when he secured control over the Bank of England. Using his own private couriers and carrier pigeons, he managed to get the news of the outcome of the battle ahead of everyone else. With this knowledge he began slowly selling stocks and bonds, which set off a panic in most of the markets. Investors, who watched closely, assumed England had lost the war. Once the stocks bottomed out, Nathan instructed his agents to begin buying everything up at give-away prices. By the time the official news of Wellington's victory arrived in London, prices shot back up. At this point Nathan was laughing, as most of the important aspects of England's commercial and financial infrastructure was now in the hands of the Rothschilds.

By the middle of the 19th century they had become the wealthiest family on the planet. In 1850 James Rothschild in France was said to be worth 600 million francs, 150 million more than all the other French banks combined. With this wealth came power, and with most or Europe's monarchs and governments in debt to the Rothschild banking cartel, they now had the power to influence policy. The lender is always master over the borrower.

Masters at organisation and control, the family now had the opportunity to direct the future course of human history. Combining their power with established European royalty and aristocracy, they united to help propel the British Empire to the next phase of global imperialistic domination. They worked together to undermine the American Republic, the German Republic, Russia under the Tsar, China, Africa and anywhere else which had ambitions of independence, The goal was globalisation under their control. They financed the Rockefellers, the Coon-Logans, the Harrimans, the Vanderbilts, the Carnegies, the Morgans and Cecil Rhodes, all acting under the direction of the lender, the House of Rothschild.

By controlling a country's private central bank and owning the majority of major stocks in the country's industrial and commercial infrastructure, some of these owners were in a position to steer those indebted nations in any direction they desired. Occasionally they would come up against a rogue leader, who wanted freedom, liberty and sovereignty for his nation. These independent mavericks were soon dealt with and brought back under control. During the First World War JP Morgan was assumed to be the richest man in America, but after his death it was discovered that he was just another agent for the House of Rothschild. Governments, monarchs and business owners throughout many parts of the world gradually succumbed to the parasitic influence of Rothschild finance, failing in their duty to shield their subjects from the ravages of debt slavery, instead turning on their people to service the interest on huge loans through various methods of unfair taxation. Much was written about the Rothschilds during the 19th century, but once they took control of the media and its outlets, they could censor what was being said about them, essentially going underground.

"The few who understand the system, will either be so interested from its profits or so dependent on its favours, that there will be no opposition from that class." - "Let me issue and control a nation's money and I care not who writes the laws." – Mayer Amschel Bauer Rothschild, 1744-1812

"History records that the money changers have used every form of abuse, intrigue, deceit, and violent means possible to maintain their control over governments by controlling money and its issuance." – James Madison (1751-1836), 4th US President.

"A power has risen up in the government greater than the people themselves, consisting of many and various powerful interests, combined in one mass, and held together by the cohesive power of the vast surplus in banks." – John C. Calhoun, Vice President (1825-1832) and U.S. Senator, from a speech given on May 27, 1836

"The Government should create, issue, and circulate all the currency and credits needed to satisfy the spending power of the Government and the buying power of consumers. By the adoption of these principles, the taxpayers will be saved immense sums of interest. Money will cease to be master and become the servant of humanity. "- Abraham Lincoln (1809-1865), 16th US President.

"These international bankers and Rockefeller-Standard Oil interests control the majority of the newspapers and the columns in those papers to club into submission or drive out of office officials who refuse to do the bidding of the powerful corrupt cliques which compose the invisible government." – Theodore Roosevelt (26th US President), as reported in the New York Times, March 27th, 1922.

"**By remaining behind the scenes, they (the Rothschilds) were able to avoid the brunt of public anger which was directed, instead, at the political figures which they largely controlled. This is a technique which has been practised by financial manipulators ever since, and it is fully utilized by those who operate the Federal Reserve System today.**" – G. Edward Griffin, (born November 1931), American political commentator, writer and documentary filmmaker.

"**The Rothschilds belong to no one nationality, they are cosmopolitan . . . they belonged to no party, they were ready to grow rich at the expense of friend and foe alike.**" - John Reeves's book *The Rothschild's: The Financial Rulers of Nations (1887)*

In the book *Bloodlines of the Illuminati,* Fritz Springmeier, suggests that the Rothschilds are the leading family within the circles of the Illuminati. Furthermore, Jim Marrs, in his book *The Illuminati: The Secret Society That Hijacked the World,* points out a possible link between the Rothschilds and members of the Illuminati.

"**Not only do I have too many eyewitnesses who have come from the inside of the Illuminati who say the Rothschilds are one of the top, but one can also point to how much control and wealth the Rothschilds exercise. The process of history has been to increase their control and wealth. The overall picture can't be denied. The Rothschilds are not flunkies for some other more powerful family.**" - Fritz Springmeier, *Bloodlines of the Illuminati*.[11]

"**The eighteen century Jewish philosopher and Bible translator Moses Mendelssohn, known as "the German Socrates", was a student of the Cabala and was a mentor to Adam Weishaupt, founder of the Illuninati. Mendelssohn may have also been a link between Weishaupt and banker Mayer Rothschild. Another link was Mendelssohn follower Michael Hess, the tutor of Jacob Rothschild's children, who later headed the philanthropist school for needy Jewish children established by Mayer Amschel Rothschild in Frankfurt.**" - Jim Marrs, *The Illuminati: The Secret Society That Hijacked the World.*[12]

The true activities and involvement of all these groups regarding the political landscape of the past 250 years is uncertain. As secret societies and private organisations, they have a vested interest in keeping their affairs and objectives out of public scrutiny. Consequently, because of the lack of transparency, within these secret groups, the level of cooperation between them will always be a exercise in speculation. What is known is that various credible individuals, throughout this time period, who have no connection or vested interest in these groups, have suspected and warned the rest of us about a possible hidden hand, a hand which may not have the interests of the majority of us at its heart, instead there appears to be a sinister hidden hand concealing overriding objectives behind the public charade of geopolitics.

At this point It is important to recap on the common objectives of all the fore-mentioned groups :

Rothschilds
- To control the world's monetary system. (The rich rule over the poor, and the borrower is slave to the lender.) Proverbs 22:7 (NIV)

Frankist Sabbateans
- To sin in order to walk among the qliphoth, down the Tree of Death.
- To destroy all existing systems of religion.
- To destroy all existing systems of government.
- To foment chaos.

Illuminati
- To abolish religious influence over public life.
- To promote rationalism and science over religious belief.
- To abolish abusive state power.
- To seek wisdom and enlightenment through knowledge.

"The very word "secrecy" is repugnant in a free and open society; and we are as a people inherently and historically opposed to secret societies, to secret oaths and to secret proceedings. We decided long ago that the dangers of excessive and unwarranted concealment of pertinent facts far outweighed the dangers which are cited to justify it. Even today, there is little value in opposing the threat of a closed society by imitating its arbitrary restrictions. Even today, there is little value in insuring the survival of our nation if our traditions do not survive with it. And there is very grave danger that an announced need for increased security will be seized upon by those anxious to expand its meaning to the very limits of official censorship and concealment. That I do not intend to permit to the extent that it is in my control. And no official of my Administration, whether his rank is high or low, civilian or military, should interpret my words here tonight as an excuse to censor the news, to stifle dissent, to cover up our mistakes or to withhold from the press and the public the facts they deserve to know." - Part of John F Kennedy's speech. Press Association 1961.

"The real menace of our Republic is the invisible government, which like a giant octopus sprawls its slimy legs over our cities, states and nation." —John Hylan, Mayor of New York City, 1922

"Behind the ostensible government sits enthroned an invisible government owing no allegiance and acknowledging no responsibility to the people."— From the Platform of President Theodore Roosevelt's Progressive ("Bull Moose") Party.

"The conscious and intelligent manipulation of the organized habits and opinions of the masses is an important element in democratic society. Those who manipulate this unseen mechanism of society constitute an invisible government which is the true ruling power of our country. We are governed, our minds are moulded, our tastes formed, our ideas suggested, largely by men we have never heard of."—Edward Bernays, the "father of public relations", writing in his influential 1928 book Propaganda.

"But quite frankly there is an outside source which we refer to as the 'deep state' or the 'shadow government'. There is a lot of influence by people which are actually more powerful than our government itself, our president." — Ron Paul, former U.S. Representative, November 2016 (following Donald Trump presidential election win).

"I merely say that, by certain processes, now well known, and perhaps natural in themselves, there has come about an extraordinary and very sinister concentration in the control of business in the country. However it has come about, it is more important still that the control of credit also has become dangerously centralized.

The great monopoly in this country is the monopoly of big credits. So long as that exists, our old variety and freedom and individual energy of development are out of the question. A great industrial nation is controlled by its system of credit. Our system of credit is privately concentrated. The growth of the nation, therefore, and all our activities are in the hands of a few men who, even if their action be honest and intended for the public interest, are necessarily concentrated upon the great undertakings in which their own money is involved and who necessarily, by very reason of their own limitations, chill and check and destroy genuine economic freedom. This is the greatest question of all, and to this statesmen must address themselves with an earnest determination to serve the long future and the true liberties of men.

This money trust, or, as it should be more properly called, this credit trust, of which Congress has begun an investigation, is no myth; it is no imaginary thing.

We have come to be one of the worst ruled, one of the most completely controlled and dominated, governments in the civilized world—no longer a government by free opinion, no longer a government by conviction and the vote of the majority, but a government by the opinion and the duress of small groups of dominant men." - W Wilson The New Freedom, Chapters 8-9, 1913.

"So you see, my dear Coningsby, that the world is governed by very different personages from what is imagined by those who are not behind the scenes." (Sidonia speaking), from Coningsby (1844) book 4, Chapter 1. Benjamin Disraeli, two time British Prime Minister (1868-1880).

In his book *Tragedy and Hope, A history of the world in our time,* 1966. Carroll Quigley discusses the great monopolies of industry and banking which dominated much of the world before World War 1.

"As early as 1909, Walter Rathenau , who was in a position to know (since he had inherited from his father control of the German General Electric Company and held scores of directorships himself), said : "Three hundred men, all of whom know one another, direct the economic destination of Europe and choose their successors from among themselves."" - Carroll Quigley quoting Walter Rathenau. *Tragedy and Hope, A history of the world in our time,* 1966. Page 61.

"Fifty men have run America and that's a high figure." - Joseph Kennedy - July 26th 1936. Purported to be from New York Times.

"Fifty men in the United States have it within their power, by reason of the wealth which they control, to come together within 24 hours and arrive at an understanding by which every wheel of trade and commerce may be stopped from revolving, every avenue of trade blocked, and every electric key struck dumb. Those fifty men can paralyse the whole country for they control the circulation of currency and can create a panic whenever they will." - Senator Chauncey M Depew (New York), and attorney for Cornelius Vanderbilt (President for the New York Central Railroad and US senator from 1899-1911).

"There exists a shadowy government with its own Air Force, its own Navy, its own fundraising mechanism, and the ability to pursue its own ideas of national interest, free from all checks and balances, and free from the law itself." - Daniel Ken Inouye (1924 - 2012), US Senator (1963 - 2012), Senate Select Committee on Secret Military Assistance to Iran and the Nicaraguan Opposition (Iran-Contra hearings) (1987).

Freemasons

The Masons are not a secret society as such, but a society with secrets, a large international organisation with an estimated 5 million members in nearly every country in the world. It is based on medieval stone mason's guilds, Old Testament symbolism, ancient Egyptian mystery religions and the construction of Solomon's Temple. They publicly refer to themselves as "morality veiled in allegory". There are many levels of Freemasonry, known as degrees, with the majority falling into the Blue Lodge Order. From here members progress up 3 degrees before splintering off to either the Scottish Right or York Lodges. The highest known level is the 33rd degree, which is the Grand Sovereign Inspector General. A significant number of the influential elite within western society were, and in some cases still are Freemasons, including politicians, lawyers, barristers and policemen, all looking out for one another as fellow Freemasons, swearing an oath to secrecy and allegiance. It could be considered as a religious order, because no one can be a fellow Mason unless they believe in the Masonic God, the God of light and universal wisdom. The Freemasons refer to their God as the great architect of the universe, which some suspect as being the Demiurge.

Oblivious to its true purpose, many Freemasons think they are just part of an old boys' network, hoping to further their own personal careers and social status, they lack the understanding of what Freemasonry is really built upon. Like all religions its core belief stems from aspects of astronomy, astrology, metaphysics, ancient mysticism and Kabbalah. This is easily identified by analysing Masonic rituals and symbolism, which also have a great deal of Judaic influence.

The Freemasons regard Nimrod as one of the founders of Masonry, he is generally considered as the one who proposed building the Tower of Babel, and directed its construction. Nimrod is often associated with the constellation of Orion. He was also renowned for his rebelliousness against God.

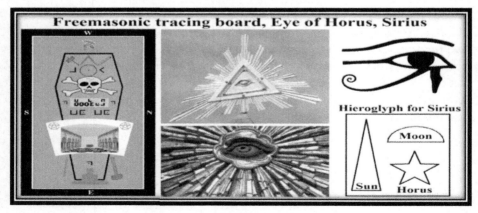

Freemasonic tracing board, Eye of Horus, Sirius

Hieroglyph for Sirius

Sirius is a star twenty times brighter and bigger than our own Sun, it was worshipped in ancient Egyptian mythology. The legend of Isis, Osiris and Horus originated from those ancestors who studied the heavens focusing on the Sirius star constellation, which became the ancient Egyptian trinity, similar to the Father, Sun and Holy Spirit of the Christians. Some scholars believe that Sirius is the sister star to our Sun, moving within a binary which completes a full cycle every 25,800 years (the Great Year). Freemasonry use Sirius symbolism throughout all levels of the fraternity, suggesting they have some affiliation to the planets, stars and luminaries. In Masonic Lodges Sirius is known as the "Blazing Star".

As the new initiate Mason progresses up the ladder of degrees, they are exposed to ancient knowledge and wisdom, in a steady process of enlightenment. As the penny begins to drop their level of understanding concerning occult mysteries and holy science becomes clearer. An emphasis is made in the holy sciences, in this case holy means holistic or whole. Once you are exposed to the whole picture, within the science of light, your chance of becoming illuminated is greatly increased. Most of man's religions, in general, do not enlighten the believer, instead they only offer part of the equation, half truths which cloud and confuse the minds of those followers who, on the whole, are righteous but spiritually stagnant within the rigid dogma surrounding these religions.

Solomon's Temple plays an important role in Freemasonry. An ancient temple, supposedly constructed by King Solomon and his Master Masons, headed by a man named Hiram Abiff. Although the legend suggests that the temple was built to hold the Arc of the Covenant, there is no archaeological evidence to support the physical existence of the first temple, only the account mentioned in the Bible.[13]

When we examine the whole concept of Solomon's Temple from an astrological perspective, it all begins to add up. Solomon is a constructed name which refers to the Sun in three ancient languages.

SOL: Latin for the Sun
OM: Aum pronounced (Om) means the Sun in Hindu Sanskrit
ON: In biblical Hebrew Heliopolis (city of the Sun) was referred to as "ON"

SOL-OM-ON is just the Sun in three ancient languages. Solomon's Temple is often depicted with two large pillars each side, just like the pillars of Kabbalah, severity and mercy, with mild equilibrium in the centre where access to the temple and the Creator can be found through its doorway.

Freemasonry, Kabbalah & Solomon's Temple

The story told by Freemasons, is that Hiram Abiff, the Master Mason, during the final stages of constructing Solomon's Temple, was approached by three lesser stone workers, who threatened him with death, unless he revealed the Master Mason's secret password, a word which they thought would grant them access to wisdom and paranormal powers. Hiram Abiff refused to divulge the password and was subsequently murdered by the three commoners.

Outraged at this, King Solomon found the body and reburied the remains in an ornate temple, commemorating Hiram as an honourable Master Mason. The murderers were eventually caught, tried and executed. The Masons hold Hiram Abiff in great esteem, as an example of honour amongst Masons, keeping their oaths and secrets even to the point of death. Hiram Abiff is mentioned in the Bible but there is no account of his murder. His name is interesting from an astrological point of view. Hi-ram refers to Aries, the ram, Aries also represents the head or the crown chakra the Hiram. Abiff starts with A and B the first two letters of the alphabet, letters associated with Aries, the beginning of the year in the ancient calendar.

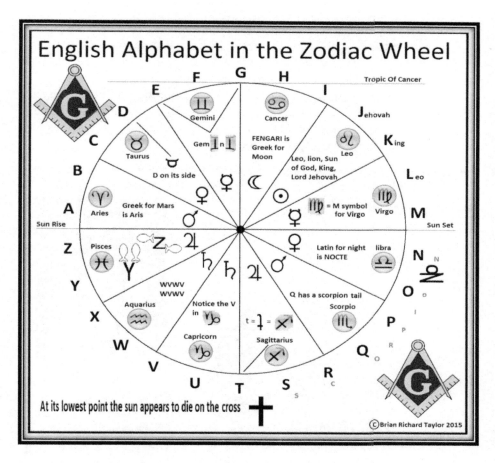

English Alphabet in the Zodiac Wheel

At its lowest point the sun appears to die on the cross

©Brian Richard Taylor 2015

The G in the centre of the famous Freemason's emblem is the highest letter in the zodiac alphabet. It could also be associated with the G in Gemini, with its twin pillars, Castor and Pollux, the pillars either side of Solomon's Temple, and the pillars found in Kabbalah.

Gemini   Solomons Temple   Masonic   Arc of the Covenant

Symbolism is very important in the process of reprogramming a belief system into the subconscious mind, aligning oneself with the energetic frequencies associated with the symbols or ceremonies used. All new recruits must take part in rituals and ceremonies attaching emotional stimulus to suggestions, transforming the individual into a pliable and useful member for future Masonic aspirations, the outer circle of fresh initiates rarely come into contact with the inner circle of established Hiram Masons, who set the direction and course of the overall organisation within modern society.

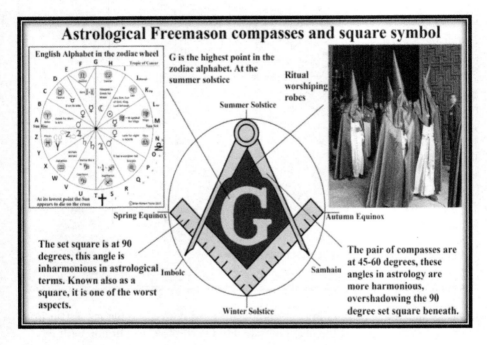

Astrological Freemason compasses and square symbol

English Alphabet in the zodiac wheel

At its lowest point the Sun appears to die on the cross

G is the highest point in the zodiac alphabet. At the summer solstice

Ritual worshiping robes

Summer Solstice

Spring Equinox

Autumn Equinox

The set square is at 90 degrees, this angle is inharmonious in astrological terms. Known also as a square, it is one of the worst aspects.

Imbolc

Samhain

The pair of compasses are at 45-60 degrees, these angles in astrology are more harmonious, overshadowing the 90 degree set square beneath.

Winter Solstice

Masonic oaths

At each level of Freemasonry, from the 1st degree to the 33rd, the Mason must perform a ritual ceremony and take an oath to keep secret passwords and knowledge within the brotherhood. The penalty for divulging these secrets can be horrific.

- 1st degree penalty: Throat cut, tongue buried in the sands of the sea.
- 2nd degree penalty: Heart plucked out, placed on highest pinnacle of temple.
- 3rd degree penalty: Disembowelled, bowels burnt to ashes.
- 7th degree York right: Top of skull taken off, brain exposed to noon day Sun.

At the 33rd degree level, it has been reported that the initiate is asked to drink wine from a human skull, symbolising Holy Communion with a Masonic twist. The oaths within the brotherhood of international Freemasonry transcend national and political allegiances, creating a powerful unaccountable and influential organisation throughout the world.

As a Mason progresses up the ranks of the fraternal order, his fellow Masons will do all they can to protect him from outside harm, even shielding his involvement in criminal activities. In 1826 a Mason by the name of William Morgan aired his intentions to publish a book exposing the Freemason's secrets, still under his Masonic oath, he found himself arrested, under spurious accusations, later to disappear, never to be seen of again. The Freemasons where blamed for his death, which, in turn, caused a huge anti-Masonic backlash, giving the Masons a bad reputation for the next few decades, with many members leaving, causing many lodges to close. However, by the end of the 19th century their numbers had recovered back to where they once were. Around the time of Albert Pike (1809-1891) any person of renown, who was respected in the circles of high society, would join one of many Freemason Lodges.

Some researchers have concluded that Jack the Ripper was a Freemason, performing Masonic ritual killings throughout London's Whitechapel district in 1888. They propose that the 2nd heir to the English throne, the Duke of Clarence, also a Freemason, had fallen in love with a common Catholic prostitute by the name of Annie Crooks. It is claimed that he married her and had a daughter. Annie was set up with a place to live along with a nanny to help take care of the baby. However, the nanny they hired eventually turned to prostitution to increase her income, and began spreading news of the royal secret amongst other Whitechapel prostitutes. Eventually some of the prostitutes threatened to expose the story to the press unless they were paid off. At the time the Prime Minister Robert Cecil who was also a Freemason, together with the police commissioner, Sir Charles Warren and Sir William Gull, the Royal Physician. It is suggested that either the Queen or the Prime Minister gave the go ahead to eliminate this threat which had the potential to undermine the royal establishment's reputation. It is claimed that the royal physician was called upon to neutralise the problem. Consequently, Gull, the Royal Physician, went on a killing rampage to protect his fellow Masons who likewise protected him. The interesting part of this case is the way the victims were murdered. It was as though they were in accordance with Masonic oath penalties, their throats were cut from ear to ear, and their bowels were ripped out of the body etc. Prior to being called Jack the Ripper, the killer referred to himself as "Leather Apron", a reference to a lamb skin or leather apron given to Master Masons. It has been suggested that the reason why Leather Apron was never caught, was because he was surrounded and protected by fellow Masons in high positions.

Jack the Ripper Duke of Clarence Robert Cecil PM Sir Charles Warren PC Sir William Gull Freemasons leather apron

Many influential figures throughout history have been Freemasons, with an allegiance taking precedence over many other aspects of their lives. Cecil Rhodes was a member of the Bulawayo Lodge in Rhodesia, in 1895 he donated some land over to the order for the construction of a temple. During World War II, both Churchill and Roosevelt were high ranking Freemasons. Brothers in war and also united within international Freemasonry.

Tehran Conference 1943

A meeting of Masons, Roosevelt and Churchill

Churchill joined the Stodholme lodge No 1591 in May 1901. A time when becoming a Mason was seen as a symbol of social status. Prince Edward, a Grand Master for 25 years, was soon to be King following the death of his mother Queen Victoria.[14] Edward, a popular monarch, gave prestige and credibility to the order, while promoting it as a tool for British imperial aspirations.

Franklin Delano Roosevelt was initiated into the Scottish Right of Freemasons in October 1911. By 1929 he had reached the level of 32nd degree, and became a Shriner in Cyrus Temple of the 'Ancient Arabic Order Nobles of the Mystic Shrine'. By the time the National Socialists came to power in Germany Roosevelt held a number of honorary Grand Master positions, one in Georgia and one in the Order of Demolay.[15]

There had been rumours and speculation about Joseph Stalin's Masonic ties ever since the war finished, but there is no conclusive evidence to support these claims. However, the fact that two of the big three, both Churchill and FDR were Freemasons leaves one to conclude that Masonic influence must have played a part in the policies of the Allies.

When a person decides that they want to join a Freemasons Lodge, they must first ask to join. If you are regarded as a suitable candidate, you may be asked to fill out a petition form. Your request for membership is then voted on by existing members using a secret ballot system. The traditional method used is based on astrological symbolism. A white ball is chosen for 'yes', and a black ball or cube is chosen for 'no'. The white ball represents Venus energy of love and liking, whereas the black ball or cube represents Saturn's serious and restrictive energy, in this case a rejection. Most members will be unaware of this, blindly accepting it as a glorified game of marbles. The planet Venus is shrouded by a layer of reflective clouds made from sulphuric acid; this gives the planet a light yellowish white appearance.

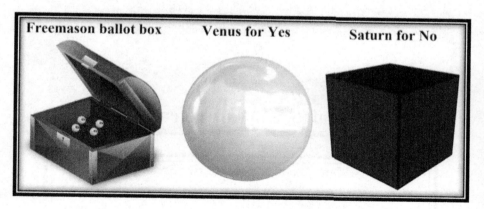

Freemason ballot box   **Venus for Yes**   **Saturn for No**

Bohemian Grove

The Bohemian Grove is a large forested area in northern California, where a 140 year old private Sanfranciscan men's art club holds a two week encampment for its members and their guests and includes some of the world's most powerful men. Senior members of the grove, with over 40 years service are elevated to the prestigious status of "Old Guard", this gives them priority and VIP treatment at seminars and ceremonies.

Like the Illuminati, the Bohemian Grove has an owl for their mascot and emblem. Standing at centre stage at the edge of the lake, in the grove, is a 30 foot concrete statue of an owl, the symbol of wisdom. Some spectators have suggested that the owl represents Moloch, one of the top demons of the underworld. At the start of the event a ceremony called "cremation of care" is performed in front of the 30 foot owl, a mock human sacrifice along with its burning takes place in front of a large audience by a selection of robed members purporting to be performing an exorcism. The reason they give is that this helps to ensure the success of the ensuing two weeks. This whole ceremony has a definite ancient occult overtone. The Bohemian club has a patron saint, John of Newpomuk, furthermore, similar to the Freemason's Hiram Abiff, their saint suffered death rather than disclose closely guarded secrets, reminding Bohemian Grove members of their expected cooperation.

Bohemian Grove

Cremation of care ceremony

Famous attendees of the Grove		
George H W Bush	Dick Chaney	Al Gore
George W Bush	Bill Clinton	Robert Kennedy
Herbert Hoover	Dwight D Eisenhower	Richard Nixon
Henry Kissinger	Gerald Ford	Colin Powel
Ronald Reagan	Henry Ford	Donald Rumsfeld
Theodore Roosevelt	Newt Gingrich	William Taft
Jimmy Carter	http://americansagainstnwo.tripod.com/id14.html	

"Democracy must be built through open societies that share information. When there is information, there is enlightenment. When there is debate, there are solutions. When there is no sharing of power, no rule of law, no accountability, there is abuse, corruption, subjugation and indignation." Atifete Jahjaga (President of Kosovo).

"There is nothing so despicable as a secret society that is based upon religious prejudice and that will attempt to defeat a man because of his religious beliefs. Such a society is like a cockroach — it thrives in the dark. So do those who combine for such an end." William H Taft, 27th President of the US (Speech to the Young Men's Hebrew Association in New York 20 December 1914).

Skull and Bones

Skull and Bones is a secret society located within the grounds of Yale University, established in 1832 by William Huntington Russel. The university was founded by Eli Yale, a wealthy opium trader with connections to the East India Company. Russel who was also involved in the drug business had a successful shipping firm which dominated the United States side of the Chinese opium trade. The Skull and Bones secret order became a recruiting ground to preserve power and commercial interests of prominent families in the area, many of whom were connected and profited primarily from the opium business. Drugs in those days were not illegal, they acted as a mechanism of control and influence, addicting people from all walks of life, while generating profit and political leverage for the sellers, people who cared not for the well being of their victims. The opium trade eventually led to the opium wars which brought about the British Empire's control over Hong Kong. Each year the Skull and Bones secret society would select a mere 15 new recruits from all those enlisting as first year students. In their final year, at Yale, they would become members of the order through an initiation ceremony. Each generation of elitist families would ensure their son's were chosen, keeping the power tight within the same circles. George W Bush was a member along with his father and grandfather, a family name synonymous with bonesmen. Being nominated a bonesman would certainly guarantee you a prominent position in the outside world, together with financial success in areas of politics, banking, law and commerce; bonesmen would take care of bonesmen. Considering only 15 new recruits are initiated each year, the number of bonesmen in top jobs is disproportionate to the rest of the population. During the 2004 presidential campaign, the electorate were given two choices, George W Bush or John Kerry, both members of skull and bones. While swearing an oath of secrecy within the secret order, they opposed each other in public as political rivals. Just like many other secret societies, the initiates go through an array of macabre occult rituals. The Skull and Bones is no exception, it has been reported that while the initiate lays helpless in a coffin, he is flanked by members dressed as the devil and others dressed as hooded skeletons, chanting words like (the hangman = death, the devil = death and death = death). In the temple itself, there is a room called the tomb which houses numerous human skulls and bones presented in decorative display cabinets; overall an unhealthy fixation of death seems to be the overriding theme. There is a rumour that Prescott Bush along with fellow bonesmen, robbed the grave of the Apache Chief Geronimo back in the early part of the 20th century, the story suggests that they took his skull and displayed it in a glass case within the tomb of their temple.

Skull & Bones Temple   Skull & Bones members   Skull & Bones 322   George Bush

The symbolism behind the society's 322 and Skull & Bones are still secret, but one can speculate as to its origins. A theory is that it represents the second chapter of a German fraternity created at Yale University in 1832. Another explanation comes from Genesis 3:22 :

Then the LORD God said, "Behold, the man has become like one of us, knowing good and evil; and now, he might stretch out his hand, and take also from the tree of life, and eat, and live forever " Genesis 3:22 The American standard Bible

Yale University and the Skull & Bones secret society has had some interesting involvements in Chinese politics, partially due to the potential within the countries active opium trade. With the exception of the Carter administration 1976-1980, all United States Ambassadors to Beijing since Henry Kissinger's initial dealings with Mao, back in the early 70s, have been members of the Skull and Bones secret society. This is quite a feat when considering that only 15 new initiates are created each year.

At the start of the 20th century Yale Divinity School established a number of schools and hospitals throughout China, known as "Yale in China". Perceived by many as another non-profit philanthropic charitable organisation, it was designed to develop educational programs in China which would further relations and understanding between the Chinese and American people. It could also be seen as a front aimed at influencing political change and to alter the beliefs of the Chinese people. Writing in the Yale Daily News, Jonathan Spence, a professor of Chinese history at Yale University, reveals that "Yale in China" supported Mao Zedong's rise to power. In 1919 when Mao was 26, the students union invited him to take over editorship of the Yale journal. Mao accepted the position where he quickly changed its format, promoting his own social criticisms and Marxist ideology.[16][17] China was in the throes of great change after the fall of the old imperialistic system, a new republic under Sun Yat-Sen could see China competing against the west, economically and militarily. The western elitists preferred a tougher approach, one which would keep China in a perpetual state of backwardness, a command and control structure which was simple and authoritarian, keeping a boot firmly stamping on China's progress for decades. Mao's communist party could do just that. Once Mao was in full control he turned China into the world's largest opium producer.

Satanic rituals and child sacrifice

Within the inner circles of some secret societies, ancient mediaeval and occult rituals take place. Behaviour and practices which most of us would find bizarre or so disturbing that we would not understand or comprehend the occult meaning of what was taking place. Without appreciating it, the majority of us live within the parameters of social norms, based around the Tree of Life and its pathways of morality with a basic sense of common decency, as though the Creator has installed, within each one of us, a basic code of morality and conduct.

**"This is the covenant I will make with the people of Israel after that time,"
declares the Lord. "I will put my law in their minds and write it on their hearts. I
will be their God, and they will be my people."** - Jeremiah 31:33 (NIV)

For those who distance themselves form the Tree of Life and the Creator, searching for material fulfilment over spirituality, will find that the Divine spark within them will slowly withdraw and become suffocated by their new perverted morality as they descend, across the Red Sea, down into the Tree of Death. Their new dark perspective of reality will be supported, confirmed and encouraged by the people they associate with, people already lost on dark pathways, as the Qliphoth opens them up to newer and greater circumstances which ultimately lead them further down into the depths of hades.

The inner circles of some dark secret societies, use blackmail as a mechanism of control over their minions in the outer circles, members who hold influential positions within society can be targeted for use to the societies overall objectives. The easiest and most effective way to compromise an average individual, of mediocre morality, who is slightly on the naive side concerning occult matters, is to subject them to an encounter with someone just under the age of consent.

This can be done in many ways.

"The rich seduce the poor and the old are seduced by the young" - Bob Dylan (When you gonna wake up)

On one side there are middle aged men who don't get much attention back home, or men with inflated egos, who could find themselves in an all expenses paid hotel, while on a business trip. On the other side there are many young people, just below the age of consent, who look older than their years, who are, not only impressionable, but also prepared to do almost anything for money. Consequently, if these young people are recruited by unscrupulous individuals to proposition those who require compromising, and if the older person takes the bait, then those with the evidence to expose them have a new obedient recruit for life. This is a popular tactic used among the elite circles, to keep those outside under control. This is one reason why so many children go missing each year, they are either groomed for use in child sex trafficking circles or used for occult satanic ritual sacrifice.

"for the highest spiritual working one must accordingly choose that victim which contains the greatest and purest force, a male child of perfect innocence and high intelligence is the most satisfactory and suitable victim". – Allister Crowley (1875-1947) English Occultist.

"The ILO (International Labour Organisation) estimates that there are as many as 1.8 million children sexually trafficked worldwide, while UNICEF's 2006 State of the World's Children Report reports this number to be 2 million. The ILO has found that girls involved in other forms of child labour — such as domestic service or street vending — are at the highest risk of being pulled into commercial child sex trafficking." - Trafficking of children, Wikipedia[18]

Recently, both Britain and America have witnessed some of the peripheral workings of these under age/paedophile sex rings. Organised crime syndicates of the most despicable kind, conducting their affairs within circles of the filthy rich and famous. A practice which appears to have been going on for decades, culminating in the exposure of two of the most notorious procurements of children for purposes of under age sex ever to be seen. I am referring to Jimmy Savile, in the UK, and Jeffrey Epstein, in the United States. Both frequent guests within the inner circles of British Royalty. An embarrassment for royalty which leaves big questions as to the actual scale of the problem.

When we are born, we come into this world as a unique expression of Divine light which emanates from the Pleroma at the centre of the galaxy. Consequently, children are closer to the Divine source than the rest of us. The jealous gods of the Qliphoth are inversions of the Creator, they will only bestow, in a material sense, if they themselves receive constant adoration together with frequent sacrifices. Unlike the Tree of Life, it is not a spiritual transaction, but a material one, requiring continuous upkeep. When a group of dark occultists get together to converse with their Satanic gods, they charge the surrounding atmosphere with psychic tension using various methods, many of which are perversions or inversions of religious ceremonies. With demonic mantra and mindful intent, together with sexual energy, they narrow the gap between this reality and that of the Qliphoth lifting the divide for whatever entities wish to integrate with their sadistic congregation. When the atmosphere is full of psychic tension, they either perform perverted sexual acts on each other, or with animals and children. Occasionally they will sacrifice a victim, after a drawn out period of torture, the victim's blood is consumed. The blood of a tortured person is said to contain natural hallucinogenics, adrenalin and stimulants which have the added potential, when consumed, of altering a person's perception of reality while promoting various connections with entities from demonic realms.

In some satanic circles, the lifeless body of the sacrificed victim is used as a vessel for summoning demonic spirits, which take over and animate the corpse while acting as a medium for communicating with the Qliphoth and their armies of demons. This is known as necromancy or death magic, an ancient practice which sheds some light on the Skull and Bone's obsession with rituals centred around human remains.

Once involved in a Satanic cult, it is not easy to get out. Although there is an inner circle, the members on the outer rings are tested and compromised to see how far they will go to impress their peers by showing their complete disregard for all forms and expressions of Divine spirit within creation. In other words these people will go to any lengths to cause death and destruction on the rest of humanity, as they descend down the left hand path defiling their own Divine spark in the process.

In a 2013 article in the Daily-extra, the author described the Bohemian Grove as :

"Former American president Richard Nixon called it "The most faggy goddamned thing you could imagine." - Bohemian Grove is a men's club that meets for two weeks in July in Monte Rio, California. The most powerful men in the world — bankers, politicians, movie stars and the elite of society — make up the guest list. There's been a lot of speculation about what goes on at Bohemian Grove, and as most conspiracy videos on YouTube will tell you, it's allegedly two weeks of the filthy rich, powerful and famous walking around naked and fucking each other, as well as gay male, female and child prostitutes. Oh yeah, in between performing occult rituals, of course." - Raziel Reid, Dailyextra[19]

It is suspected that so many people within the higher cogs of politics, the legal profession and the media are so heavily compromised by nefarious organisations that any investigation leading to their exposure will never get far enough to cause any damage due to their loyalty towards one another.

Cases of Satanic rituals

Below are some extracts and quotes from cases in which police and government agencies have found compelling evidence to support claims of Satanic Ritual Abuse (SRA) from all over the world.

"Perth police say they have proved a link between organised child sex abuse and devil worship, following the conviction on Monday of a young man on 22 charges of indecent assault and dealing and of evil intent. The head of WA's child sex abuse unit, Detective-Sergeant Roger Smart, said the conviction of Scott Brian Gozenton demonstrated the link. Satanic practices "and the associated abuse perpetrated on children is prevalent in the United States and Britain and no-one can now doubt that the link can be made here", Sergeant Smart said. Gozenton, 20, pleaded guilty to all charges and was remanded until April 5 for sentencing after the District Court was told that 13 witchcraft covens operated in Perth. Judge Kennedy was told that Gozenton had been a victim of sex abuse as an eight year-old and had been recruited as a teenager into a satanic cult where adults practised bizarre sex with each other, their own children and teenage recruits." - Sydney Morning Herald, March 13th 1991[20]

"Police have uncovered evidence of central coast sites used in satanic rituals, to which drawings made by children who claim to have been abused, bear an

eerie resemblance. One mother's traumatised child tells of adult groups hanging him from a cross, killing animals, performing sexual acts on cult members and watching orgies. A child from a separate family, who does not know the other child, tells an identical story. The Sun-Herald has seen evidence of the rituals. One mother, Genevieve, who has fought a four-year campaign to have authorities probe her claims said her case was similar to 33 other cases reported to the Department of Community Services. Medical evidence has proved that both Genevieve's children have been abused.

"I'm coming across more and more women who tell the same story," she said. "I've spent years trying to get help for my children, but there are people who don't want this to come out."" - Sun Herald, Australia, 8th August, 1999.[21]

"In 2003, five members of the Superior Universal Alignment cult in the Amazonian town of Altamira were convicted for the ritualistic murders of three children and the castration of two others. The victims were aged between eight and thirteen years, and they were kidnapped, tortured or killed between 1989 and 1993. Their genitals were removed and used in Satanic rituals by 75-year old village clairvoyant, Valentina de Andrade, the leader of the Superior Universal Alignment cult. De Andrade had previously been sought by police in Argentina and Uruguay prior to her arrest in Brazil on suspicion of involvement in other satanic ritual killings" - List of satanic ritual abuse allegations, Wikipedia[22]

"In 2003 allegations by three children in Lewis, Scotland resulted in the arrest of eight people for sexual abuse occurring between 1990 and 2000. A 2005 investigation by the Social Work Inspection Agency found extensive evidence of sexual, physical and emotional abuse and neglect. Police investigation resulted in allegations of an island-wide "Satanic paedophile ring", though charges were dropped nine months later following an inconclusive investigation.

A key witness who had implicated her family in the abuse and whose evidence was "vital" to the case of satanic abuse recanted her testimony in 2006 and the media raised questions about the nature of the police interviewing techniques. With a police spokesperson replying that the witness was questioned appropriately and that allegations were made by numerous witnesses." - List of satanic ritual abuse allegations, Wikipedia[22]

When these Satanic cults sodomise and torture children, they are taking part in the ultimate sin, the desecration of the closest connection to Divine light. Furthermore, to participate in the communal blood drinking of their victims compromises the participants to such an extent that it cements their place within the cult itself. As they all witness one another's involvement in the murder of innocence, they collectively defile the Divine spark which once occupied their own hearts and gave them life.

In 2018 an ex illuminati banker, by the name of Ronald Bernard, gave a testimony in front of a audience of representatives of his community, including clergy, local authority and law officials. During the course of his testimony, he admitted to being drawn deeper into a network of Satanists, who included him as part of their corrupt business affairs together with various Satanic rituals. After many years of living a lavish lifestyle, from the proceeds of crime he was asked to take part in a ritual involving children being sacrificed. At this point he realised he had become too deeply involved and no longer had the stomach for it. Subsequently, he made the decision to walk away. This wasn't easy for him, it took him over 10 years, costing him almost everything he had. However, he was determined to do whatever was necessary to break away from his dark and sinister past. At the end of his testimony he said :

"Its about a dark force who enjoys destroying all life on this planet, and its still going on." – Ronald Bernard 2018[23]

"This is the verdict: Light has come into the world, but people loved darkness instead of light because their deeds were evil. Everyone who does evil hates the light, and will not come into the light for fear that their deeds will be exposed. But whoever lives by the truth comes into the light, so that it may be seen plainly that what they have done has been done in the sight of God." – John 3 : 19-21 (NIV)

Notes for Chapter 7.

(1) Frank, Jacob and the Frankists, Encyclopedia.com,
https://www.encyclopedia.com/religion/encyclopedias-almanacs-transcripts-and-maps/frank-jacob-and-frankists

(2) Robert Akers, *Sibling Rivalry on a Grand Scale: The Devil's in the Details*. 2011.
https://www.amazon.co.uk/Sibling-Rivalry-Grand-Scale-Details/dp/B009AN85H8

(3) Isabel Hernandez, Meet the man who started the Illuminati. History Magazine.
National Geographic. https://www.nationalgeographic.com/archaeology-and-history/magazine/2016/07-08/profile-adam-weishaupt-illuminati-secret-society/

(4) Gershom Scholem, Redemption Through Sin, was published in 1936 and then
appeared in English in 1970.
https://archive.org/stream/REDEMPTIONTHROUGHSIN/REDEMPTION%20THROUGH%20SIN_djvu.txt

(5) Dominus ac Redemptor, Wikipedia,
https://en.wikipedia.org/wiki/Dominus_ac_Redemptor

(6) Illuminati, origins, Wikipedia, https://en.wikipedia.org/wiki/Illuminati

(7) Schneider, Heinrich (2005) [1947]. Quest for Mysteries: The Masonic Background
for Literature in 18th Century Germany. Kessinger Publishing. p. 24 n.49.
ISBN 1419182145.

(8) Einige Originalschriften Des Illuminaten Ordens 1787, Archive.org.
https://archive.org/details/EinigeOriginalschriftenDesIlluminatenOrdens1787/page/n5

(9) Michael Howard, New Dawn Magazine, The Enlightened Ones: The Illuminati and
the New World Order, https://www.newdawnmagazine.com/articles/the-enlightened-ones-the-illuminati-and-the-new-world-order

(10) Adam Weisehaupt quotes, Wikiquote, "Greeting to the newly
integrated illuminatos dirigentes", in Nachtrag von weitern Originalschriften vol. 2
(1787) p. 45. https://en.wikiquote.org/wiki/Adam_Weishaupt

(11) John Robison, A. M. Professor of natural philosophy, and secretary to the Royal
Society of Edinburgh. 1798. *Proofs of a conspiracy against all the religions and
governments of Europe, carried on in the secret meetings of Freemasons, Illuminati,
and reading societies.* https://www.gutenberg.org/files/47605/47605-h/47605-h.htm

(12) Fritz Springmeier, *Bloodlines of the Illuminati.* https://www.docdroid.net/7MC1nJr/bloodlines-of-the-illuminati-by-fritz-springmeier.pdf

(13) Jim Marrs, *The Illuminati: The Secret Society That Hijacked the World. Visible ink press, 2017.* https://www.amazon.com/Illuminati-Secret-Society-Hijacked-World-ebook/dp/B06Y92XKW4

(14) Science and Nature, Horizon, BBC, 17/9/14, http://www.bbc.co.uk/sn/tvradio/programmes/horizon/solomon_qa.shtml

(15) W. Bro. Yasha Beresiner, Winston Churchill a famous man and a Freemason, Masonic Papers, http://www.freemasons-freemasonry.com/beresiner7.html

(16) FDR and the Masons, Roosevelt history, 2011, https://fdrlibrary.wordpress.com/tag/freemasons/

(17) Jonathan Spence, Yale Daily News no. 96 February 29 1972, http://digital.library.yale.edu/cdm/compoundobject/collection/yale-ydn/id/135148/rec/14

(18) Yale China Association, Wikipedia, https://en.wikipedia.org/wiki/Yale-China_Association#cite_note-1

(19) Trafficking of Children, Wikipedia. https://en.wikipedia.org/wiki/Trafficking_of_children

(20) Raziel Reid, The 'faggy' Bohemian Grove: Satanism, rent boys and gay orgies. 2013. https://www.dailyxtra.com/the-faggy-bohemian-grove-satanism-rent-boys-and-gay-orgies-48834

(21) David Humphries, 1991 - CHILD SEX ABUSE LINKED WITH SATANISM: POLICE. Sydney Morning Herald, March 13th 1991. https://ra-watch.livejournal.com/4950.html

(22) Miranda Wood And Martin Chulov, Evil In The Woods, Articles on ritual abuse in Australia, 8 August 1999, Sun Herald. https://ra-watch.livejournal.com/25145.html

(23) List of satanic ritual abuse allegations, Wikipedia, https://en.wikipedia.org/wiki/List_of_satanic_ritual_abuse_allegations.

(24) Ronald Bernard, Satanic Child Sacrifice - ex Illuminati Banker Testimony, Youtube Video. Dec 6th 2018. https://www.youtube.com/watch?v=rgESZ1_9J2o

Chapter 8.

The left and right hand of politics

The concept of left and right wing within the spectrum of politics is probably far older than mainstream academia would have you believe. The orthodox view suggests it originated from the period surrounding the French Revolution, where the King and his supporters were considered as right wing, while those on the side of the revolution were seen as left wing.[1] This is all very well. However, when analysing this concept from a metaphysical and astrological perspective, additional clues to its true origin begin to reveal themselves.

First it is necessary to view the zodiac as two polarities. The first six signs, from Aries to Virgo, represent the right wing of the political spectrum, while the remaining signs, from Libra to Pisces, are the left wing.

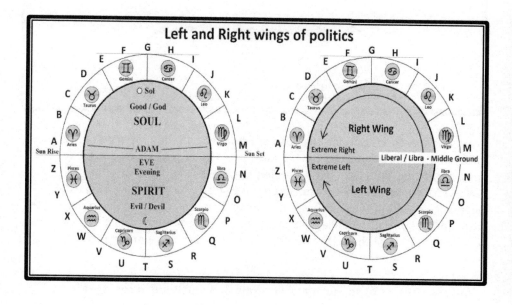

As can be seen from the previous diagram, the middle ground, within this political structure, is on the cusp of Libra, the balancing scales. The further we deviate from this position the more extreme the political system becomes, in either direction. The top blue half of the zodiac is traditionally viewed as masculine, while the bottom half is feminine and red, reflecting the standard colours adopted by the political left and right within modern politics. When each half is examined, in closer detail, some remarkable coincidences stand out.

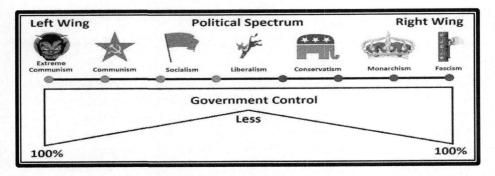

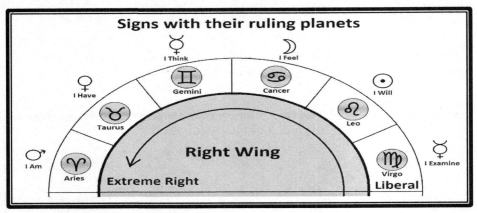

From the liberal position, on the cusp of Libra, we can see how the political spectrum, on the conservative right wing arm, tallies, as we make our way towards the extreme right, with the first six houses of the zodiac. The basic concept of conservatism is to conserve the traditions and social practices of people living within their communities. Respecting the rights of the individual to own land and property while sustaining values and traditions which they are familiar with, giving them the freedom necessary to participate unmolested within society and the political process.

"Conservatism is not so much a philosophy as an attitude, a constant force, performing a timeless function in the development of a free society, and corresponding to a deep and permanent requirement of human nature itself" - Quintin Hogg, the chairman of the British Conservative Party in 1959.

Leo and Cancer are the only signs in the zodiac ruled by the two luminaries, the Sun and the Moon. Here they represent the whole establishment of monarchy, the kings and queens within traditional patriarchal conservatism, where the male heir takes precedence over the female. Cancer is also the fourth house of the zodiac associated with the home environment. Here the traditional patriarchal

217

structure attributes great significance to the institution of home and family values.

As we move further right, away from the rule of the monarchs, we enter into thinking territory influenced by Gemini, the twins. Here we have a small group of minds underpinning the traditional values of conservatism. Similar to Geniocracy, where the greatest minds of a community are promoted as rulers, where traditional conservative values are upheld by two or more intellectuals with the necessary compassion to generate wisdom.

In Taurus 'I have', we move closer to extreme conservatism, where even less people have a say in the political system. Being the second house of the zodiac, concerned with personal wealth and material possessions, we find the wealthiest member of the community taking the reins of power. The idea being that with wealth comes responsibility, so those with the most would have the most to lose. Consequently, in order to keep hold of their wealth, who ever becomes ruler, must conserve traditions by implementing sensible policies.

On the far right we have the 'I am' of Aries, where one overriding ruler, usually the most authoritarian and marshal (Mars) like takes command. Traditional politics placed fascism at this end of this scale. However, there are different types of fascism, either socialistic or conservative in outlook. Most people's idea of fascism is Nazi Germany or Mussolini's Italy of the 1930s. In the case of Germany we saw a combination of a fascistic leader with a national socialistic agenda. Bringing elements of the far right, in line with their leader's concept of socialism. It is also worth pointing out that Hitler and the Nazis used the idea of the Aryan (Aries) master race to underpin their own brand of superior national socialism. As Hitler was born on the 20th April 1889, on the cusp of Aries and Taurus, it made him the perfect choice as leader for this Aryan/Aries Ideology.

Far right, fascism. Mars ruler of Aries (Aryan)

There is another aspect of the left and right to consider, one in which can be defined as either rational or emotional. The first six houses of the zodiac, considered here as right wing conservatism, is the masculine half of the chart, ruled by the Sun and the focal consciousness. This represents the rational and logical side of the mind, whereas the left wing socialistic side of the zodiac, the feminine side, ruled by the Moon and the subconscious, represents the emotional side of human thinking. Furthermore, the colours of blue and red, which represent masculine and feminine polarities, are also used to represent either conservative or socialistic values.

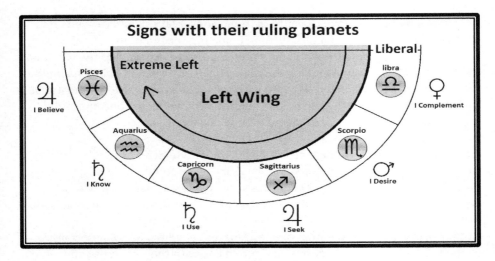

The left wing of politics is comprised of socialism and communism, where the views and aspirations of the individual become subordinate to the society or community as an organisation, with its overriding ideologies and objectives paramount. Here the state makes all the important decisions concerning a person's life, owning most of the land and infrastructure, while the individual is given privileges by the state for services rendered to the state.

As we progress past the liberal left of politics we come to Scorpio, the scorpion and the house of sex, death, rebirth and transformation. Its motto is 'I desire', ruled by Mars, the planet of proactive energy. This is a doorway into socialism and the temptations offered by Lilith in the form of sexual promiscuity and free love for all. It is where traditional values and old school cultural behavioural patterns can be transformed by socialistic ideologies.

"In Europe and North America, the free love movement combined ideas revived from utopian socialism with anarchism and feminism to attack the "hypocritical" sexual morality of the Victorian era, and the institutions of

marriage and the family that were alleged to enslave women. **Free lovers advocated voluntary sexual unions with no state interference and affirmed the right to sexual pleasure for both women and men, sometimes explicitly supporting the rights of homosexuals and prostitutes."** - Socialism and LGBT rights, Wikipedia[2]

As socialism gains ground and develops, it moves into the realm of Sagittarius, the house of higher learning, philosophy and long distance travel. This house and sign is ruled by Jupiter, the planet of expansion and optimism. Here socialism will promise more than it can deliver, by being over optimistic as it seeks to expand new horizons into neighbouring cultures, infesting institutions of higher learning and the traditional social and philosophical norms of the day.

""long march through the institutions of power" to create radical change from within government and society by becoming an integral part of the machinery." - Rudi Dutschke (1940-79), religious socialist[3]

Aquarius and Capricorn represent communism, an extreme version of socialism, where the state has almost full control over the lives of its citizens. The motto's for these two signs are 'I know' and 'I use', a perfect reflection of how a communist state views its people, it knows better and it uses them to further its own political agenda. These two signs are ruled by the planet Saturn, a planet synonymous with control, restriction, pessimism, frustration, loss, depression and misery. Satan is the personification of this planet, together with Moloch they rule the crown Qliphoth down the Tree of Death, on the left hand path. The glyph for Saturn is the cross of materialism over the crescent of spirituality, reflecting Saturn's metaphysical orientation. A similar configuration as the hammer and sickle which is commonly used to represent various forms of communism.

At the extreme end of left wing politics we find socialistic totalitarianism, where the state has 100% control over its subjects. This is essentially hell on Earth, where every person becomes a slave to the system. Like George Orwell's *1984* or Aldous Huxley's *Brave New World*, the people would only be allowed to live if they submit to their rulers completely. The motto for this house and sign is 'I believe', because only someone indoctrinated and programmed to believe, without question, in the system, as a utopian concept, would serve it.

"Diet, injections, and injunctions will combine, from a very early age, to produce the sort of character and the sort of beliefs that the authorities consider desirable, and any serious criticism of the powers that be will become psychologically impossible. Even if all are miserable, all will believe themselves happy, because the government will tell them that they are so." - Bertrand Russell, *The impact of science on society*, 1953.

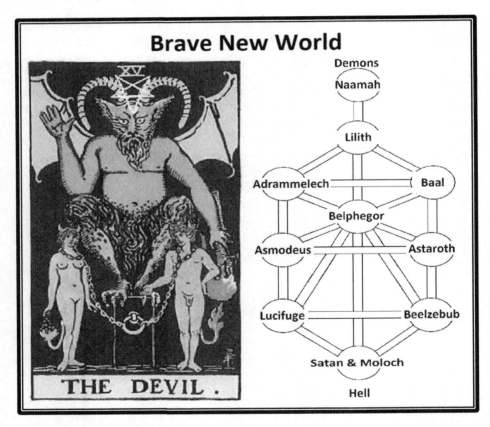

The modern two party system

Throughout history humanity has tried nearly every kind of political system on offer, with some disastrous results. The further society deviates from the balancing scales of Libra, the more extreme consequences are inflicted on those people who are unfortunate enough to live under the conditions created. Consequently, as a result of years of trial and error, modern political systems have generally centred around the middle ground, with only marginal differences between their left and right perspectives, this is usually referred to as the two or three party system.

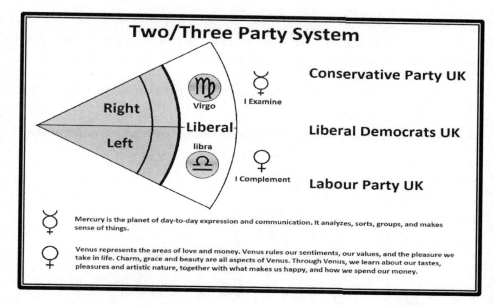

The two party system, in general, has promoted stability and steady prosperity within its centrally based parliamentary platform, drifting only marginally from left to right, as each round of political theatre eventually loses favour with its disgruntled voters. These parties, on the whole, work together to quash and alienate extreme ideologies which have the potential to cause havoc by undermining the objectives of this system's strategy towards globalisation.

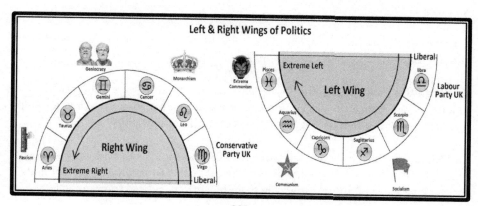

While the extreme left wing of the political spectrum can be viewed as a journey down the left hand path, equally, the extreme right must therefore be a journey up the right hand path, towards the Creator. A situation where we see monotheism as a theocratic dictatorship imposing the law of the one true God or Creator, expressed through various Abrahamic religions. Bearing in mind that God said to Moses "I Am that I Am", the same motto as the first sign of the zodiac, Aries 'I am', a sign ruled by Mars (Marses/Moses).

"And God said unto Moses, I Am That I Am: and he said, Thus shalt thou say unto the children of Israel, I Am hath sent me unto you." - Exodus 3:14 (KJV)

The name Abraham can be viewed as an expression of the first zodiac house of the ram, Aries, as AB-ram.

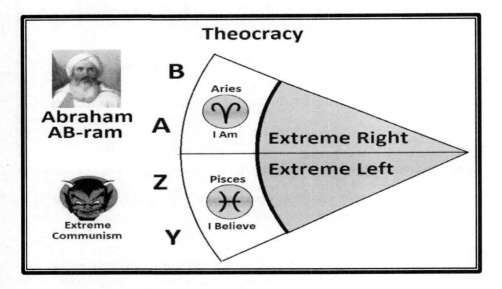

Karl Marx

"Thus Heaven I've forfeited, I know it full well. My soul, once true to God, Is chosen for Hell." - Karl Marx, *The Pail Maiden* (poem)

Although the above quote from Karl Marx was taken from one of his early poems, where poetic licence allows for detachment and free expression, one can't help but wonder how much of it is a reflection of his inner workings.

Karl Marx was born in Trier, Germany in 1818, the son of a middle class lawyer, who owned a number of Moselle vineyards. He was ethnically Jewish, coming from a long line of Rabbis, especially from his fathers side of the family. His father converted over to Protestantism because laws in Prussia at that time prevented Jews from working in certain professions. As a young adult he followed in his father's footsteps by studying Law at Bonn and Berlin universities. His first year at Bonn was not all that successful, spending more time socialising in bars than attending classes. Consequently, his father moved him to Berlin, away from the temptations of Bonn. At this time he developed a deep interest in philosophy and politics, admiring the works of the great German philosopher Georg Wilhelm Hegel. After graduating he went on to successfully attain a PhD in Philosophy. However, by this time he had become so radicalized by his left wing views and associations with various extreme groups that his natural progression into the realms of academia were restricted, he therefore turned towards journalism as a way to survive. In 1841 he began plans to start a journal called 'Atheistic Archives', however, the project never took off and was forgotten about. The following year Marx moved to Cologne, to work for the 'Rhineland News', a radical publication which suited his political persuasion, giving him plenty of room to express his socialistic views, while at the same time criticizing and venting his disdain for the right winged establishment of the day. Consequently, his reporting and views attracted the attention of the Prussian authorities. Marx wrote :

"Our newspaper has to be presented to the police to be sniffed at, and if the police nose smells anything un-Christian or un-Prussian, the newspaper is not allowed to appear." - Karl Marx, writing for the *Rhineland News*.

This radical attitude towards the right wing establishment culminated in a critical publication about the Russian monarchy. After reading the article, Tsar Nicholas I asked the Prussian government to remove it from sale, which they did in 1843. Later that year Marx moved to Paris to co-edit a new radical leftist Parisian newspaper with the German philosopher and political writer Arnold Ruge. The newspaper was called *'Deutsch-Französische Jahrbücher'* (German - French Annals). This publication and partnership didn't last long and by the following year Marx had moved over to begin writing for the *Vorwärts!* (Forward), the only uncensored, bi weekly, radical German language newspaper still in circulation at that time. It was a publication with strong links to a secret socialist society, full of workers and artisans, known as 'League of the Just'. It was around this time Karl Marx refined his views on dialectical materialism, a theory based on the Hegelian dialectic (dialectic = dialogue between two or more different points of view, to establish the truth) of a thesis, an anti-thesis and a synthesis. Whereas the Hegelian dialectic is primarily dependent upon the mind's perception of reality, incorporating a creator, Karl Marx's materialistic dialectic is based around the assumption that human consciousness is a response to the material world not the creator of it. This is very much understandable when considering Karl Marx was an atheist, someone who did not conceive the Creator as the benchmark of all creation, instead he was very much a materialist, denying the existence of a Creator, while promoting his vision of a socialistic utopia. This all fits together neatly, when using the zodiac as a template for political persuasion, where extreme socialism, in the form of communism, is found in the houses ruled by Saturn, the planet associated with materialism. Saturn, of course, has the same glyph orientation as the famous communist hammer a sickle, the cross of materialism over the crescent of spirituality.

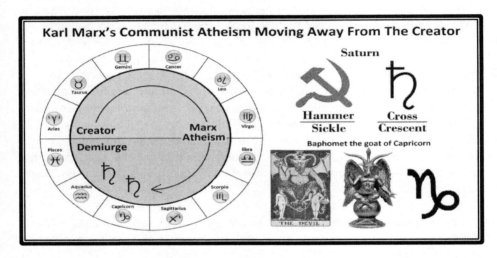

Karl Marx's Communist Atheism Moving Away From The Creator

While Marx was working on *Vorwarts* (Forward) he met Fredrick Engels, another German socialist philosopher, who he formed an alliance with, both eventually becoming life long friends. Unfortunately, at this time, in 1845, the Prussian King Fredrick William IV took a keen interest in neutralising the threat which was coming from radical leftist movements throughout Europe. This ultimately led to the closure of the *Vorwarts*, together with Marx's expulsion from France. Losing almost all his capital, Marx fled to Brussels to begin all over again, this time with the support of Engels, who also shared the view that the proletariat (working class) would, one day, rise up and overthrow the bourgeoisie and ruling classes. Engels later joined Marx in Brussels where they worked together on numerous projects. In the summer of 1845 they both went to England to study the living and working conditions of the country's working class. On their return they believed that the time was right for the working classes of Europe to rise up and liberate themselves with a working class revolution. They renamed the 'League of the just' into the 'Communist League', promoting it forward from just an underground secret socialist society, into an outward political movement. Together they worked on the parties manifesto, which would later become one of Karl Marx's best known writings, the *'Communist Manifesto'*. Published in 1848, its release coincided with a great deal of political turmoil at that time. It was a year, especially in France, of republican revolts against European monarchs, ending with the Second French Republic and overthrow of the monarch. Riding on the wave of revolution Marx was accused of being personally involved by the Belgian authorities, he subsequently fled to France before heading to Cologne, hoping the socialist revolution would spread throughout Germany. The king of Prussia, once again, introduced sever counter measures against leftist revolutionaries and Karl Marx was ordered to leave Germany. After months of avoiding the authorities he eventually found refuge in England where he spent the rest of his days stateless, living in London.

Marx and Engel's *Communist Manifesto* became the benchmark for almost all the world's far left socialist and communist movements throughout the twentieth century. It is worth pointing out that the sign of Aquarius has a shared ruler-ship. In old astrology Saturn ruled the whole sign, but recent astrology gave the first 1000 years to Uranus, the planet of rebellion and revolution.

"The Communists disdain to conceal their views and aims. They openly declare that their ends can be attained only by the forcible overthrow of all existing social conditions. Let the ruling classes tremble at a Communistic revolution. The proletarians have nothing to lose but their chains. They have a world to win. Working Men of All Countries, Unite!" - Karl Marx, Communist Manifesto, chapter 4.

"The theory of the Communists may be summed up in the single sentence: Abolition of private property. We Communists have been reproached with the desire of abolishing the right of personally acquiring property as the fruit of a man's own labour, which property is alleged to be the groundwork of all personal freedom, activity and independence." - Karl Marx, Communist Manifesto, chapter 2.

"Anybody who knows anything of history knows that great social changes are impossible without the feminine foment. Social progress can be measured exactly by the social position of the fair sex (the ugly ones included)." - Marx-Engels Correspondence 1868

"Religion is the sigh of the oppressed creature, the heart of a heartless world, and the soul of soulless conditions. It is the opium of the people. The abolition of religion as the illusory happiness of the people is the demand for their real happiness. To call on them to give up their illusions about their condition is to call on them to give up a condition that requires illusions. The criticism of religion is, therefore, in embryo, the criticism of that vale of tears of which religion is the halo." - Karl Marx, Works of Karl Marx 1843, A Contribution to the Critique of Hegel's Philosophy of Right.

In 1914, at the start of world war one, a Marxist revolutionary movement sprang up in Germany, attempting the overthrow the old order in favour of a communist revolution. However, although they tried three times the right wing opposition in Germany was too strong. The name they chose for their organisation was 'The Spartacus League'. The same name Adam Weishaupt gave to himself as head of the Illuminati.

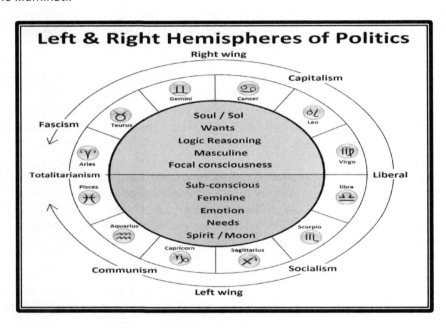

For socialism / communism to thrive all those values, traditions and ideologies associated with the right need to be replaced by leftist values. This is one of the main reasons why traditional concepts of masculinity, logic and rationality are attacked and undermined in favour of feminism and emotional rhetoric when promoting socialistic policies. This is exactly what we see throughout the world as the globalisation project moves into high gear undermining old nation states together with their traditional values concerning gender and the role of the family as a whole. As a collective our wants and needs are also coming into question, being socially engineered, as the globalists program of sustainable development (Agenda 21) is expanded throughout the world.

The number of leftist organisations and movements, dedicated to either undermining the right or promoting the left is on the rise. A new form of politics is emerging, one in which emotions are taking precedence over truth, facts and rational arguments. It is becoming fashionable to take offence at the slightest form of displeasure, opinions which do not fall in line with the lefts latest view of how their perfect socialistic utopia should be. A vision of a brave new world, offered to them by various sponsored groups and think tanks working for left wing interests. Many forms of united spirituality, especially those attempting to climb the Tree of Life, find themselves being targeted for division, decimation and finally elimination, confirming Karl Marx's suggestion that religion is no friend to the overall happiness of those living within a communist system. Leftists who rely on emotion to bolster their political argument also rely on the expansion of state power to protect their fragile emotions. The underlining purpose behind cultural Marxism is to make society so divided (Diabolos, divide & abolish) that it can be easily conquered by state forces, a situation which ultimately leads to totalitarianism.

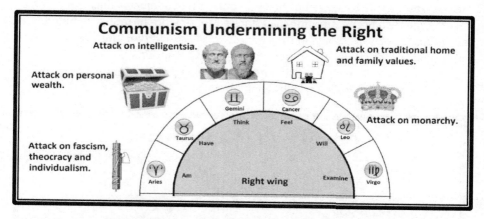

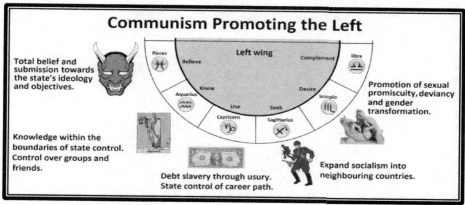

Feminism

As can be seen from the previous diagrams, the top half of the zodiac can be viewed as masculine, representing a patriarchal political system, within the realms of traditional conservatism. Where the majority of monarchs would place the first male child as heir to the throne, essentially demoting females as second class citizens. Over time, as many societies evolved becoming more sophisticated, some people began to question unfair discrepancies between the sexes in certain aspects of life. This gave rise to a variety of feminist movements, prompted by certain issues of the day. Although liberal feminists adopted a balanced approach towards an end to patriarchal rule, radical feminists, aligned with the far left, demanded that their liberation should pervade over all aspects of society. Consequently, because some of these left wing movements, were deeply rooted in socialistic ideologies, they were utilised and sponsored by outside interests who were trying to undermine the power base and values of the traditional right. There are now so many feminist offshoot movements that many fight among themselves, unable to agree on the vast spectrum of subjects which some have become fanatically and emotionally attached to. Any organisation demanding recognition and/or a change in the law, especially concerning the overturning of traditional conservative values, generally fair better under a powerful regulated socialistic system than they would under right wing policies. This is the main reason why you rarely see far right wing feminism.

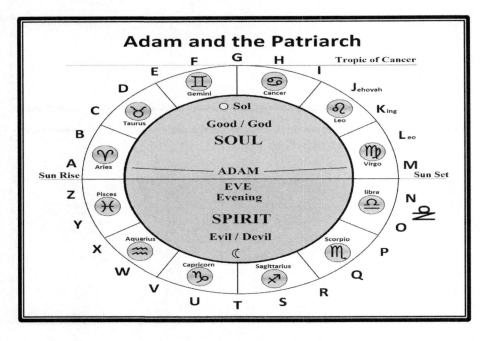

The ultimate goal of the Demiurge is to draw humanity away from the traditional laws of nature, laws put in place by the Creator, which led to a variety of expressions of Divine consciousness. The Demiurge along with his Archonic entourage, being empty husks and cyborgal in nature, naturally require the human species to evolve into entities like them. A prospect where we would drift so far from the Creator that all our natural variations and differences would be ironed out, creating a mono culture of gender neutral automatons, living in an open air prison, a communist utopia of self imposed self regulatory political correctness.

Fabian Society

During the latter half of the 19th century, a number of collectivist movements and groups of socialists began to appear, believing that human civilisation would only survive and advance under a global collectivist system, a system which would be organised top down and controlled by people like themselves. In this future world, the majority of the citizens have no inalienable rights, instead they are given privileges by those in control. Essentially they are only born to serve the greater good of the collective. There were two basic camps of socialists, both with similar goals but with entirely different approaches. The Marxists group saw a fast revolutionary approach as the best way to bring about change within society. However, this method was only suitable in countries where democracy was weak, where the people had already acclimatised to mild forms of dictatorships. The other camp preferred a slower approach, using various methods of covert persuasion, these included propaganda, legislation, education and media to socially engineer a nation's population around to their way of thinking. They understood that societies with strong participatory democracies would put up resistance to rapid changes which would erode their basic rights and freedoms away. Therefore they concluded that most of these old democracies were to be infiltrated slowly, adopting a slow march through the institutions, where changes would go unnoticed by the majority, who were preoccupied with sport and entertainment. This group are known as Fabians, a semi secret socialist society who adopted two symbols to reflect their organisation's overall strategy, a turtle and a wolf in sheep's clothing. Named after the Roman Quintus Fabius Maximus Verrucosus, a general who became famous for avoiding direct military engagements, instead preferring wars of slow indirect attrition. Fabianism or Fabian strategy has come to mean a gradual slow cautious approach to a political solution.

Both these groups work together to control world populations, aiming to bring about a unified global collectivist society. The Marxists/Leninist camp made great gains throughout the east, sponsored by international financiers, using communism as an expression of their socialist collectivism, predominantly in the Soviet Union and China. The Fabians', on the other hand, had to be patient, they had to develop strong influences at all levels of government and society, based in London they nurtured many offshoots and socialist organisations, groups which sprang up across the globe promoting collectivism. The Fabians are wolves in sheep's clothing, whereas Marxist/Leninists are wolves in wolve's clothes. Many prominent labour party politicians have been members of the Fabian Society including, Ramsey McDonald, Clement Attlee, Tony Benn, Harold Wilson, Tony Blair and Gordon Brown. Other famous Fabians include George Bernard Shaw, HG Wells and Bertrand Russell.[4]

Collectivists see the state as the new God, the new emperor, the new religion. Their aim is to mould your individuality to fit within the parameters set out by the state, you must serve the state to justify your existence otherwise you would be viewed as an unworthy misfit or a home-grown terrorist, a threat to the legitimacy of statism and the overall collective. Their new definition of extremist would become anyone who challenges their established order no matter how extreme that order becomes. All subjects within this new social order would be restricted within a narrow band of experiences offered to their perception of reality, limiting the natural biological relationship they could have with the Creator who offers an endless stream of unlimited possibilities. These restrictions would limit freedom, liberty and most unique forms of self-expression. To achieve their objectives the collectivists have their members actively perverting media, politics, education, history and science, with the aim of advancing their ideology, firmly believing that the final end product justifies their interim lies, manipulations and deceptions. We are told that man is responsible for climate change, we are told who our new enemies are, those who we should fear and fight, we are told that we must give up our freedoms for security, give up our sovereignty for harmony, we are told that austerity is necessary, that there is no more money for our communities but on the other hand we see plenty of money for war. We are told to be vaccinated and that GMO's are safe, we are conditioned to accept the official versions of events and not to question anything, just keep on shopping, watching TV and eating, and eventually everything will be just fine. The problem associated with all variations of collectivism, whether it is communism, socialism or globalism, is that they all eventually resort to brute force to maintain power and to perpetuate themselves. David Rockefeller an agent for the international financiers expressed his admiration for the collectivist experiment in China under Chairman Mao, fully aware that at least 45 million people had been worked, starved or beaten to death in the process, Mao is possibly the greatest mass murderer in history.

"Whatever the price of the Chinese Revolution, it has obviously succeeded, not only in producing more efficient and dedicated administration, but also in fostering a high morale and community purpose. The social experiment in China under Chairman Mao's leadership is one of the most important and successful in human history." - David Rockefeller, New York Times, 1973.

To the globalist, the human cost involved in this collective experiment is not an issue. This is why George Bush and Tony Blair can take their countries to war on lies. They are not interested in the truth or the lives of those killed in the process. Their overall mission is to force through the next phase of globalisation, making it plausible to the public. It is their job, they are just public relations men for the real power behind what we call our governments, they are henchmen of the Demiurge. They would not have been allowed to occupy their place in the political system if their views and thinking ran contrary to the globalisation project.

Since the fall of the Berlin wall, the west has become more like the east and the east has become more like the west, merging the two variations of collectivism towards unification. Once practical parity has been achieved, sometime in the near future, a new level of global administration will emerge from some manufactured crisis, a new tier of bureaucracy, out of reach of most people whom it will supposedly represent and control.

In 1948 another Fabian George Bernard Shaw wrote:

"I am a communist, but not a member of the Communist Party. Stalin is a first rate Fabian. I am one of the founders of Fabianism and as such very friendly to Russia" - George Bernard Shaw 1948[5]

"The Bolshevik leaders here, most of whom are Jews and 90 percent of whom are returned exiles, care little for Russia or any other country but are internationalists and they are trying to start a worldwide social revolution." - David Francis, American Ambassador to Russia at the time of the Revolution - U.S. National Archives[8]

"The schemes of the International Jews. The adherents of this sinister confederacy are mostly men reared up among the unhappy populations of countries where Jews are persecuted on account of their race. Most, if not all of them, have forsaken the faith of their forefathers, and divorced from their minds all spiritual hopes of the next world. This movement among the Jews is not new. From the days of Spartacus-Weishaupt to those of Karl Marx, and down to Trotsky (Russia), Bela Kun (Hungary), Rosa Luxemburg (Germany), and Emma Goldman (United States), this world-wide conspiracy for the overthrow

of civilisation and for the reconstitution of society on the basis of arrested development, of envious malevolence, and impossible equality, has been steadily growing." - W Chirchill, Zionism v Bolshevism, Sunday Herald (1920)[9]

"This enabled Jewish financiers to become the agents of national loans, a form of business which they encouraged wherever possible. The Jew has always desired to have nations for his customers. National loans were facilitated by the presence of members of the same family of financiers in various countries, thus making an interlocking directorate by which king could be played against king, government against government, and the shrewdest use made of national prejudices and fears, all to the no small profit of the fiscal agent. And this tendency, which served the race so well throughout the troublous centuries, shows no sign of abatement. Certainly, seeing to what an extent a race numerically so unimportant influences the various governments of the world today, the Jew who reflects upon the disparity between his people's numbers and their power may be pardoned if he sees in that fact a proof of their racial superiority." - Henry Ford (Ford Motor Company), The international Jew.[10]

Albert Pike, WW1,2 & 3

At the same time Karl Marx was making his presence felt within the political chaos spreading throughout Europe, an American author, journalist, lawyer, Brigadier General and prominent 33rd degree Freemason, by the name of Albert Pike (1808 – 1891), was also forging an impressive legacy westwards, in the new world of the American colonies. Apart from having a decorated military career Pike became one of the most senior members of the Scottish Right of freemasonry, holding the title of Sovereign Grand Commander for 32 years. In this capacity he would be fully aware of the overall agenda and objectives of international Freemasonry as a whole. For decades it has been alleged, by numerous researchers throughout the alternative media, that a letter dated 15th August 1871, was sent by Albert Pike to Giuseppe Mazzini (1805-1872), an Italian politician, the then head of the Illuminati, who took over from Adam Weishaupt (1748-1830). Purported to have been displayed in the British Library up until 1977, after which the letter was never seen again. However, the British Museum denies these allegations. The correspondence are said to have outlined plans for three major global conflicts, which were necessary to bring about a one world government. Although it is likely that the existence or authenticity of these letters are bogus, whoever wrote them appears to have an informed understanding of the overriding objectives of the globalisation project.

- **The document allegedly suggested World War One was planned to overthrow the Tsars in Russia and make the country a communist stronghold.**

- The Second World War was sparked as a catalyst to destroy Nazism, according to the letter, so communism could take over wearier governments and for a sovereign state of Israel to be set up in Palestine.

- The Third World War must be fomented by taking advantage of the differences caused by the 'agentur' of the 'Illuminati' between the political Zionists and the leaders of Islamic World. The war must be conducted in such a way that Islam (the Moslem Arabic World) and political Zionism (the State of Israel) mutually destroy each other. Meanwhile the other nations, once more divided on this issue will be constrained to fight to the point of complete physical, moral, spiritual and economical exhaustion. We shall unleash the Nihilists and the atheists, and we shall provoke a formidable social cataclysm which in all its horror will show clearly to the nations the effect of absolute atheism, origin of savagery and of the most bloody turmoil.[6]

"We must pass through the darkness, to reach the light." - Albert Pike

"Masonry, like all the Religions, all the Mysteries, Hermeticism and Alchemy, conceals its secrets from all except the Adepts and Sages, or the Elect, and uses false explanations and misinterpretations of its symbols to mislead those who deserve only to be misled; to conceal the truth, which it calls light from them and to draw them away from it." - Albert Pike, *Morals and Dogma of the Ancient and Accepted Scottish Rite of Freemasonry.* Page 104-5

The Protocols of the Elders of Zion

The Protocols of the Elders of Zion is a book which was first published in Russia in 1903. The unknown authors claimed that it contains and is based around minutes taken from a meeting of Jewish leaders, sometime at the end of the 19th century, who were discussing a plan for global Jewish hegemony, through the subversion of gentile social structures which dominated most societies at that time. To achieve this they needed to control the world's economies; the world's media and almost all its institutions. Although the book was taken seriously at that time, by a large number of influential figures, one of which was Henry Ford, who funded the printing and distribution of half a million copies throughout the United States, the book was eventually exposed as a fraud, from the perspective of its purported origins. However, the book was not alone, much of the *The Protocols of the Elders of Zion* was plagiarised from earlier works , largely written by authors with a grudge against aspects of Judaism and Jewish communities as a whole. Many of these authors were convinced of an international Jewish conspiracy to take over and control the world. This coincided with the creation of organised political Zionism, championed by Theodore Herzl (1860 – 1904), a movement which tried to unite the Jews towards aspirations of returning to the Promised (Holy) Land. The anti Zionist movement which sprung up in opposition to the Russian Zionist Congress of 1902, was suspected of being the mastermind behind *The Protocols of the Elders of Zion*. Initially designed as an internal parody memo mocking Jewish ideology, it was later modified into book form.

In the mid 19th century a Russian Jew from Minsk by the name of Jacob Brafman fell out with a number of members of the local qahal (autonomous government of Ashkenazi Jews). As a result, he turned against Judaism converting instead to Russian Orthodox Christianity. Being a writer, he authored many polemics against Judaism, the Talmud and the qahal. In 1868 he published a book called *The Local and Universal Jewish Brotherhood,* stating that the qahal still exists in secret, as an international conspiratorial network, with the ambition to undermine Christianity and take control of all property while seizing power. The following year he published another book entitled *The Book of The Kahal*, exposing more about this secret shadow government working as a state within a state. The book was translated into English, French and German, and was taken seriously by a number of influential figures and officials. This ultimately added more fuel to the already fragile relationship between Jews and Gentiles living in Russia and Eastern Europe. Consequently, many Jews suffered harsh treatment through various pogroms which erupted around this time. Other books plagiarised by the *The Protocols of the Elders of Zion* were Osman Bey's 1878 book *The Conquest of the World by the Jews*, and Hippolylus Lutostansky's *The Talmud and the Jews* (1879), in which he claimed the Jews wanted to divide Russia amongst themselves.

It is inevitable that under our new laws governing anti-Semitism together with today's coordinates concerning political correctness and hate speech that old books of this nature should be recategorised in an attempt to distance today's readers from the perspective and circumstances of the times they were written. At that time the rise of Communism was of great concern to most systems of governance with ageing Monarchs putting contingency plans in place against future socialist revolutions and communist takeovers.

Quotes from *The Protocols of the Elders of Zion*

"Meantime, however, until we come into our kingdom, we shall act in the contrary way: we shall create and multiply free masonic lodges in all the countries of the world, absorb into them all who may become or who are prominent in public activity, for in these lodges we shall find our principal intelligence office and means of influence. All these lodges we shall bring under one central administration, known to us alone and to all others absolutely unknown, which will be composed of our learned elders. The lodges will have

their representatives who will serve to screen the above-mentioned administration of masonry and from whom will issue the watchword and programme. In these lodges we shall tie together the knot which binds together all revolutionary and liberal elements."

"In order to give the GOYIM no time to think and take note, their minds must be diverted towards industry and trade. Thus, all the nations will be swallowed up in the pursuit of gain and in the race for it will not take note of their common foe. But again, in order that freedom may once for all disintegrate and ruin the communities of the GOYIM, we must put industry on a speculative basis: the result of this will be that what is withdrawn from the land by industry will slip through the hands and pass into speculation, that is, to our classes."

"We must compel the governments of the GOYIM to take action in the direction favored by our widely conceived plan, already approaching the desired consummation, by what we shall represent as public opinion, secretly promoted by us through the means of that so-called "Great Power" - THE PRESS, WHICH, WITH A FEW EXCEPTIONS THAT MAY BE DISREGARDED, IS ALREADY ENTIRELY IN OUR HANDS."

"The GOYIM are a flock of sheep, and we are their wolves. And you know what happens when the wolves get hold of the flock?"

"The citizens of nations are stupefied with alcohol and drugs; their youth have grown stupid on classic literature and novels, and from immorality learned at early ages. That immorality was taught to them by our special agents - teachers, mindless servants, governesses in the houses of the wealthy, by ecclesiastics and others; also by our women in the places of dissipation commonly used by the citizenry".

"In all corners of the earth the words 'Liberty, Equality, Fraternity,' brought into our ranks whole legions who bore our banners with enthusiasm - all thanks to our blind agents. ... "...That abstract illusion called freedom that we have used to infect the minds of the mob in all countries, we have used to convince them that they are the ones that choose their government. It has also enabled us to make the mindless mob think that they are the true owners of their country, and that their government is only their elected servant and can be replaced like a worn-out glove whenever they desire."

"In order that the masses themselves may not guess what they are about we further distract them with amusements, games, pastimes, passions.... Soon we shall begin through the press to propose competitions in art, in sport of all kinds: these interests will finally distract their minds from questions in which we should find ourselves compelled to oppose them. Growing more and more disaccustomed to reflect and form any opinions of their own, people will begin to talk in the same tone as we, because we alone shall be offering them new directions for thought."

Anti-Semitism

"Hostility to or prejudice against Jews." – Oxford dictionary definition of Anti – Semitism.

"I know thy works, and tribulation, and poverty, (but thou art rich) and I know the blasphemy of them which say they are Jews, and are not, but are the synagogue of Satan." – Revolation 2:9 (KJV)

Jews are described as an ethno-religious group, this means they are an ethnic group of common ancestry (race), who share the same religious beliefs, that of Judaism. Their origins go back a long way, and some traditional scholars believe they are the descendants of Shem, one of Noah's three sons, hence the term Shemites or Semites. Prior to WWII they made up 0.7 percent of the world's population, around 16.7 million people. In reality they are a mix multitude of people from many areas, converging under the umbrella of Judaism. In recent times the term Semite has evolved from being a racial concept into the more preferred linguistic and cultural classification.

The descendants of Adam and Eve eventually led to Noah, who at the age of 500 became father to his three sons Shem, Ham and Japheth. As the population of the Earth at that time increased, the son's of the Gods saw that the daughters of the humans were beautiful, and they would marry who ever they desired. As time went by, and the human population increased, the god gene or spirit became diluted, they essentially became less godly and more animalistic.

Then the Lord said, "My Spirit will not contend with humans forever, for they are mortal; their days will be a hundred and twenty years." The Nephilim were on the earth in those days—and also afterward—when the sons of God went to the daughters of humans and had children by them. They were the heroes of old, men of renown. The Lord saw how great the wickedness of the human race had become on the earth, and that every inclination of the thoughts of the human heart was only evil all the time. The Lord regretted that he had made human beings on the earth, and his heart was deeply troubled. So the Lord said, "I will wipe from the face of the earth the human race I have created—and with them the animals, the birds and the creatures that move along the ground—for I regret that I have made them." But Noah found favour in the eyes of the Lord. - Genesis 6 : 3-8

When analyzing the different types of Jews, it becomes clear that the term ant-Semitic is slightly misleading, because the original Semites only make up a very small percentage of the overall world wide Jewish population. The majority, around 80%, of those who consider themselves as Jews are from the Ashkenazi lineage, which by all accounts appear to be no more genetically related to the original Semites than the rest of us. However, this is still a topic of debate, even among some of the best scholars in the world. The other aspect to consider is that the original descendants of Shem, who initially lived in the region of Canaan, became known as the Canaanites, a group of people who also consisted of many variations of Arabs. The Bible refers to the original inhabitants of this area as a mixed multitude.

"So it was, when they had heard the Law, that they separated all the mixed multitude from Israel." – Nehemiah 13:3 (NKJV)

"Biblical scholar Mark Smith notes that archaeological data suggests "that the Israelite culture largely overlapped with and derived from Canaanite culture... In short, Israelite culture was largely Canaanite in nature."" – Canaan, Wikipedia[7]

This suggests that the original term Semite includes a number of Arab inhabitants who also lived within the area at that time. Consequently, the phrase anti-Semite has been redefined in recent years to specifically refer to Jewish people as a whole. The problem with this is that many of today's Jews no longer practice the old religious traditions associated with Judaism, adhering to its strict teachings of the Torah. Instead, many of today's Jews have evolved into living more of a modern secular life style, while still considering and labelling themselves as Jews. However, the Bible suggests that being a Jew is more to do with a state of mind than an outward appearance. This tallies with the teachings of Kabbalah where the individual has to make a conscious decision whether to walk the pathways within the Tree of Life or descend down into the realms of the Qliphoth, towards a dark materialistic and spiritless existence on the Tree of Death.

"For he is not a Jew, which is one outwardly; neither is that circumcision, which is outward in the flesh: But he is a Jew, which is one inwardly; and circumcision is that of the heart, in the spirit, and not in the letter; whose praise is not of men, but of God." – Romans 2 : 28 – 29 (KJV)

As traditional Judaism is associated with Binah, the Messianic Sefirot, within the Supernal Triad on the Tree of Life, expressed on Earth as various areas within the Holy Lands of Israel. It is in the interest of Atheistic and Satanic cults to undermine all forms of spirituality associated with all aspects of the Tree of Life, especially traditional Judaism located within the Holy Land.

We have already established that Frankest and Sabbatean Jews, who could be referred to as Qliphotic Sabbateans were essentially in opposition to traditional values of righteousness and spirituality, which underpinned orthodox Judaism, and that many of their offshoots infiltrated high society through secret organisations in order to undermine right wing conservatism and replace it with a new global socialistic collective. Zionism appears to be another one of these organisations, a political ideology hiding behind Judaism, for the purpose of building a new Temple in Jerusalem to their materialistic God, the Demiurge.

Zionism

The majority of people either have no idea of what Zionism is, or they have a distorted view of its true nature and history. A call for a return of Jews to Palestine has a long history. Modern Zionism was created by elements within the British establishment to further the ambitions and aspirations of the British Empire/international financial cliques partnership. Their objective was to create a colonial controlled outpost in the Middle East, populated by Jews who would see it as a return to their ancestral homeland. The outpost would be a strategic commercial and military base for further imperialistic expansion using the Jews as a mechanism to drive a wedge between the Arab Muslims and other colonial powers in the area, all seeking to advance their own political or religious ambitions.

Palestine is situated between Asia and Europe, whoever controls that area would control trade routes between the two; they would also have access to important oil fields. The only problem was how to get the Jews to go along with the idea. Zion is a term used to describe the area around Jerusalem, Zionism is a political philosophy, a call to relocate Jews from all over the world and place them back to where they supposedly came from, the Promised Land, mentioned in the Old Testament, between the Nile and the Euphrates.

In the middle of the 19th century the British Empire, at the height of its power, was concerned about economic advancements being made by its competitors. The empire had become master of the seas, protecting their trade routes and defending their ports with a superior navy, which ultimately controlled 1/3 of the Earth's surface. Their competitors on the other hand were industrialising inland, the United States, France, Germany and Russia all posed a potential threat to the British economic dominance, especially if they all united against her. The French had completed the Suez Canal in 1869, enabling goods to flow easily between Europe and Asia. Bismarck had unified Germany in 1871 which encouraged the industrialisation of internal transport links making it easier for other empires and republics to compete with the British. The Empire would do all they could to keep themselves in control, especially by undermining competition in specific areas. Palestine was one of those strategic regions. Its importance became more pronounced after the Suez Canal was opened.

The idea of Jews returning to their homeland is an old one, from the Exodus out of Egypt to the Babylonian conquest of Judea in 641 BCE; Jews have been encouraged to go along with this notion. Even during the annual Passover celebrations, some Jews end their prayers with "next year in Jerusalem". Daily prayers, another powerful repetitive mechanism used to cement a belief system, include references to:

"Your people Israel; your return to Jerusalem; and a redeemer shall come to Zion".

The persecutions of Jews also has a long history, in Spain and Portugal many were persuaded to adopt the Christian faith, while secretly keeping the Judaic traditions alive. The Catholic Church suspicious and intolerant initiated the inquisition and by 1492 had expelled the remaining Jews. In 1516 Venice decided that Jews had to live in secure ghettos, they also had to pay a tax for the privilege, and by 1555 the Pope, in Rome, followed suit. Jews had already been expelled from England in 1290, only to be allowed back in 1649 under Oliver Cromwell. At the end of the 17th century, Judah he-Hasid Segal ha-Levi, a Jewish preacher, travelled from one Jewish community to another persuading a number of Jews to participate in a new ALIYAH (The immigration of Jews from the diaspora to the Promised Land of Israel). By 1700 he had assembled 1,500 for the long journey, but a third of them died along the way. When they reached their destination they were broke and found they were not altogether welcome. At that time there were only around 1,200 Jews living in the city, so the sudden arrival of another 1000 new Ashkenazi Jews created a massive problem. The newcomers, viewed with hostility, got into debt trying to build a new synagogue and by 1720 their Arab creditors set fire to the building and took back control of the land. The Turkish authorities blamed all the Jews collectively for the mess and banned the Ashkenazi Jews from the area.[12] The Jewish population within the Holy Land steadily increased after the Christian persecutions of the Reconquista. Following Napoleon's conquest, laws were brought in to emancipate Jews throughout Europe which helped in the decline of their persecution. Britain gave Jews equal rights in 1856 and so did Germany in 1871. During the competitive Age of Nationalism and expanding empires, Jews ceased to be persecuted for their religious beliefs, but instead were seen as a different race altogether, anti-Semitism took over from the simple disapproval of Judaic/Saturn worship. The British established a consulate in Jerusalem in 1838, which at the time was ruled by the Turks and governed from Istanbul, the following year a report was published about the conditions of Jews in the area, a memorandum followed which encouraged European monarchs into supporting the idea of restoring Jews back to Palestine. In August 1840 the Times of London reported that the British government was considering the restoration of a Jewish homeland, and that both Lord Shaftsbury and Lord Palmerston were instrumental in its promotion.[13] Lord Shaftsbury was a proactive advocate for Zionism as early as the 1820s, motivated by an Evangelical revival, which took place between the 1820s and 30s. Napoleon in 1799 saw the strategic importance of the area for his own empire, he considered helping the Jews back to Palestine and prepared a proclamation to this effect. It was only his defeat at Waterloo which put an early end to this proposal.[14] There was also the Muslim threat under Muhammad Ali, who by 1832 had united much of Palestine and Syria, he also began to industrialise the region with the intention of turning it into a modern state, Ali also established an Egyptian/French alliance which made it necessary for the British to champion the cause for relocating the Jews back to the Promised Land in order to gain a foothold.

Benjamin Disraeli was a British politician and writer, who came from a wealthy family of Sephardic Jews. He was British Prime Minister twice, once in 1868 and again from 1874 – 1880. As a pro Zionist, with close ties to the House of Rothschild, he was able to bring the Zionist dream closer to fruition. Lord Stanley, a Freemason and Conservative Party politician mentions visiting Disraeli in his diary in January 1851, he talks about " Disraeli's ideas for the restoration of the Jews to Palestine".[15] With a string of pro Zionist and pro Rothschild writings behind him, Disraeli seemed to be the ideal candidate to turn this idea into a reality. In 1862 the Prince of Wales (future King Edward VII), a Freemason, made a visit to Palestine and the Holy Land, not only representing the state but also to do some ground work. After the defeat of the British backed Confederates in the American Civil War, momentum gained for the Zionist project. In 1865 the Foreign Office began preparations for resettlement, a fund called 'The Palestine Exploration Fund' was created backed by both Oxford and Cambridge universities, along with money from Freemasonry. This exploration fund produced a practical plan to make the country habitable for resettlement. With the construction of the Suez Canal, the potential threat to British pre-eminence was aired by Lord Palmerston (two times British Prime Minister).

"I must tell you frankly that what we are afraid of is losing our commercial and maritime pre-eminence, for this Canal will put other nations on an equal footing with us. At the same time I must own that we are not quite easy on the score of the designs of France. Of course we have every confidence in the loyalty and sincerity of the Emperor, but who can answer for those who will come after him?" - Lord Palmerston, Tuchman, Barbara, Bible and Sword, 1956 p 258

In 1862 Moses Hess, a German, French, Jewish philosopher and associate of Karl Marx wrote a book called 'Rome and Jerusalem, the last national question', in which he calls for the creation of a Jewish socialist state in Palestine. In the latter half of the 19th century various socialist movements sprang up, each one targeting different social and political aspects of society. The Fabians, the Marxists and Hess's Zionist Socialism, were all organised ventures promoted to influence the future direction of humanity. In an effort to control the Suez Canal, Disraeli and the Rothschilds arranged to purchase the Egyptian ruler's portion of shares, placing them under the control of the British government. In the late 1870s Jewish philanthropists helped to finance an agricultural resettlement program for Russian Jews who were desperately trying to flee persecution in Eastern Europe. The Rothschilds came to their aid, sponsoring many new settlements in Palestine. In 1877 Disraeli created a blueprint for a Zionist State, which would be under British rule, ensuring political and economic penetration in the region. In his book *Alroy*, Disraeli reveals what was on his mind.

"Sire, bear with me. If I speak in heat, I speak in zeal. You ask me what I wish: my answer is, a national existence, which we have not. You ask me what I wish: my answer is, the Land of Promise. You ask me what I wish: my answer is, Jerusalem. You ask me what I wish: my answer is, the Temple, all we have forfeited, all we have yearned after, all for which we have fought, our beauteous country, our holy creed, our simple manners, and our ancient customs." - Benjamin Disraeli, *Alroy* 1828, part 8 chapter 6.

An interesting point to make regarding Suez, is that its name is Zeus spelt backwards. When dividing the whole globe into twelve signs of the zodiac, using the old prime meridian of Giza as the benchmark, Pisces falls west of Giza and Aries to the east. Jupiter/Zeus is the ruler over Pisces, ruling the land west of Giza. Aries to the East and the opposite end of the zodiac. Suez is a reflection of that opposition. The British with the will and financial backing needed a man who would promote their Zionist cause, a man who would successfully convince the Jewish community of the merits for returning to the Promised Land. The man they approached was Theodore Herzl.

Theodore Herzl was born Benjamin Ze'ev Herzl in Pest, East Budapest, Hungary in 1860. His parents were German speaking assimilated Jews, his father Jakob Herzl was a successful business man. Theodore's conversion to Zionism was purported to be around the time of the Dreyfus affair in 1894. While he was working as a reporter in Paris he witnessed anti-Semitic protests erupt following the arrest and conviction of a French Jewish Army Captain who was accused of spying for the Germans. This persuaded him to reject Jewish emancipation and embrace the notion of moving all Jews out of Europe and into Palestine. In 1889 Theodore Herzl married Julie Naschauer, the daughter of a wealthy Jewish business man, and moved to Vienna. In those days high society in Vienna socialised in a network of salons set up by Julie Rothschild, the daughter of the Viennese branch of the banking dynasty. These salons were recruiting grounds for secret societies and Isis cults. Herzl was known to be a regular patron. On March 10th 1896 Herzl was visited by Reverend William Hechler, an Anglican Minister working for the British Embassy; Hechler was familiar with Herzl's publications on Zionist issues. This meeting would be the turning point in Herzl's career. He wrote in his diary:

"Next we came to the heart of the business. I said to him: (Theodor Herzl to Rev. William Hechler) I must put myself into direct and publicly known relations with a responsible or non-responsible ruler – that is, with a minister of state or a prince. Then the Jews will believe in me and follow me. The most suitable personage would be the German Kaiser." - Theodore Herzl

Hechler arranged Herzl to meet Frederick I in 1896, which led to an audience with Wilhelm II in 1898. This gave credence to Herzl's movement in the eyes of the Jewish community. Before Hechler's intervention most Jews considered Herzl as a lunatic or even a British agent, the majority of Jews considered Zionism to be an assault on Jews and Judaism. This created a split within the Jewish community, with those against the homeland and those for it. The problem was that most Orthodox Jews believed that a homeland could only be given to the Jews by a new Messiah. As Jesus (Jupiter/Zeus) was not considered as their Messiah, this instruction to go back, had not yet happened. This meant a homeland for Jews throughout the Piscean Age was not an option. As Saturn worshippers, their Messiah was not to appear until the New Age of Aquarius. It could be argued that the new pseudo or false Messiah for the Zionist movement came in the form of finance from the House of Rothschild, enabling Zionist projects to move forward. Opposition was expressed in the "Pittsburgh Platform", a position adopted by the Central Conference of American Rabbis in 1885.

"We consider ourselves no longer a nation, but a religious community, and therefore expect neither a return to Palestine, nor a sacrificial worship under the sons of Aaron, nor the restoration of any of the laws concerning the Jewish state." - Pittsburgh Platform.[16]

Herzl came to the conclusion that anti-Semitism would be advantageous for the Zionist movement, in the sense that it would make life unbearable for Jews living in Europe, and out of desperation they would eventually move to Palestine to escape persecution. He wrote in his diary :

"The anti-Semites will be only too happy to give Zionism publicity." - Theodore Herzl

"The anti-Semites will become our most dependable friends, the anti-Semitic countries our allies." - (The Complete Diaries of Theodor Herzl. Vol. 1, edited by Raphael Patai, translated by Harry Zohn, page 83-84)

"Herzl regarded Zionism's triumph as inevitable, not only because life in Europe was ever more untenable for Jews, but also because it was in Europe's interests to rid the Jews and be relieved of anti-Semitism: The European political establishment would eventually be persuaded to promote Zionism. Herzl recognized that anti-Semitism would be harnessed to his own--Zionist-purposes." - (Benny Morris, Righteous Victims, p. 21)

During the late 19th century Herzl made regular visits to England. He once again wrote in his diary :

"Get at one stroke ... ten million secret but loyal subjects active in all walks of life all over the world.... As at a signal, all of them will place themselves at the service of the magnanimous nation that brings long-desired help.... England will get ten million agents for her greatness and influence." Theodore Herzl

Herzl and his colleagues established 'The World Zionist Congress', an organisation which would rally the Jewish people into pushing for resettlement in Palestine. The first congress was held in Basel Switzerland in 1897, attended by 200 participants, who created the first political Zionist agenda known as the "Basel Programme".

"Zionism seeks for the Jewish people a publicly recognized legally secured homeland in Palestine." - Statement from the first world Zionist congress.

Herzl wrote in his diary : "Were I to sum up the Basel Congress in a word - which I shall guard against pronouncing publicly - it would be this: At Basel I founded the Jewish State." Theodore Herzl

When Herzl was looking into other possibilities for resettlement, Argentina was one of the options mentioned, when considering this he wrote :

"We shall try to spirit the penniless population across the border by procuring employment for it in the transit countries, while denying it any employment in our country." - Herzl, considering Argentina as a homeland.

He died at the young age of 44 on July 3rd 1904, from cardiac sclerosis. His remains were moved from Vienna to Mount Herzl in Jerusalem in 1949. Before the creation of Israel, with money supplied from wealthy backers, the Zionists bought up all the land available for Jewish settlements. This was known as 'land redemption or Jewdifying the land'. In 1917, during World War 1, the British conquered Palestine from the Turks, and legalised the Jewish national homeland concept with the Balfour Declaration. The pro-Zionist British dismantled all Palestinian paramilitary groups, leaving them defenceless and leaderless, paving the way for further Zionist settlements.

In Simon Schama's book *'Two Rothschild's and the Land of Israel'*, Schama speculates that the Rothschild's, through various commercial enterprises, own approximately 80% of the land within Israel.[11] The British/Rothschild/Zionist outpost known as Israel is essentially another commercial and military base for the empire and the House of Rothschild, the richest and most powerful banking consortium on the planet. Spreading its tentacles throughout the world while avoiding criticism by controlling media outlets and shielding itself behind Jewish Holocaust victim status. Zionism is just another tool being used to bring about world unity, a global socialist society under the complete control of the hidden hand, an international banking consortium headed by the House of Rothschild. Israel today has become the 11th most powerful military force on the planet and one of four countries holding nuclear weapons not recognised by the NPT (Nuclear Non-proliferation Treaty). They maintain a policy of ambiguity, although their nuclear weapons program was exposed back in 1986 by a Mordechai Vanunu, an Israeli nuclear technician, who ended up in prison for what they considered as treason.

"Palestine belongs to the Arabs in the same sense that England belongs to the English or France to the French. It is wrong and inhuman to impose the Jews on the Arabs... Surely it would be a crime against humanity to reduce the proud Arabs so that Palestine can be restored to the Jews partly or wholly as their national home" — Mahatma Gandhi

"People who call themselves supporters of Israel are actually supporters of its moral degeneration and ultimate destruction." — Noam Chomsky

"If every single Jew born anywhere in the world has the right to become an Israeli citizen, then all the Palestinians who were chucked out of Palestine by the Zionist Government should have the same right, very simple." — Tariq Ali

"When modern political Zionism emerged around the turn of the twentieth century, most Orthodox Jews opposed it." - David Novak

As a buffer against criticism, the Sabbatean and Frankest Jews aligned with Zionism use anti-Semitism as a tool to quash descent. Even though some of their greatest opponents and critics are traditional Torahic Jews. Who, being on the spiritual and righteous path are regarded by Qliphotic Sabbateans as a threat to their inverted ideologies and objectives towards the globalisation project. To the average person, all Jews come under the same umbrella, and anyone criticising any of them, in any way, can easily be discredited by being labelled as anti-Semitic. Hiding behind victim status, the Qliphotic Sabbateans keep the historical persecutions of both righteous and Qliphotic Jews alive as a defence mechanism against all their opponents. It is worth pointing out here the old motto used by Mossad, Israel's secret intelligence agency, a motto which can be translated in a way which underlines the Sabbatean mentality, a motto which was recently changed.

"By way of deception, thou shalt do war". – Victory Ostrovsky (former Mossad case officer 1982 – 1986) & author of *By Way of Deception: The Making of a Mossad officer.*

The other motto which needs mentioning here is the one used by 33rd degree Freemasons, 'Ordo ab chao' which translates as 'Order out of chaos'. This can be found within the grand decorations of the Order of the Sovereign Grand Inspectors General. One of the highest rankings to be bestowed on any Freemason. I would suggest that order out of chaos relates to the order they intend to impose from the chaos they help to create. Whereas order over chaos relates to man's ability to tame nature while trying to live in harmony with it. Many of these secret organisations and orders work together, by sharing information with common objectives.

"Some even believe we are part of a secret cabal working against the best interests of the United States, characterizing my family and me as 'internationalists' and of conspiring with others around the world to build a more integrated global political and economic structure — one world, if you will. If that is the charge, I stand guilty, and I am proud of it." – David Rockefeller (1915-2017), American Banker and statesmen. Memoirs (2003), chapter 27, p 406

Notes for chapter 8

(1) Norberto Bobbio, Left and Right: The Significance of a Political Distinction, 1997, University of Chicago Press. https://www.amazon.com/Left-Right-Significance-Political-Distinction/dp/0226062465

(2) Socialism and LGBT rights, Wikipedia, https://en.wikipedia.org/wiki/Socialism_and_LGBT_rights

(3) Rudi Dutschk, wikipedia, https://en.wikipedia.org/wiki/Rudi_Dutschke

(4) Fabian society, New World Encyclopaedia, http://www.newworldencyclopedia.org/entry/Fabian_Society

(5) Evening Herald (Dublin, Ireland), February 3, 1948, reprinted in Economic Council Letter (National Economic Council), Issue 278, Part 397 (1952), p. 290.

(6) Selina Sykes, Chillingly accurate 200-year-old letter predicts WW3 and final battle against Islam. Express newspaper. March 10th 2016.v https://www.express.co.uk/news/uk/650822/Letter-WW3-200-year-old-islam-final-battle

(7) Canaan, Wikipedia, https://en.wikipedia.org/wiki/Canaan

(8) David Francis, American Ambassador to Russia at the time of the Revolution - U.S. National Archives. https://en.wikipedia.org/wiki/Talk%3AJewish_Bolshevism%2FArchive_5

(9) Winston Churchill, Zionism v Bolshevism, Sunday Herald, Feb 1920, Wikiquotes, https://en.wikiquote.org/wiki/Winston_Churchill

(10) Henry Ford, The international Jew, 1920, publication. P.8 http://www.americannaziparty.com/about/InternationalJew.pdf

(11) Simon Schama, Two Rothschild's and the Land of Israel (Collins, London, 1978), http://www.abebooks.co.uk/Two-Rothschilds-Land-Israel-Schama-Simon/14948680363/bd

(12) from the Sephardic Dispersion, Page 38, The Jewish publication society, Philadelphia. https://books.google.co.th/books?id=vW 9E_fFSOUC&pg=PA39&dq=%22the+hurvah+synagogue%22&lr=&cd=10&redir_es c=y#v=onepage&q=%22the%20hurvah%20synagogue%22&f=false

(13) Gerhard Falk, The Restoration of Israel: Christian Zionism in Religion, Literature and politics. Page 17, http://www.amazon.com/The-Restoration-Israel-Literature-University/dp/0820488623

(14) Napoleon Bonaparte, Letter to the Jewish Nation from the French Commander-in-Chief Bonaparte, (translated from the Original, 1799). http://www.napoleon-series.org/ins/weider/c_jews.html#Appendix 2

(15) Benjamin Disraeli, John Alexander Wilson Gun, Benjamin Disraeli Letters: 1848-1851,volume 5, page 404, University of Toronto press incorporated, 1993. http://www.jstor.org/stable/10.3138/9781442671287

(16) Pittsburgh Conference in 1885, Reform Judaism. https://www.jewishvirtuallibrary.org/jsource/Judaism/pittsburgh_program.html

"Believing he was the only true God of the material realm, Yaldabaoth (Demiurge) moved away and created other realms and subservient Archons for himself. He was described as an artificial non-organic life form with machine like qualities." – Taken from chapter 2, Logos and the Demiurge.

Humanity is at an unprecedented cross roads, a turning point in history in which it may permanently lose its spiritual connection to Creator consciousness. A prospect of such alarming magnitude, the consequences of which could be disastrous for all of humanity for a very long time. Those in control of this latest bout of globalisation are pushing for, at an alarming rate, artificial intelligence, which will become the foundation and core of their brave new utopian collective. A digital control grid linking every man, woman and child up to their new God in the form of artificial intelligence. A feet which, from all accounts of official lineal history, has never occurred before. The majority of people are so wrapped up with the day to day task of making ends meet, that they are powerless to stop this all pervasive artificial control grid consuming them. Most people are under the illusion that their political representatives have all the necessary information to make well informed decisions on their behalf, believing that those decisions have humanity's overall best interests at heart.

What many people don't realises is that there has been an ongoing battle between the spiritual Creator God, at the centre of the pleroma, and the material God or Demiurge, ever since time began. Those of us alive now are here to witness the next round, where the Demiurge appears to be gaining ground over the Creator.

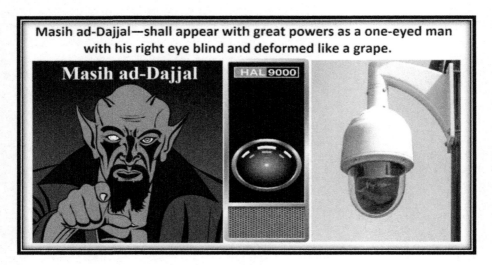

Masih ad-Dajjal—shall appear with great powers as a one-eyed man with his right eye blind and deformed like a grape.

According to Muslim scripture, the false messiah—anti-Christ, Masih ad-Dajjal—shall appear with great powers as a one-eyed man with his right eye blind and deformed like a grape. Although believers will not be deceived, he will claim to be God, and to hold the keys to heaven and hell, leading many people astray. In reality, his heaven is hell, and this hell is rapidly coming to our earthly realm. The Dajjal will be followed by seventy thousand Jews of Isfahan (city in Iran) wearing Persian shawls. This is one of the major signs to appear prior to judgement day from the perspective of Muslim eschatology.

The automation of society has been under way for a very long time, slowly detaching humanity from their hands on involvement over a system of control which they will ultimately become slaves to. Humanity has essentially been building its own open air prison for generations, being steered covertly by hidden political agendas, far out of the common man's reach. The only thing which held back absolute control over humanity, in the past, was the level of technology available. Full automation was never possible before, as various levels of human involvement was always necessary to keep whatever technology they had in operation. However, now we have reached a tipping point, where the level and speed of technological advancements are so breath taking, we are either at a point, or not far off, when the machines will, not only think for themselves, but will be able to maintain and evolve themselves. We truly are entering the realms of the Terminator (Hollywood movie). Those of us who lived prior to the start of the Computer Age of the 1980s, where human interaction was necessary to perform almost every task imaginable, occasionally find ourselves, in today's world, out of place, and out of touch, even when tackling some of the most basic automated procedures. Tasks which once took minutes, through human interaction, can now take hours of frustrating tail chasing when trying to navigate automated on-line purchasing procedures. Void of the most basic human contact, we are slowly detaching ourselves from the mechanisms which control us. Although the majority of those born post 1990 have been socially engineered to accept that an overriding artificial intelligence is a necessary step in the right direction of progress, they are oblivious to the possibility that they are being groomed and conditioned to accept a society ruled by an integrated technological control grid with possible sinister motives. When people give up their independence within a interactive community of proactive human participants, to alternatively embrace a society of individual automatons, serving an artificially created management system, their social cohesive skills will deteriorate to a point where the purpose of their overall existence comes into question. What the technocrats and their followers fails to appreciate is that many people are not just human beings seeking a spiritual dimension, but spiritual beings having a human experience. And to dilute traditional three dimensional ways in which we interact, could ultimately trap us within a controlling web of artificial intelligence, undermining our natural connection to universal spiritual consciousness, essentially pulling us further away from the Creator.

5G is the fifth generation of digital cellular network technology, designed to improve all forms of digital communication with greater speed when accessing the internet, planned to be fully operational by 2021. To achieve this, a wider spectrum of band widths are being made available for transmitting and receiving data. Utilising higher frequencies within the lower realms of the Infra red spectrum, known as microwaves. Although these frequencies are generally considered safe when emitting non ionising radiation, the potential for biological and cellular damage is becoming a growing concern. While microwave ovens utilise microwave technology to cook food, the level of power used to achieve this is enormous compared to the microwaves used within 5G technology. However, the accumulative and long term effects on human health is unknown. It is already well documented in scientific research papers that the existing technology of 3 and 4G have already contributed to a number of health issues.

"Wireless radiation has biological effects. Period. This is no longer a subject for debate when you look at PubMed and the peer-review literature. These effects are seen in all life forms; plants, animals, insects, microbes. In humans, we have clear evidence of cancer now: there is no question we have evidence of DNA damage, cardiomyopathy, which is the precursor of congestive heart failure, neuropsychiatric effects…5G is an untested application of a technology that we know is harmful; we know it from the science. In academics, this is called human subjects research." – Dr Sharon Goldberg MD, Internal Medicine / General Internal Medicine, Complementary and Integrative Medicine.

"In my judgement, we already have clear evidence for elevations in brain and other cancers resulting from excessive exposure to mobile phone, Wi-Fi and other sources of electromagnetic fields," - **"there has not been adequate study**

of the adverse effects of electromagnetic fields in general and there has been almost no study of the specific higher frequencies to be used in 5G". - David Carpenter, professor and director of the Institute for Health and the Environment, University at Albany.[1]

In 1996 a new Telecommunications Act was passed in the United Stated, designed to free up the industry for corporations to compete with one another for business without too much government interference, designed to encourage the rapid development and implementation of new technology concerning telecommunications.

"No State or local government or instrumentality thereof may regulate the placement, construction, and modification of personal wireless service facilities on the basis of the environmental effects of radio frequency emissions to the extent that such facilities comply with the Commission's regulations concerning such emissions." - Section 704 of The Telecommunications Act of 1996

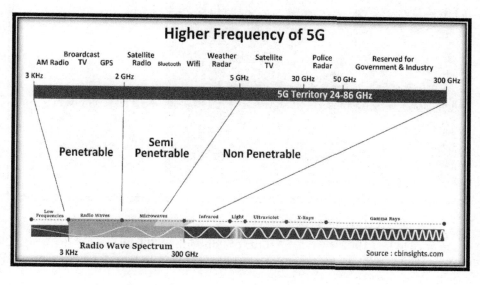

We are, as a species, about to undergo an experiment, where all of us are essentially being used as guinea pigs for the profits of a handful of individuals, running the telecommunications corporations. To roll something out on a global scale without adequate testing, is akin to playing Russian roulette with the whole human race, an experiment which we may never recover from. Although the speed of this new generation of technology is attractive, one can't help but suspect the potential and opportunity for abuse by malevolent forces is always a possibility.

After 5G we should see 6G, an even more sophisticated technological control grid. Six is of course the number associated with Saturn, the planet of control, restriction, limitation and frustration. When they link humanity with electronic devices through their fleet of satellites (Saturn-lights), there will be nowhere to escape and nowhere to hide. This ultimate control grid will, no doubt, be rolled out, in the name of keeping humanity safe, as a counter measure against terrorism and other threats. Dangers created as a mechanism to influence public opinion in the direction required for an endless array of overreaching controls.

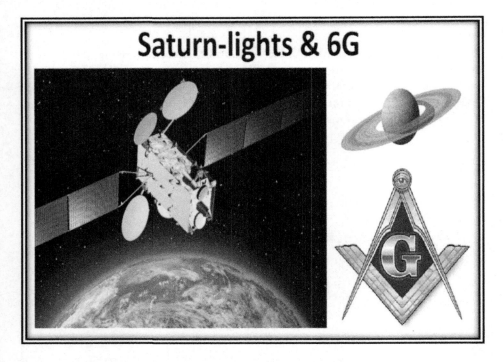

It is ironic that the first ever geosynchronous satellite broadcast, which took place back in July 1962, carried pictures of Pope John XXIII, all around the world. A Saturn-light which looked more like the death star from Star Wars than the satellites we are use to seeing today.

"John XXIII made a momentary appearance on the world's first geosynchronous satellite, Telstar I, in 1962." – Robert Kaiser, A Church in Search of Itself: Benedict XVI and the Battle for the Future.[2]

It is important to point out that the global smart grid, which will run in tandem with cyber security technologies, is a grid designed to spy on almost every aspect of our lives, growing exponentially in the country of Israel faster than any other country on the planet. Some analysts have suggested that in a few short years Israel will be at the centre of all AI surveillance technology throughout the world. A point will come when nothing will happen in this world without the knowledge of the Israeli intelligent services.

"Israel's longstanding position as a leader in the global effort to prevent cyber-crime remains indisputable," - The Times of Israel, Cybersecurity investment in Israel surges 47% to over $1b in 2018.

Our unique individual consciousness interfaces with this physical reality with our five basic senses. These senses are stimulated through various frequencies of electromagnetic energy decoded by our brains. We were designed or have evolved in such a way as to function in harmony with our natural environment. Ever since the birth of man, we have lived in tune with nature's rhythms and cycles, responding to the energetic frequencies emanating from our surroundings together with transits occurring from all the magnificent planets and luminaries gracing our solar system. Lately, human arrogance, has decided to submerge every one of us in an artificial ocean of electromagnetic pollution. This, in my opinion, is an attack on human consciousness itself, driving into the very heart of who we are. An artificial reality is being created which could potentially replace our natural subconscious collective which is tethered to the spiritual realm and the Creator. I suggest that the overriding objective of this electromagnetic control grid is to cut us off from our 6th and 7th senses together with restricting our connection to the spiritual collective, giving us over, hook, line and sinker to the artificial machine like God of the underworld, the Demiurge.

One has to wonder where did this rapid expansion of artificial intelligence technology come from, and why are we in such a hurry to promote it as the solution to all our worldly problems? Could it be that human history has been deliberately distorted to hide the existence of an ancient society once ruled by the Demiurge and his Archons. Who were indeed the Gods of the ancient world, using our human ancestors as slaves and objects of abuse and amusement.

"There were giants in the earth in those days; and also after that, when the sons of God came in unto the daughters of men, and they bare children to them, the same became mighty men which were of old, men of renown." – Genesis 6:4 (KJV)

Could it be that the ancient megalithic remains, which we see in abundance, all over the world, are the remains of a once powerful and materialistic civilisation, brought to an end by a global cataclysm, which ultimately reset human consciousness. A cataclysm which gave freedom back to humanity, as the Creator had intended.

Although the consciousness, at the centre of the galaxy, is the ultimate power out in this part of the universe, Its creation (us), here on Earth, was, in my opinion, intended to have fee will, therefore, it appears that the Creator was never in any hurry to interfere with this evolving project, all the way out here at the edge of the galaxy. However, it could be the case that when society is either all good or all bad that some form of cosmic intervention resets the Earth on a biblical scale, allowing humanity to, once again, reset itself. Plato gives an interesting account of how the Atlanteans, once on a righteous path, deviated into materialism and corruption, which ultimately led to their downfall.

"For many generations, as long as the divine nature lasted in them, they were obedient to the laws, and well-affectioned towards the god, whose seed they were; for they possessed true and in every way great spirits, uniting gentleness with wisdom in the various chances of life, and in their intercourse with one another. They despised everything but virtue, caring little for their present state of life, and thinking lightly of the possession of gold and other property, which seemed only a burden to them; neither were they intoxicated by luxury; nor did wealth deprive them of their self-control; but they were sober, and saw clearly that all these goods are increased by virtue and friendship with one another, whereas by too great regard and respect for them, they are lost and friendship with them. By such reflections and by the continuance in them of a divine nature, the qualities which we have described grew and increased among them; but when the divine portion began to fade away, and became diluted too often and too much with the mortal admixture, and the human nature got the upper hand, they then, being unable to bear their fortune, behaved unseemly, and to him who had an eye to see grew visibly debased, for they were losing the fairest of their precious gifts; but to those who had no eye to see the true happiness, they appeared glorious and blessed at the very time when they were full of avarice and unrighteous power. Zeus, the god of gods, who rules according to law, and is able to see into such things, perceiving that an honourable race was in a woeful plight, and wanting to inflict punishment on them, that they might be chastened and improve, collected all the gods into their most holy habitation, which, being placed in the centre of the world, beholds all created things. And when he had called them together, he spake as follows -" (The rest of the Dialogue of Critias has been lost.)[3] Excerpt from "Critias" By Plato circa 428-347BC

Edgar Cayce

Edgar Cayce (1877 – 1945), the sleeping prophet, is one of America's most famous clairvoyants, he became famous for his ability to diagnose illnesses from a sleep like trance. Throughout his life he produced over 14,000 psychic readings, much of which was recorded, referenced and stored in a dedicated research library. During many of these readings he would remote view periods of time throughout human history, going all the way back to the time of Atlantis. He explained that around 210,000 years ago human consciousness descended into dense matter in a place know as Atlantis, to experience a material reality from their basic etheric form. At this time humanity was thought to be in harmony with nature and closer to the Creator. It is believed that they were illuminated and enlightened beings, with a sophisticated society, of high technology and etheric tools, enabling them to perform incredible feats of engineering. However, as time went by, Cayce states that, this society rebelled against nature to become more egocentric, detaching themselves from their spiritual roots and to develop a hierarchical system of governance. Dark energies began to fragment their once magnificent society, and as they descended into factional fighting, they lost much of their technology along the way. Around 50,000 – 28,000 BC the great continent of Atlantis broke up into five smaller islands, creating more division and disunity. Again in 28,000 – 22,000 BC other Earth changes submerged two of those islands, leaving only three. This was thought by Cayce to be the Great Deluge mentioned in the Bible. Prior to this, three groups of Atlanteans went out to three separate locations over the Earth, looking for a place to bury 32 stone tablets containing the history of the human race, now referred to as the hall of records. Cayce suggests one group buried their records in the Yucatan region of South America. Another was buried in Egypt and the third was in an unknown location. Finally, around 10,600 BC what was left of the Atlantis islands sank due to massive Earth changes brought about by the impact of a disintegrating comet, setting off a rise in sea levels and a new Ice Age.[4]

It is also worth pointing out that Cayce gave an impression of Lemuria (lost continent in the Pacific/Indian ocean) suggesting the inhabitants were so spiritually in tune with nature, that their society advanced in a very different way. Allowing them to manipulate some of the most difficult aspects of the material world, achieving things which we would struggle with today. As they had only partially devolved from their etherical bodies into full matter, the name Lemuria, (Latin 'lemures'), was used which means ghost of the departed.

The lesson we can learn from this is simple. The further humanity deviates from the righteous path of respecting one another, together with respect for their environment by being in harmony with nature, the more difficult their lives seem to become. When humanity rebels against nature, nature will rebel against us, quickening our descent into chaos. It is possible that one or more of the sets of stone tablets making up the hall of records have already been recovered. Offering those who found them a valuable perspective of human history together with records possibly containing information about advanced technology. Giving them the opportunity of replicating the same technology which ultimately led to a previous societies destruction.

The Serapeum

Beneath the sands of Saqqara, North West of the Djoser pyramid, near the ancient city of Memphis is a labyrinth of underground passageways. Connected to these passageways are numerous alcoves containing 25 huge granite boxes weighing around 100 tons each. These boxes are made from a single piece of hard granite, 4m long, 2m wide and 3.3m high, granite which came from a quarry 500 miles away. The staggering precision and craftsmanship is breath-taking, leaving any observer puzzled and perplexed as to how and why these boxes were made. The surfaces are totally smooth, a tolerance of within 2/10000 of an inch, the sides are perfectly parallel and each granite top weighs approximately 30 tons alone, a design and feat which would be almost impossible be replicated today. Rediscovered in 1850 by the French archaeologist, Auguste Mariette (1821-81), who had the foresight to use the writings of Strabo, a Greek geographer, from around the time of Christ to locate the boxes. This gave Mariette clues enabling him to stumble across the entrance to a labyrinth with all its underground passageways, a place which Napoleon had searched in vain for during his long extended expedition in Egypt. When Mariette first entered the Serapeum, he reported the boxes to be already empty, looted in a previous Age, left with their lids opened. The official explanation by mainstream Egyptologists suggest the boxes were sarcophagi, tombs for Apis Bulls, placed there during the Ptolemaic period, mummified bulls locked away in these giant granite boxes for all time. The only problem with this explanation is the sheer size of the boxes. Mummified bulls have been recovered in tact elsewhere, found in wooden tombs a fraction of the size. Bulls are usually mummified in the kneeling position and don't take up anywhere near the space we see inside these granite sarcophagi, they would only reach 1.6 m from the ground. The other problem with this hypothesis is that no bulls were ever found in the boxes, not a single one. The word Serapeum comes from the Graeco/Egyptian God Serapis, a politically created religion, designed to unify the Greeks and the Egyptians under the rule of Ptolemy I, during the 3rd century BC, derived from the Egyptian Gods of Osiris and Apis, along with attributes from Greek deities such as Hades and Dionysus. The cult of Serapis continued until 391 AD when pagan religions were suppressed under Theodosius I. Under Ptolemy's deliberate policy to spread the cult of Serapis, a Serapeum was built in Alexandria. The discovery of the Serapeum at Saqqara altered the course of Auguste Mariette's life. He was initially commissioned by the Louvre museum to find Syrian and Coptic manuscripts for the leaders of various monasteries. Unfortunately, for Mariette, at that time, the English were going around snapping up everything before he could get his hands on it. Once his work on the Serapeum was under-way Mariette devoted the rest of his life to Egyptology, making detailed notes on the Serapeum, together with all his other findings. Unfortunately, in 1878, while Mariette was in France, the Nile experienced the greatest flood of the century, flooding the basement of the Egyptian Museum in Cairo, where most of Mariette's notes and manuscripts were stored. His life's work lay underwater for months, much of it destroyed beyond repair. The scale of the catastrophe took its toll on him, leading to his death 3 years later. As for the Serapeum no one has come up with a credible explanation, no one knows what they are, who made them, how or why. The only thing we can be sure of is that the Dynastic Egyptians did not possess that level of technology.

100 ton granite boxes at the Serapeum, Saqqara

"Let me tell you that Mariette's first reports - the detailed discovery of each sarcophagus, each grave, each new underground passage, all through several years - have completely disappeared. This again will not surprise you if you've been following my writings for a while. Everything significant on the Giza plateau tends either to disappear, or if it can't be moved, to be closed to the public" - Antoine Gigal

Extra Terrestrials

From the perspective of this book, it is possible that what many consider to be extra terrestrial beings from other planets, could in fact be the henchmen of the Demiurge. Archons and demons which support and reside in the dark recesses of the Qliphoth down the Tree of Death. An array of ungodly creatures resembling lizards, cyborgs and red eyed monsters who occasionally manifest within our physical reality and spectrum of visible light.

Being the prince of darkness and the lord of the underworld, Satan/Saturn rules over anything under the ground, including rocks and stones. This is one of the reasons why in traditional Judaism stoning someone to death was a favoured punishment.

In the late 1970s Philip Schneider, a geologist and structural engineer, became involved in building underground military bases for the US government. He stated that different races of alien beings lived deep underground, and have been with us for thousands of years.[5] Schneider also stated that the United States has 131 active deep underground military bases (DUMBs), and there are well over 1400 in various locations all over the world. Many people are aware that billions of dollars are siphoned off from the US tax payer's coffers each year, funnelled into black budget and secret military operations by the internal mechanisms within the US government, and because the US holds the world's reserve currency, they have a bottomless pit of funds to tap into. On September 10th 2001, the day before 9/11, the then Secretary of Defence, Donald Rumsfeld, admitted to losing $2.3 trillion of the Pentagon's money, with absolutely no idea as to its whereabouts.[6]

In August 1979 Philip Schneider was working on a new deep underground military base down in New Mexico, when the drilling machine his team was using repeatedly broke. His suspicion that something unusual had taken place, was later confirmed when dozens of green and black barrette soldiers showed up to investigate the tunnels for themselves. When his team was sent down to inspect the drilling machine all hell broke loose.

"I was involved in building an addition to the deep underground military base at Dulce, which is probably the deepest base. It goes down seven levels and over 2.5 miles deep. At that particular time, we had drilled four distinct holes in the desert, and we were going to link them together and blow out large sections at a time. My job was to go down the holes and check the rock samples, and recommend the explosive to deal with the particular rock. As I was headed down there, we found ourselves amidst a large cavern that was full of outer-space aliens, otherwise known as large greys. I shot two of them. At that time, there were 30 people down there. About 40 more came down after this started, and all of them got killed. We had surprised a whole underground base of existing aliens. Later, we found out that they had been living on our planet for a long time, perhaps a million years. This could explain a lot of what is behind the theory of ancient astronauts. Anyway, I got shot in the chest with one of their weapons, which was a box on their body that blew a hole in me and gave me a nasty dose of cobalt radiation. I have had cancer because of that." – Philip Schneider 1995

Schneider was one of only a handful of people with level one security clearance, and possibly the only one who spoke out publicly about what he knew. He says there were nine underground bases in and around area 51, employing 18,000 people in shifts, developing and testing technology shared by non-human entities. The act of speaking out publicly put Schneider in a compromising position, he was essentially breaking his official oath and therefore the law. This could have contributed towards his mysterious and premature death back in January 1996, a few months after going public with this information.

Together with AI, this planet, as a whole, appears to be under some form of artificially stimulated geoengineering program. A covert project designed to interfere with nature's own balancing mechanisms. The reason for this is unknown, however, it could be part of an attempt to make the planet more favourable for the Demiurge and his entourage, while at the same time making it more difficult for the Divine spark to exist in harmony with nature through its variety of expressions within the human genome.

"Extremely high quantities of aluminum, barium, strontium, and other metals and chemicals are showing up in rainwater, surface water and air. - This data matches data from other citizen and environmental groups testing nationwide as well as Europe. Dangerous levels of aluminum, barium and other contaminants have saturated most surface waters in much of the US and all NATO countries. The metals found exactly match the primary elements listed in a host of "geo-engineering patents". - Recent soil testing and analysis reveals that soil PH's are now changing tremendously. A number of studies state conclusively that bio-available aluminum is highly detrimental to countless organisms, including conifers." – Geoengineering proof from NOAA, Geoengineeringwatch.org

"Whatever the country, capitalist or socialist, man was everywhere crushed by technology, made a stranger to his own work, imprisoned, forced into stupidity. The evil all arose from the fact that he had increased his needs rather than limited them; . . . As long as fresh needs continued to be created, so new frustrations would come into being. When had the decline begun? The day knowledge was preferred to wisdom and mere usefulness to beauty. . . . Only a moral revolution - not a social or political revolution - only a moral revolution would lead man back to his lost truth." – Simone de Beauvoir, French writer and intellectual.

Notes for chapter 9.

(1) Mobile phones and health: is 5G being rolled out too fast? Computer weekly, 24th April 2019. https://www.computerweekly.com/feature/Mobile-phones-and-health-is-5G-being-rolled-out-too-fast

(2) Robert Kaiser, *A Church in Search of Itself: Benedict XVI and the Battle for the Future*. 2007, https://www.amazon.com/Church-Search-Itself-Benedict-Battle/dp/030727814X

(3) Critias, By Plato, Written 360 BCE, Translated by Benjamin Jowett. http://classics.mit.edu/Plato/critias.html

(4) John Van Auken, Edgar Cayce Everything You Ever Wanted to Know About Atlantis 2018, radio interview, Earth Ancients.com. September 2018. https://www.youtube.com/watch?v=5dc1RYf7YhE

(5) Philip Schneider, Preparedness expo 95, Presentation. 1995. https://www.youtube.com/watch?v=xedmfAgx8eg

(6) ALEEN SIRGANY, CBS January 29, 2002, The war on waste, CBS evening News. http://www.cbsnews.com/news/the-war-on-waste/

Conclusion

"The race of man, after its miserable fall from God, the Creator and the Giver of heavenly gifts, "through the envy of the devil," separated into two diverse and opposite parts, of which the one steadfastly contends for truth and virtue, the other of those things which are contrary to virtue and to truth. The one is the kingdom of God on earth, namely, the true Church of Jesus Christ; and those who desire from their heart to be united with it, so as to gain salvation, must of necessity serve God and His only-begotten Son with their whole mind and with an entire will. The other is the kingdom of Satan, in whose possession and control are all whosoever follow the fatal example of their leader and of our first parents, those who refuse to obey the divine and eternal law, and who have many aims of their own in contempt of God, and many aims also against God." – "At this period, however, the partisans of evil seems to be combining together, and to be struggling with united vehemence, led on or assisted by that strongly organized and widespread association called the Freemasons." - To the Patriarchs, Primates, Archbishops, and Bishops of the Catholic World in Grace and Communion with the Apostolic See. HUMANUM GENUS ENCYCLICAL OF POPE LEO XIII ON FREEMASONRY.

So who's side are you on? Are you walking among the pathways upon the Tree of Life, or are you a pleasure seeking, self serving, egocentric individual, rapidly descending into the well worn corridors down into the belly of the beast and the Tree of Death?

The endgame is approaching, it is a showdown of biblical proportions, on one side there are those devoting their lives, trying to ascend up the Tree of Life. These are the righteous few, pockets of individuals who adhere to the righteous path, desiring unity with the Creator. They can by found among Traditional Judaism, Christianity, Islam and other forms of spiritually orientated people. They are targets of Satan and his many henchmen, all those who find themselves walking amongst the Qliphoth. They have, in some cases, unwittingly been led down the left hand path to become useful idiots and servants for the Demiurge and his entourage of disciples.

A new world order is under way, one which will ultimately outlaw all forms of spirituality, uniting humanity within a technologically controlled grid, a socialistic collective of transhuman automatons, obeying their masters and serving all aspects of the system they are helping to underpin. United in a material sense but devoid of nature's Divine spark of spiritual diversity. I suspect humanity has been down this road many times before, a cyclical loop of rising and falling civilisations, some of which steered their citizens towards the righteous Tree of Life and others down the Tree of Death. Competing factions, endlessly sparring against one another, occasionally reset by an overriding benevolent consciousness, a Divine spark which through cosmic circumstance smashes everything the Demiurge creates back into dust bringing forth a new Stone Age and a fresh beginning for humanity. The Tower of Babel is good example of this.

"A united humanity in the generations following the Great Flood, speaking a single language and migrating westward, comes to the land of Shinar. There they agree to build a city and a tower tall enough to reach heaven. God, observing their city and tower, confounds their speech so that they can no longer understand each other, and scatters them around the world." – Tower of Babel, Wikipedia

It appears that the spiritual God, will only tolerate His creation becoming too materialistic to a certain degree, before some Divine intervention takes place. And the Material God will do all in his power to undermine those trying to become more spiritual. Hence why we see major conflicts throughout the Holy Land, wars with an extra dimension, where the Demiurge desires the Supernal Triad within the Holy Land to be under his yoke. Kicking out all forms of spirituality to favour his disciples, with a new temple devoted to him. It has been an ongoing ambition of the globalists to base their new world order out of Israel, to create the right environment for their Archonic Messiah to rule from the old Supernal Triad within the Holy Land. It recently came as no surprise to see Donald Trump, on the 6th December 2017, relocate the United States Embassy, from Tel Aviv to Jerusalem (foundation of the God Shalim). Possibly in an attempt to promote Jerusalem as the future capital of the NWO. To desecrate this historic spiritual area, by handing over Israel to the Demiurge and his henchmen, will undoubtedly, restrict the Divine spark from having any influence over the future of humanity, locking each new generation into a artificial reality of transhumanism and technological folly. The wars we see unfolding throughout the Middle East, are multi faceted, mercenary armies disguised as Muslims trying to undermine unity within traditional Islam in an attempt to promote western/Qliphothic Sabbatean interests over that of the Muslims. The ultimate goal is to divide and rule (Diabolos), all the old systems to make way for a new form of global governance.

According to the Hebrew prophet Zachariah, who saw the dark days at the end of this Age, wrote about the redemption of Israel, a time when all the nations of the world would attack Israel at the battle of Armageddon. Zach 14 : 2-5 (KJV)

- **For I will gather all nations against Jerusalem to battle; and the city shall be taken, and the houses rifled, and the women ravished; and half of the city shall go forth into captivity, and the residue of the people shall not be cut off from the city.**

- Then shall the LORD go forth, and fight against those nations, as when he fought in the day of battle.

- And his feet shall stand in that day upon the mount of Olives, which is before Jerusalem on the east, and the mount of Olives shall cleave in the midst thereof toward the east and toward the west, and there shall be a very great valley; and half of the mountain shall remove toward the north, and half of it toward the south.

- And ye shall flee to the valley of the mountains; for the valley of the mountains shall reach unto Azal: yea, ye shall flee, like as ye fled from before the earthquake in the days of Uzziah king of Judah: and the LORD my God shall come, and all the saints with thee.

Zachariah suggests that during the last days, the Mount of Olives will split leaving a huge valley, in which residing Jews will be safe and protected. He also suggests that during Armageddon 2/3 of Israel will perish.

"In the whole land," declares the Lord, "two-thirds will be struck down and perish; yet one-third will be left in it. This third I will put into the fire; I will refine them like silver and test them like gold. They will call on my name and I will answer them; I will say, 'They are my people,' and they will say, 'The Lord is our God'." - Zech 13 : 8-9 (KJV)

After this it is thought that the nation of Israel will prosper far beyond anything every seen before.

What were the pyramids for? Were they frequency generators, designed to keep spirituality dormant? or on the contrary to keep the destructive influence of the Demiurge away from a society desiring righteousness? What we do know is that there are enormous factions here on Earth right now, some aligned with the Demiurge, some aligned with the Creator and some neutral, three great tectonics gearing up for one all mighty show down. The unsettling aspect of all this is that this showdown, which is unfolding before our very eyes, is almost in line with Albert Pike's description of world war three. And to make matters worse, an informed interpretation of astrological cycles also leans in this direction. The three tectonic factions rubbing against one another, creating friction, are the three variations of globalisation. The first one is an economical version of globalisation, based on western economics, with the debt based monetary system at its heart. This is a materialistic approach, one which could be viewed as being in opposition to spiritual values, a left hand path to globalisation, with the Demiurge at its helm. It is interesting to note that many Muslims within the world of Islam, 24% of the worlds population, consider the United States to be the Great Satan.

264

The second form of globalisation is a spiritual one, predominantly made up by the world of Islam. However, since the Saturnisation of much of the Christian world, Russian Orthodox Christianity (Mosco Patriarchate) is still considered by some Muslims as authentically spiritual. Together with traditional Judaism this spiritual version of globalisation is based around theological ideologies as they try to walk a righteous path and ascend up the Tree of Life.

The third tectonic faction grinding against the other two, is from a Kabbalistic perspective, a neutral form of globalisation. However, although the Chinese aspirations of expansion, based around Beijing, do not have a theological approach, or an extreme materialistic slant, they do base their society around a communistic/socialistic model, heavily influenced by Karl Marx. These three variations of the globalisation model could eventually collide, with a new world order emerging from the ashes. Whether this Armageddon type of conflict happens by accident or by design, through the geopolitical three dimensional underwater chess game that our political classes like to play, is unimportant. At the end of the day, it is still part of the ongoing battle between the Creator and the Demiurge. Consequently, which ever faction prevails, implementing their version of globalisation, they could still continue the human integration with artificial intelligence, locking future generations into an artificial reality, ultimately controlled by the Demiurge. Nothing can change society quicker than a war, so if great global changes are required, by those behind our nation's governments, then a great global problem, in the form of a war, may be arranged to bring about all the changes necessary. Unfortunately, many people alive today have become so domesticated and dependent upon government institutions for their day to day survival and security, that they have relinquished independent responsibility and handed it over to big brother institutions, allowing them to do their thinking for them. Focusing instead on excessive consumption and fashionable mundane entertainment.

"For we wrestle not against flesh and blood, but against principalities, against powers, against the rulers of the darkness of this world, against spiritual wickedness in high places." – Ephesians 6:12 (KJV)

The reason why astrology is so important during great times of upheaval, is because it gives us a reference point, a benchmark of cosmic cycles, in which our connection to universal consciousness and the Creator is represented. As we enter the New Age of Aquarius, the level of disinformation is increasing, to a point where most of us do not know what or who to believe. Various factions compete with one another for pole position, as the cosmic clock steadily takes us from the Piscean Age into Aquarius, a new Age of knowing. Like all new cycles, this new Age starts in Aries, ruled by the old God of war. Just like the Piscean Age began with military conquests brought about by the expansion of the Roman

Empire. This Age will go through some similar cosmic influences. For the first 180 years Mars will promote its proactive energy as the globalisation project kicks into high gear.

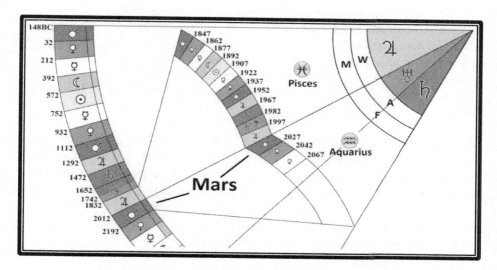

To add to this expectation of military escalation. This time period, which we are entering, also coincides with cyclical returns of both Uranus, the planet of revolution and rebellion, and Pluto, the planet of transformation, death and rebirth. Consequently, the near future in going to be a very rocky ride, where we could see the demolition of old social systems in favour of a new one. Every 84 years Uranus completes a full orbit around the Sun, this is Uranus' revolutionary cycle. Beginning with its discovery, between the American and French revolution. We are now coming into yet another 84 year cycle.

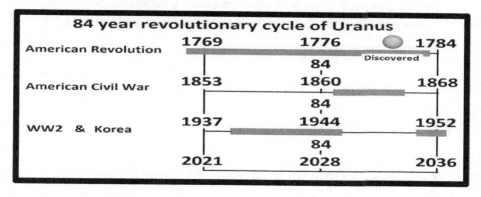

Pluto takes 248 Earth years to complete a full orbit around the Sun. Therefore, in the year 2024, it will be in the same position relative to the Sun, that it was when the American Revolution transformed the country. All in all our future is uncertain, but it all makes for very interesting times. Under the circumstances a wise man will prepare for the worst while hoping for the best. However, it is also a time when we, as members of the human race, have to stand up and be counted. Now is the time, before it is too late, to make changes, it is important to asses one's own life and decide which side you are on, and which path are you walking. Many good people are, without realising it, blindly walking or supporting the left hand path. They have allowed themselves to become useful idiots or pawns in a huge global game of three dimensional underwater chess, believing they are doing God's work, while in-fact, they have essentially become unwitting henchmen for the Demiurge and his array of Anchons.

The final book of the New Testament, written by the Apostle John, back in the first century, is an apocalyptic vision of the end times, or at least an end to what most people would regard as their normal lives within an accepted status quo. From an astrological perspective these revelations refer to the transition period from the Piscean Age into Aquarius. A period of profound change described in the Bible as a time of tribulation. In Revelation 6, four living creatures observe a lamb open seven seals of prophesy regarding this transition period.

"In the centre, around the throne, were four living creatures, and they were covered with eyes, in front and in back. The first living creature was like a lion, the second was like an ox, the third had a face like a man, the fourth was like a flying eagle." - Revelation 4 : 6-7 (NIV)

This revelation refers to the solstices and equinoxes of the new Aquarian Age. The lion and ox being Leo and Taurus, while the eagle and man represent Scorpio and Aquarius (the water bearer).

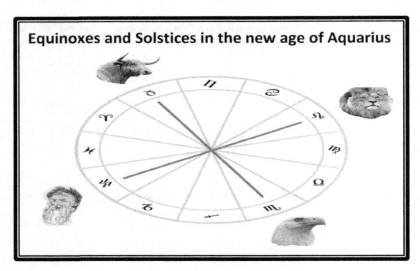

Equinoxes and Solstices in the new age of Aquarius

As the seals are opened four apocalyptic horsemen appear, each representing specific events throughout this time period.

"I watched as the Lamb opened the first of the seven seals. Then I heard one of the four living creatures say in a voice like thunder, "Come!" I looked, and there before me was a white horse! Its rider held a bow, and he was given a crown, and he rode out as a conqueror bent on conquest." - Revelation 6 : 1-2 (NIV)

Each of the four horses are different colours, they represent the colour of the sky at various times of the day, and from this we can determine the season in which these horses and their riders refer to. Depictions of horses in the ancient world usually represented a journey from either one place to another or one time period to another. In this case the white horse refers to the mid day sun and consequently, the summer solstice. Lambs in astrology usually represent Aries or the Spring equinox, and as the lamb is the one opening each seal it could be referring to a period beginning around the spring equinox. Therefore, this white horse could depict a period of time between March 21st to June 21st. This rider is wearing a crown (corona) as he rides out as a conqueror bent on conquest.

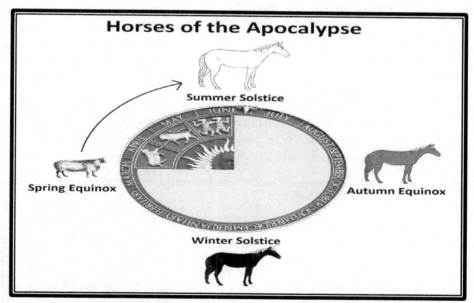

"When the Lamb opened the second seal, I heard the second living creature say, "Come!" Then another horse came out, a fiery red one. Its rider was given power to take peace from the earth and to make people kill each other. To him was given a large sword." - Revelation 6 : 3-4 (NIV)

"When the Lamb opened the third seal, I heard the third living creature say, "Come!" I looked, and there before me was a black horse! Its rider was holding a pair of scales in his hand. Then I heard what sounded like a voice among the four living creatures, saying, "Two pounds of wheat for a day's wages, and six pounds of barley for a day's wages, and do not damage the oil and the wine!" - Rev 6 : 5-6(NIV)

"When the Lamb opened the fourth seal, I heard the voice of the fourth living creature say, "Come!" I looked, and there before me was a pale horse! Its rider was named Death, and Hades was following close behind him. They were given power over a fourth of the earth to kill by sword, famine and plague, and by the wild beasts of the earth." - Revelation 6 : 7-8 (NIV)

From these visions recorded by the Apostle John we can assume that major changes are likely to occur, with a spectrum of different interpretations as to what practical effects and challenges this will bring. However, most agree that big changes are coming, and those smart enough to recognise this should prepare for the worst while hoping for the best. Maybe it is a good time to get back in tune with nature and the garden.

As we go about our daily business we must constantly ask ourselves which side are we on and which path are we walking?

Although various forms of monotheistic religions, throughout the years, have tried to unite their followers on a path of righteousness, with each religion adopting a different Sefirot, upon the Tree of Life, the Demiurge will do all in its power to undermine each religion by corrupting its followers and discrediting them in the eyes of the secular world. It is likely that some time in the future all religions of a spiritual nature will be outlawed, limiting the Creator's connection to his creation, leaving humanity to the mercy of the Demiurge. The ongoing demonisation of Islam, by the west, is all part of this agenda.

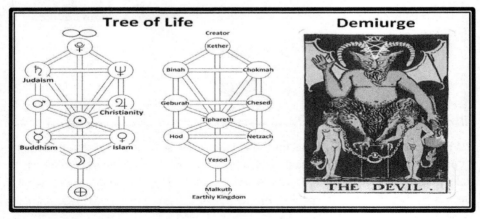

As traditional Judaism is aligned with the Sefirot Binah, part of the Supernal Triad and the Sefirot of the Messiah, it is no wonder that expectations of the new coming Messiah should be associated with the Holy Land and Jerusalem, making that area of land even more of a target for the Demiurge and his Archons to undermine and control. Through their nihilistic programs of infiltration and subversion, the Qliphotic Sabbateans sabotage many forms of Divine unity within society, hoping to bring forth their Archonic Messiah, who will rule the material world from the Supernal Triad within Israel.

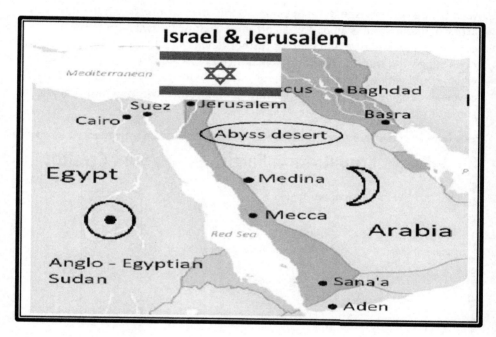

Many modern social critiques regard today's society as sole-less, where in fact it is becoming the exact opposite, spiritless. The sole is primarily concerned with the focal consciousness and the material world, whereas the spirit is our connection to Divine universal consciousness. And as we move away from our spiritual roots, the soul will take precedence aligning itself with Archonic principles. There is a great deal of rhetoric, in the world of the occult, concerning Lucifarianism, labels banded around, without a comprehensive understanding of the term. Lucifer is the Latin name for the planet Venus, the morning star or shining one. Its association with Satan is misguided and questionable. However, what we do know is the corresponding Qliphoth Satariel, down the Tree of Death, to Binah on the Tree of Life, the Messiah Sefirot, is a Qliphoth ruled by the a demon called Lucifuge. This demon is one who flees from the light, promoting atheism as he shuns the Divine spark. It could be argued that Lucifuge is the true source behind the real Lucifarian doctrine.

270

Some esoteric scholars are of the opinion that the Archons created the solar system independent from the Earth, Sun and Moon, as inorganic places where they could dwell. And it is their ultimate goal to turn the Earth into another one of their inorganic habitats. To balance the fall and manifestation of Sophia, out in this dense part of the galaxy, the Aeons, within the pleroma, manifested the Sun and the Moon, as a way to create divine harmony and balance here on Earth. it is therefore vitally important to keep one's biorhythms in tune with these important celestial luminaries, as a way to harmonise with nature and connect with Divine consciousness. It appears that the drive to interface humanity with artificial intelligence is all part of an attempt to draw us away from our connection with nature and send us further down the left hand path. It has also been suggested that the Archons have difficulty existing in our physical reality, which could very well be one of the reasons why our planet has been under a covert geoengineering program promoting unnatural environmental changes for some time.

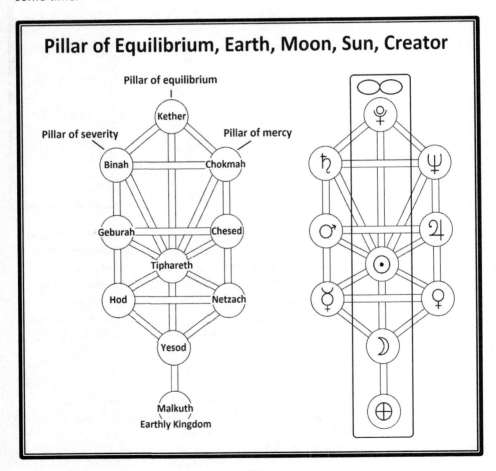

Pillar of Equilibrium, Earth, Moon, Sun, Creator

Mastering the art of meditation is one of the best ways to begin the process of ascending the Tree of Life. As the first pathway, from Malkuth, the Earthly Kingdom, leads to Yesod, ruled by the Moon, it is possible to utilise the Moon's natural cycles and phases to stimulate communication with our spiritual subconscious, aiding the overall process of righteous ascension. Monks (moonks) have been doing this for thousands of years. A new moon is nature's way of initiating a new cycle, giving those who understand its metaphysical importance an ideal opportunity to make necessary changes to the direction of their lives, making it easier to break old habits in favour of new ones. Consequently, where ever you find yourself in life, what ever path or stage you are at, every month there is an opportunity to turn your situation around. We all have choices available to us. If enough of us put into practice the changes we want to see in the world, hopefully we can leave this potential paradise in a better state than we found it.

As humanity progresses towards its uncertain future, it is worth examining what our expectations are concerning our view of progress. Most people assume that the progressive direction of humanity is being managed by humanitarian groups and organisations with our best interests at heart. This may not be the case. If the motives behind the future technological control grid is intrinsically sinister, designed to enslave humanity within an artificial web of Archonic control, then today's generation has a duty, to future generation. A duty to protect basic human freedoms, by preserving humanity's ability to influence their own future direction, without the burden of non human interference leading them away from Divine potential towards the left hand path.

Author's Bio

Brian Taylor was born in a small town in the suburbs of Nottingham, England during the late 1960s. After graduating with BSc (Hons) in construction management from Leeds Polytechnic in 1992, he spent most of his time working as an engineer. After many years fascinated by the bigger questions of life, he chose to take time away from western society, to pursue a journey of discovery. With an open mind and an optimistic belief in himself, he decided to see where destiny would take him.

During his many years travelling mostly throughout Southeast Asia, he discovered the answers to many of the questions which he had been carrying for years. At this time he wrote two books, the first one entitled *'Language of the Gods'*, was a comprehensive breakdown of how the controlling elite divide and rule humanity from a physical perspective, with an astrological overtone. His second book *'Metaphysics of the Gods'* looked into how universal energies are the building blocks for our perception of reality, within a feed-back loop of human consciousness. At this stage in his journey, he began to understand the mechanisms in play relating to how we influence our reality. A profound moment, and the most important and valuable lesson an individual can learn in a limited lifetime. From this core knowledge he revisited history to see if it made more sense. This was when he wrote *'Metaphysics of WW2'*.

As the years progressed Mr Taylor noticed an increase in obesity in western tourists visiting Southeast Asia. American and British tourists in particular, appeared to have developed some unhealthy eating habits in comparison to the Asians, who, on the whole, ate a relatively healthy and modest diet. This prompted Mr Taylor to investigate the subject from a metaphysical perspective, not only to benefit others, but also himself. This resulted in the book *'The Metaphysical Diet'*. To add to the series of books on metaphysics and suspecting that humanity was being steered in a direction which was not entirely righteous Mr Taylor next decided to investigate Kabbalah in relation to astrotheology and the globalisation project. This resulted in his book *'The Left Hand Path'*.

Finally, after more years of travelling and still evermore fascinated and puzzled by life's deeper questions, Mr Taylor focused on research regarding our connection to the spirit realm. This resulted in the book *'When The Spirit Takes Over'*.

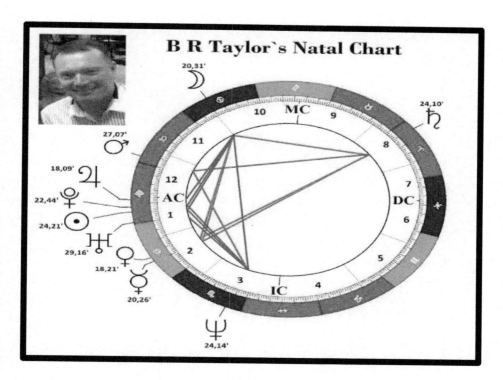

B R Taylor`s Natal Chart

Other books by this author

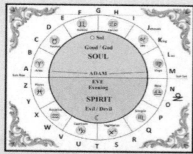

This book sets out to challenge the way we see the world, our adopted belief systems and coordinates within world history. It exposes how the potential of a united humanity has been suppressed by various forms of control over thousands of years, elites which have used division in both our physical and spiritual realms. The book is a journey of discovery into our true connection to the universe, and the relationship between the macrocosm and microcosm. The reader will come away with a fresh empowering view of how planetary cycles and energies along with human consciousness are the drivers behind geopolitical events and the ever changing fortunes of time.

"We are what we think. All that we are arises with our thoughts. With our thoughts, we make the world." Buddha

Language of the Gods

B R TAYLOR

Metaphysics of the Gods

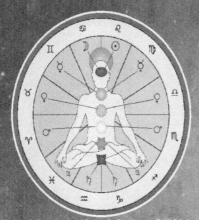

"And i saw in the right hand of him that sat on the throne a book written within and on the backside, sealed with seven seals."
Revelation 5:1

Metaphysics of the Gods

B R Taylor

B R Taylor

Metaphysics of WW2

If you think you understand WW2, think again! Until you have looked into the metaphysical (beyond the physical) aspect of the subject, together with the astrological timing in which it took place, you really are only scratching the surface. Many war historians and scholars concern themselves with the people, places and events surrounding WW2, but neglect the bigger picture. This is the only book of its kind to give you the big picture.

Metaphysics of WW2

B R Taylor

B R Taylor

The Metaphysical Diet

The Metaphysical Diet

B R Taylor

Only recently has the three meal a day mentality become accepted as the norm. We are a generation overeating. Our habitual nature has been hijacked and steered in a sinister and unhealthy direction, in order to underpin and support a corporate system reliant on excessive consumption. Most diets fail because they focus on momentary solutions to deep rooted problems. This is the only book of its kind to explain the astrological and metaphysical mechanisms at play behind obesity, and how, without spending a fortune, one can learn to sow new seeds of health, wealth and happiness within the powerful mind of the subconscious.

B R Taylor

When The Spirit Takes Over

When The Spirit Takes Over

B R Taylor

This book explores the spiritual aspect of consciousness, and what we can expect when the physical body expires and our conscious perspective transcends into an alternative reality. The book also explores our relationship with other realms, entities and dimensions, together with the possibility of reincarnation being a plausible concept.

B R Taylor

Websites by this author

www.BRTaylorMetaphysics.com

Metaphysics and astrology are the foundations to understanding universal consciousness, 360 degrees of holistic wisdom as opposed to 1 degree of compartmentalised academic knowledge.

B R Taylor's Youtube channel

https://www.youtube.com/channel/UC6Ic7_8H0JGdrDhpQWuvfBQ

https://www.bitchute.com/channel/O60Mhc33iUmU/

https://brandnewtube.com/@BRTaylor

https://odysee.com/@BRTaylorMataphysics:b

https://twitter.com/BRTaylor14

Printed in Great Britain
by Amazon

44470100R00159